THE
ORGANIZING SOURCEBOOK

THE
ORGANIZING
S O U R C E B O O K
Nine Strategies for Simplifying Your Life

Kathy Waddill

Contemporary Books

Chicago   New York   San Francisco   Lisbon   London   Madrid   Mexico City
Milan   New Delhi   San Juan   Seoul   Singapore   Sydney   Toronto

Library of Congress Cataloging-in-Publication Data

Waddill, Kathy.
    The organizing sourcebook : nine strategies for simplifying your life
/ Kathy Waddill.
        p. cm.
    Includes bibliographical references and index.
    ISBN 0-7373-0424-3
    1. Home economics. 2. Time management.   I. Title: Organizing sourcebook.
II. Title.

    TX147.W23 2001
    640—dc21

                            2001028451

Contemporary Books

A Division of The **McGraw·Hill** *Companies*

1 2 3 4 5 6 7 8 9 0 AGM/AGM 0 9 8 7 6 5 4 3 2 1

ISBN 0-7373-0424-3
This book was set in Minion, Formata, and Nueva by Robert S. Tinnon Design
Printed and bound by Quebecor—Martinsburg

Cover design by Laurie Young
Interior illustrations by Randy Miyake
Interior design by Robert S. Tinnon

Contents

This book is dedicated to the bright, lively, creative,

courageous people who are my clients.

Each one of you has taught me so much.

Thank you.

I owe special thanks to Will, Alyssa, and Anna

for their unwavering support and

love during the life event of this book

and to Christine for her editorial brilliance.

Without the help of these very special people,

this book would never have been written.

Acknowledgments

The ideas presented in this book were distilled from things I learned from many wonderful people. I'd like to acknowledge and extend my heartfelt gratitude to:

My father, Tony Downs, for instilling in me his passion for ideas—thinking about them, writing them down, and sharing them with others

My mother, Kay Watson Downs, for teaching me essential life skills and being my close friend

My longtime best friends, Rachel Young, Deirdre Pulgram Arthen, and Susan Pinsky for their love and support and for putting up with all my stories and musings about what it means to be organized

All my clients, who taught me everything I know about organizing

Nick Reinhardt, for his friendship, ingenuity, and generous support

Angela Wallace and the VOS Circle (Judy Ott, Sandy Stelter, Mary Rossow, and Lynn Gross-Cerf) for holding me accountable for actually sitting down and writing

Allison Van Norman, for a fortuitous comment she made during a meeting

Kate Chambers-Maher, who gave me valuable editorial advice at the beginning of this project and has been a wonderful, thoughtful friend

Jane Roberts and Hudson Perigo, who helped me negotiate a much better contract than the one I started with

Jim Watson, for his enthusiastic devotion to the challenge of creating a card-stock version of the Eyes of a Stranger

All the family members and close friends who read different parts of the manuscript and gave me invaluable and much-appreciated feedback: Darian Downs, Dave and Carol Stahl, Phyllis Watson, Tracy

Roberts McCollam, Nicki Rose, Eileen Klatsky, Katherine Korlacki, and the Pink Hill Book Club (Victoria Smith, Charly Guidry, Cheri Etheredge, and Karin Sharp)

Caroline Lovell, for her generosity and talent with a camera

All my colleagues at NAPO-SFBA (especially Kelly Galvin and the after-meeting crowd) and NEPO (especially Helene Papanastassiou)

Maria Magallanes of Contemporary Books, for her excellent suggestions about how to improve the manuscript

And Milian Castillo and Jorge Ramos, for keeping things running smoothly in and around my house while I was distracted by this big project.

Many people contributed to this book in small ways, but four individuals deserve special recognition:

My sister, Christine Mann, who read every word and helped me make sure each chapter actually said the things I was trying to convey.

My beautiful daughters, Alyssa and Anna, who relinquished their mommy for months on end while I holed up in my office and wrote like mad.

And my fabulous husband, Will Waddill, who did all my jobs as well as his while I was writing, read excerpts and gave me feedback, cooked a whole Thanksgiving dinner by himself, and still loved me when I was finished with the book.

I am profoundly grateful for your love and support. Thank you.

Introduction

What does it mean to be organized? What is the difference between an organized person and a *dis*organized person? How can you tell them apart? Is it the way they look? The state of their home or office? Whether or not they're always on time? If people are messy, are they necessarily disorganized? Does a pristine and clutter-free desk automatically make its owner organized?

When I started my career as a professional organizer, I had definitive opinions about the answers to these questions. Organized meant neat, clean, and in control. Clutter, of course, bespoke disorganization. How could a person live in a messy environment and still function effectively in the world? And clearly, immaculate neatness was a requirement for anyone who wanted to be considered organized.

I wasn't the only one operating under these assumptions. American culture prizes neatness and equates it with a high level of organization. Just look at the characters on TV and in the movies. Are there piles of stuff on their flat surfaces? Do they have clothes draped over every chair in their bedrooms? Are their desks overflowing with papers? Do they ever have trouble finding their keys? No. Even shows touted for their "realistic" depiction of life show only carefully staged and minimal clutter when it relates to the plot. Advertising is another insidious influence. Catalogs and magazines idealize neatness by depicting spare, immaculate rooms devoid of any trace of human occupancy. Of course, we all know movies, television, and ads are not the same as real life. Yet the powerful visual images they project can make us compare ourselves unfavorably to the homes and lives we see in their virtual world.

So how does this cultural ideal affect real people whose operating style is eclectic or messy or a bit rumpled around the edges? They constantly find themselves under pressure to "clean up their act." The pressure comes not only from the culture, but from those around them—family members, friends, coworkers—and (most insidiously) from inside themselves. Even people who outwardly sneer at the idea that neatness equals efficiency often secretly punish themselves because their style doesn't conform to the cultural ideal. How many times have you heard someone say (or said to yourself), "I should get this mess under control" or "This year, I'm finally going to get organized" or "If I could just get this place cleaned up, my whole life would be better."

A person who feels disorganized gets one message continuously reinforced: "There must be something *wrong* with you. If you'd only *do* something different or *be* someone different or be a better *person*, your life would be organized. Your disorganization is *your fault*. You must be (gasp!) a Disorganized Person." This message is so pervasive that when I started my business in 1993, it was the foundation for my expectations about who my clients would be and what they would need.

Then I met Leo, and my whole perspective changed.

On the surface, Leo was a Disorganized Person *par excellence*, a poster child for clutter and chaos. He called me because he wanted help setting up his office. When I arrived for our first consultation, I found a three-bedroom house chock-full of stuff. Every flat surface was covered with papers, gizmos, equipment, office supplies, tools, piano music, plants, and knickknacks. In the two extra bedrooms (one of which he wanted to transform into an office), boxes and beer flats littered the floor, leaving only paths for getting in and out. The living/dining room floor was free of clutter, but the furniture was haphazardly arranged and a piano and a marimba were both being used as tables. One of the two bathrooms was unusable because of a broken toilet and a large wad of moldy carpeting in the bathtub. In the carport, an enormous blue tarp covered a car-sized pile of boxes. A second kitchen was made completely inaccessible by the piles of lumber in the hallway leading to it. And the laundry room cum pantry was so crowded its floor had to be cleaned up every time Leo needed to get to the washer and dryer. Because he had no attic, basement, or covered garage, he also rented a storage area and a 900-square-foot workshop in a nearby town. In short, by any standard, the place was a disaster. And throughout the tour, Leo apologized profusely, disparaged himself, and told me how ashamed he felt to be living in such an unbearable mess.

Yet, in the midst of the chaos, there were definite signs of organization and systematic thinking. Leo's bedroom and clothes closet were reasonably neat and functional. The working bathroom was clean and uncluttered. All the dishes in the kitchen were clean, and the cabinets seemed organized. One closet contained an elaborate, well-labeled, much-used file system holding all kinds of easily retrievable technical information. And the two spare bedrooms, while hard to maneuver in because of the boxes and items on the floor, contained numerous homemade shelving units cleverly designed to hold multiple drawers fashioned creatively from cardboard beer flats (the tray under a case of beer cans).

Starting with our first visit, Leo and I worked together once a week to rearrange his furniture, set up his desk and work space, weed through piles and piles (and piles!) of boxes and equipment and memorabilia and papers, empty out the storage locker so he could stop paying for it, and generally get things into a reasonably workable semblance of order. It took months. As we worked, he told me his story, and it began to be clear to me that popular assumptions about organization and disorganization are inaccurate, incomplete, harsh, and unfair.

Leo was not, it turns out, a Disorganized Person. He was an electrical engineer who had worked on numerous government projects, invented and patented several technical gadgets, built an international reputation on his knowledge of vacuum tubes, cofounded a company, and created an upper-middle-class lifestyle for himself and his family. They had lived in a fourteen-room Victorian mansion with attic and basement, as well as a carriage house where he kept his tools and had his workshop. He and his wife married in the 1950s, raised two children, and had an altogether normal, well-organized, lovely life. Then, a series of events beyond his control turned Leo's life upside down.

First, electronic chips appeared in the marketplace, making the vacuum tube obsolete. Work dried up. Then Leo's wife went back to school, became a feminist, developed other interests, and divorced him. Next his father, also an inventor, died, leaving him huge piles of miscellany to weed through. Then his mother died, too, also leaving behind a multitude of things. Finally, the large house he loved had to be sold because he could no longer afford it. Leo used the proceeds to buy the much smaller, storage-less house he lived in when I met him.

It is common knowledge that each of these life events—unemployment, divorce, death of a parent, a move—is an emotionally draining experience for anyone. What is less understood is that each of these types of changes has a tremendous impact on one's organizing systems. Not only did these events rob Leo of the resources he was used to having—money, space, family support, employment—they also left him with piles and piles of additional stuff in a dramatically smaller space.

No wonder the place was a mess! But it wasn't because Leo had a flaw in his character. It was because his life had changed drastically, and his new life was not set up to accommodate the debris these immense changes left behind.

Once I recognized that the real cause of Leo's organizing problems was a drastic change in his life circumstances, I started looking at other client situations to see if similar life-transforming events had made a disorganized person out of an organized one. I was astounded to discover that practically every single one of my clients could trace the varying levels of mess in their lives back to specific life events. The more dramatic the events, the more extreme the ensuing chaos.

Sometimes, the events are clearly negative and difficult. When Lucia hired me to organize her two-car garage, it was so full of boxes, papers, clothes, furniture, and books that she couldn't park her car in it. She wanted help because she was emotionally unable to deal with the garage herself. It contained all the remaining traces of her marriage, which had dissolved the year before. Her wedding souvenirs, the travel brochures from her honeymoon, the love letters she had received from her former husband were all too painful for her to go through alone. The garage also held her beloved brother's precious books. He had died as a result of injuries he sustained in a car accident. The longer she was able to put off going through the boxes, the longer she could pretend her divorce and her brother's death had never happened.

For Maria, the problem was papers. She had a well-indexed, extensive file system that had stood her in good stead for years, yet her office was overflowing with papers she hadn't filed. It turned out the cause of the pile on her desk was a different type of traumatic life event: She had been diagnosed with multiple sclerosis and was suffering from the flagging energy and loss of memory that go with this debilitating disease. The file system, her pride and joy, turned out to be much too complicated to use easily, and she didn't have the energy to continue maintaining it. It needed to be simplified and overhauled so she could still manage it in her new condition. The idea of changing it was daunting not only because it took time and energy, but because it underlined her declining health and diminishing strength.

Virginia had always loved decorating her house for the succession of holidays that marked each year: Christmas, Valentine's Day, Easter, Fourth of July, and Halloween. Another passion had been changing her linens, curtains, and rugs to reflect the changing seasons. Her attic was overflowing with decorations, window treatments, sheet sets, and seasonal household items. So she called me to ask for ideas on how to store her things better so she could get in and out of the attic. What I discovered was that Virginia hadn't been able to redecorate for the holidays for several years. Her desire for a seasonal home had waned along with her physical strength. Yet relinquishing the decorations was painful because it was a tacit acknowledgment of her slow physical decline and the approach of death.

When people experience difficult events like divorce, illness, disability, unemployment, and the death of a loved one, it is easy for others, especially those who have suffered significant losses of their own, to sympathize with their feelings of stress, grief, and loss. Onlookers are happy to step in and offer help, support, and resources. It's also easier for people in obvious grief to ask for assistance when they need it. If people in this kind of situation let their organizing systems slip for a while, everyone is forgiving. But when someone who is going through *happy* life-changing events backslides into disorganization, other people are not as sympathetic. It is much harder to recognize that positive life transitions *also* can cause stress, grief, and feelings of loss. Even the people going through them may not realize that changes they welcome, such as marriage, the arrival of a baby, sudden wealth, or a glitzy new job, can wreak their own brand of emotional and organizational havoc.

Terese and her husband scrimped along while he finished medical school, internship, and a residency in internal medicine. When he started working, they bought a house, and Terese stayed home to care for their small daughter. Soon, they discovered their second child was really triplets, so they used their burgeoning wealth to buy a huge, brand-new house in the country. Just before they moved, new babies in tow, Terese broke her leg and was immobilized. Someone else supervised the move, including getting all the furniture, closets, cupboards, and systems set up in the new house. As soon as Terese could get around, every ounce of her energy was taken up in caring for her children. Her home went to hell in a handbasket. By the time she called me, the triplets were happy ten-year-olds, but the immense house was in total chaos. It took us twelve hours just to clean out the enormous master bathroom so they could use it properly. It turned out that Terese had been trying to manage her new, large home containing a family of six using the same tactics she had employed in her smaller house with only one child. Also, their affluence had enabled them to provide every opportunity to their children, but by the same token, it had allowed them to accumulate far more belongings than one lone person could possibly manage on her own. Terese's intense desire to care for her family by herself, as she had done in her former, simpler life, made it hard for her to relinquish control and get the help she needed to properly handle her current situation.

Madeline was expecting twins, not triplets, for her first childbirth experience. She and her husband were renovating their home, turning two flats into a single apartment in order to make room for their growing family. The problem was Madeline's clothes. During her twenty-five-year career, Madeline had accumulated a vast wardrobe of stylish, high-quality work clothing, which filled two bedrooms on wall-to-wall hanging racks. The hallway and living room were lined with dressers and storage bins brimming with lingerie, sweaters, and accessories. Despite the fact that these clothes would be mostly useless to her as a stay-at-home mother of two and that the family would need the space currently being occupied by clothes, Madeline was having a hard time letting go of anything. The clothes were symbolic of her life as an independent, successful woman. Giving them up would be like giving up a part of herself.

Another less drastic illustration of the organizing challenges that can come from positive life events is found in the story of Tricia and Paul. When I met them, these two forty-somethings had just bought a house and were about to get married. Along with wedding planning, they had to worry about a six-year-old daughter from a previous marriage who would be staying with them on weekends, an aging dog, and a yard full of mud and weeds that desperately needed landscaping. But the biggest dilemma was the daunting task of squeezing two households and two home-based businesses into one four-bedroom house. For a person used to living alone, learning to accommodate the physical presence and belongings of another person, even a much-loved and welcomed one, requires time and resources. Although the new, shared life is compelling and desirable, there is often a real sense of loss for the independence and freedom of the single life left behind.

Every client story is not as dramatic as the ones I've described so far. Most of them involve fewer simultaneous life changes and difficult adjustments. Sometimes, the biggest organizing dilemma is the heap of papers on the desk or the jumble of boxes in the garage. But the spectacular, multifaceted case histories are the ones that really challenged my assumptions and brought new light to my understanding of the answer to the question, "What does organized mean?" Once I recognized the impact of life events in a situation like Leo's or Terese's, I was able to uncover and address similar issues in less dramatic client situations.

In every life, any unpredictable or extraordinary event, large or small, can throw one's organizing systems out of whack at least temporarily (see sidebar on page 9 for a list of life events). What really happens in people's lives goes something like this:

1. A person or family or business sets up organizing systems that are designed to function well in a certain set of circumstances.
2. The circumstances change, usually in small increments, but sometimes in a sudden and drastic manner.
3. The organizing systems either don't keep up with the life changes, or they don't change at all. In the latter case, it is often

MAJOR LIFE EVENTS	MINOR LIFE EVENTS
Setting up housekeeping	Short-term illness
First employment	Clothing seasons
Marriage/partnership	Vacations
First child	Promotion
Each subsequent child	Inheritances
Job changes	Redecorating
Career changes	Remodeling
Starting a business	Sports seasons
Working from home	School begins
Moving	School ends
Divorce	Holidays
Merging families	Trips
Financial success	Family reunions
Bankruptcy	Special projects
Empty nest	Social events
Unemployment	Personality conflicts
Disability	Changes of work schedule
Major illness	Child care problems
Accidents	Car trouble
Natural disasters	Competitions
Being victim of a crime	Unexpected guests
Illness of loved one	Storms
Downsizing move	Anything unexpected
Retirement	Anything extraordinary
Death of spouse	
Death of other loved one	
One's own impending death	

because the systems are too complicated to be easily modified.

4. The end result in either scenario is that the systems and the life they are supposed to be organizing don't match. This is a surefire recipe for disorganization.

5. The further removed the organizational system is from the actual life being lived, the more overwhelming, chaotic, and hard to fix the situation gets.

6. The disorganization and feeling of being overwhelmed create a sense of limbo (often for good reasons).

7. Organization cannot return until the organizing systems are reworked to fit the actual life being lived—*not* the life the person used to have in the past and *not* the life she or he would like to have in the future.

8. The greater the life changes and the longer the feelings of limbo remain, the more energy, time, and resources it takes to return to a state of organization (see Figure I.1 for a graphic illustration of this divergence between life and organizing system).

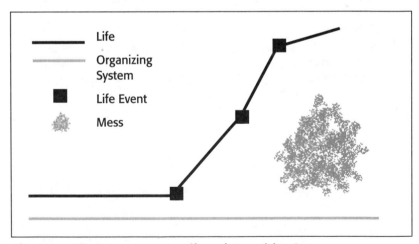

Figure I.1 Divergence Between Life and Organizing System

The real key to being organized is not a set of character traits, but rather a state of existence. You are organized when your systems fit your life as *you're living it right now*. Your life functions smoothly and efficiently. You can do what you have to do and what you want to do without wasting time or effort. Conversely, when your life *and* your systems are out of sync, you are "disorganized." You spend time and energy on activities that do not contribute to the substance of your life. In this state, it's very hard to get everything done.

Throughout their lives, people move back and forth between being organized and being disorganized. The length of each "disorganization" period depends on the magnitude of the changes life throws at you, the complexity of the systems you need to change, the number of resources at your disposal to help you get your systems back in line, and the organizing strategies you choose as you move forward. People whose systems and strategies are simple, flexible, tailored to their lives in the present moment, and include frequent and honest evaluations are those most likely to stay organized over time.

This book focuses on how to set up such a system for yourself. It will teach you nine strategies that, taken together, form a blueprint for creating and maintaining simple, flexible, functional organizing systems. Each strategy will be explained and illustrated using real-life examples of what happens when someone *doesn't* use it. You'll see how the application of each strategy can turn a dysfunctional situation around. And you'll learn the questions to ask yourself to figure out how to apply these simple principles to *your* life.

This book will *not* help you achieve a state of perfect organization. Perfection is an impossible standard, especially for busy people whose lives are constantly evolving; it leads to systems that are too complicated to withstand change. Instead, we'll focus on helping you be *organized enough* to keep your life running smoothly over the long term. Then, when your circumstances change, it will be easier to bring your systems up-to-date.

The Nine Strategies of Reasonably Organized People

The Nine Strategies of Reasonably Organized People are simple habits anyone can learn. Taken together, they form the recipe for an organized life. Over time, they will help you understand and manage the changes life inflicts on you.

The Nine Strategies of Reasonably Organized People are drawn from my experiences as a professional organizer. For me, the underlying mystery in each new situation has always been fascinating. "*Why* did things get this way? *How* can they be fixed?" The Nine Strategies surfaced as I worked to resolve these questions for people in a wide variety of life circumstances. I continually found myself giving clients the same two answers:

1. *Why did things get this way?* "Your life has changed since you set up this system, and you're having trouble with some of the fallout from those changes."
2. *How can they be fixed?* "We'll turn things around by using basic organizing principles to address each problem."

Although each client's situation is unique, pivotal life events are always in the background when things are in disarray. And while it's impossible to predict which life change will have precipitated the next person's organizing challenge(s), the organizing *principles* remain the same from one client to another.

Eventually, it dawned on me that I should put those principles in writing. So I created a tip sheet to use as a diagnostic tool with each new client. When we sat down for our first consultation, I'd show them which principles on the list needed to be applied to their situation to make things work better. In the beginning, this sheet had ten items on it so I could call it my "Top Ten" rules for getting and staying organized. Then, as I put it in practice, it got modified, refined, and consolidated into nine principles—no more, no less—with a more accurate new title: The Nine Strategies of Reasonably Organized People.

As the word *strategy* implies, every item on this list is a straightforward, uncomplicated action. Each one plays an essential role in managing the five elements of an overall organizing system: space, things, information, time, and relationships (see What Is an Organizing System?, page 14, for definitions). If you practice all nine of them throughout your organizing system, you can transform your life.

Let's look at the Nine Strategies in detail:

1. *Make Your Systems Fit You and Your Life:* The elements that make up your overall organizing system must be designed to fit the way you actually live, or they won't work. Getting them to function smoothly *for you* is the foremost consideration. Other values, such as aesthetics, expense, sentiment, or fashion, need to come *after* utility.

2. *Sort Everything by How You Use It:* Sorting is a basic mechanism for creating order. Effective sorting is based on how each item is used. Things that are used together belong together. Store the items in a collection in one place so you know what you have. Keeping like with like is more functional in every regard than a jumble.

3. *Weed Constantly:* Aside from the personal reasons people hang on to things, our materialistic culture pressures us to have more than we need. Every day, we're barraged with paper, news, advertising, and information. When you keep things you're not actively using, they get in your way and create work for you. It requires constant vigilance to prevent

What Is an Organizing System?

An organizing system is the structure you put in place to help you manage these five key organizable elements of your life:

1. **Your Space** The settings in which you live and work. Space includes fixed objects like buildings and rooms, heavy movable objects like furniture, and interior design elements like color and light.
2. **Your Things** Your portable belongings. Your things are the items you own, use, and care about. You manage them as they flow in and out of your space.
3. **Your Information** The data you keep track of. Information includes what you know and what you want to learn about.
4. **Your Time** Your schedule. The way you allocate your time determines what you accomplish, both day-to-day and in your whole life.
5. **Your Relationships** The way you interact with the people you care about. Your organizing choices affect your family and friends at every level, and vice versa.

Everything in your life can either be broken down to fit into these categories or can't be organized at all. An example from the first group is money. You manage money as Time (the schedule for your money-making activities) and Information (the way you keep track of your money once you make it). If you have an actual pile of cash lying around, you also manage money as a Thing. On the other hand, some phenomena are impossible to organize. Weather is a prime example. It affects you all the time, but you are powerless to affect it.

yourself from being overwhelmed by the onslaught. Keep everything weeded down so you can retain a semblance of control over your life.

4. *Use the Right Containers and Tools:* Effective containers allow you to keep track of things and use them easily. Bad containers make things hard to manage. The right tools help you accomplish necessary tasks quickly and efficiently. The wrong tool can keep you from accomplishing anything.

5. *Label Everything:* Labeling is essential for remembering what and where everything is once it's put away. Good labels help you retrieve things and share them with others. Something left unlabeled is likely to just disappear from your radar screen. Something labeled incorrectly is almost guaranteed not to work well.

6. *Keep It Simple:* Figure out what you want to do, then do it with the fewest possible steps. If you can do something in two steps, why waste time and effort doing it in four? The more steps it takes to do something, the less likely it is to get done. Take on only what you can handle, and no more. Simplicity is the key to efficiency.

7. *Decide to Decide:* Make decisions instead of putting them off and letting them pile up. Sometimes it takes longer to write a task on your to-do list than it takes to just do it. Other tasks never get done, no matter how long they've been on your list. Give yourself permission *not* to do them. Lessen the mess and your stress level by making decisions and carrying them out.

8. *Get Help When You Need It:* If you don't have to do all the work yourself, why should you? Share the responsibility for tasks by delegating them. Hire people to do things you aren't good at or don't want to do. Consult experts. Avoid the trap of self-sufficiency.

9. *Evaluate Honestly and Often:* Organizing your life is like hitting a moving target. Even when things are working smoothly, it's reasonable to expect life to change. Pay attention as life evolves, and change your system to make it keep up. Maintain your system so it's lean, flexible, and attuned to your life.

The power of this list comes, not only from its content, but also from the way it's used. As soon as I adopted the list as my main diagnostic tool, something dramatic began to happen. Just as my work with Leo opened my eyes to the ways that life events wreak havoc on people's organizing systems, applying the Nine Strategies led me to a second flash of insight. When I compared the list to a client's life, I could see not only how the principle would *fix* things, but how the *lack of it* had interacted with a life event to cause the problems in the first place.

Do you remember Madeline, the woman expecting twins whose work clothes were taking over her home? She was in the throes of two major life events (birth of twins and a change from working outside the home to being a stay-at-home mom) and one minor life event (remodeling) when she first called me. She asked for help figuring out how to set up her home for her babies. When I got there, I found clothes filling rows of wall-to-wall racks in two bedrooms, and inhabiting numerous dressers and bins in the hallway and living room. Madeline had not been following *Strategy #3, Weed Constantly,* for a long, long time. Yet even though her wardrobe was excessive from any reasonable standpoint, it hadn't caused her a problem because there were only two people living in the apartment, the clothes were neatly put away, and there was room for everything. When Madeline got pregnant, the exact same situation became an instant nightmare. With clothes taking up two of the three bedrooms, there was no place to put the babies! The life event of pregnancy turned a tolerable bad habit into an intolerable one overnight.

Even if all the other strategies were working perfectly for Madeline, her attachment to her clothes and her inability to keep her wardrobe in proportion to her life set her up for a crisis when her life changed. Her system was out of balance, inflexible, and difficult to change. The result: She and her husband faced the massive task of clearing out heaps of clothing at a time when their resources were diminished due to the high-risk twin pregnancy and when they might have preferred to spend their time setting up the nursery and going to baby showers. Instead of making it easy for them to concentrate on becoming new parents, their organizing system *added* to their stress during this major transition.

Madeline's story clearly illustrates the interaction between one of the Nine Strategies (*#3, Weed Constantly*) and a life event. There was a direct cause-and-effect relationship between Madeline's choice to keep her clothes (whether she wore them or not) and the concrete, tangible, hard-to-fix impact of that choice when she got pregnant. My job as consultant was to help her understand the cause-and-effect connection between the missing strategy and its consequences. Until we correctly identified the root cause of the problem, we could neither fix it nor prevent it from happening again.

The Mess Is Not the Problem

The power of the Nine Strategies of Reasonably Organized People comes when they're used to help people understand what is *really* causing their organizing dilemmas. Invariably, someone calls me for a consultation because there is a tangible, physical mess making life difficult for them. They say, "The problem is this pile on my kitchen counter that won't go away" or "My clothes are overflowing from my closet" or "There are papers all over the house." They identify the *mess* as the problem.

Usually, they've already tried to clean things up themselves. And what happens? The mess comes back. Then they get a few organizing books from the bookstore or the library. The books focus on ways to clean up specific kinds of messes. So they follow the tips in the books—"Here's what to do if you have a pile on your kitchen counter" or "The way to organize your closet is . . ." or "The perfect paper filing system is . . ."— and they clean things up again, a little better. And what happens? The *mess comes back again.* By the time they make the decision to hire me, they're convinced their mess is incorrigible, they feel like a failure, they're desperate for a solution, and they're ready to pay for it.

What causes this vicious cycle? Why does the mess return again and again? Why won't it stay cleaned up? The mess comes back because *the mess is not really the problem*! It is only a symptom of the real problem. And cleaning up a mess without addressing the source of the problem is like taking an aspirin for a strep throat. It makes things better for a while, but it doesn't cure the underlying infection. As soon as the aspirin wears off, the sore throat is back.

The real problem behind a mess is that *something is missing.* A pile or a heap or a muddle is a symptom that one or more of the Nine Strategies is not being followed. The type of pile or heap or muddle it is will tell you which strategy isn't in place. Just as an experienced trapper can tell which animal has come and gone at a watering hole, a trained eye can identify a missing strategy by the trail it leaves behind. When multiple strategies are missing, the tracks are more tangled, but it's still possible to correctly unravel and interpret each one.

Fortunately, the Nine Strategies can remedy any organizing challenge, even in the face of overwhelming change. By cleaning up the mess *and* putting the missing strategy or strategies into practice, you can make even the most persistent organizing problems go away and stay away. When Madeline and her husband realized they only had six months to get their home ready for twin infants and possibly a live-in nanny, they Evaluated (*Strategy #9*) and called me (*Strategy #8, Get Help When You Need It*). Madeline Decided to Decide (*Strategy #7*) about her clothes, and the weeding began. Their remodel included a huge new closet (*Strategy #1, Make Your Systems Fit You and Your Life*), and the practice Madeline was getting as she weeded through her enormous pile of clothing gave her a good head start for adopting *Strategy #3, Weed Constantly*, as an ongoing habit. Using the strategies to identify the underlying problems and then to correct them, Madeline and her husband were well on their way to getting their systems in line with their new life as parents.

So far, we've talked about the Nine Strategies of Reasonably Organized People in relation to a person in crisis. It's easy to see that something needs to be done when a baby is on the way and there's no room for a crib. But what's the value of these nine activities when there's no crisis? Are you thinking to yourself, "Why should I spend time and

The Nine Strategies of Reasonably Organized People

#1. Make Your Systems Fit You and Your Life
#2. Sort Everything by How You Use It
#3. Weed Constantly
#4. Use the Right Containers and Tools
#5. Label Everything
#6. Keep It Simple
#7. Decide to Decide
#8. Get Help When You Need It
#9. Evaluate Honestly and Often

energy to put these strategies in place? Things are going relatively smoothly for me right now. There are a few piles lying around, but they're not in my way, so they're not a problem. Why bother?" (This, of course, is what Madeline used to think about her clothes.)

The first reason to put the Nine Strategies in place goes back to the old saying, "An ounce of prevention is worth a pound of cure." If Madeline had taken time here and there to sort through her clothes and let go of the things she was no longer wearing, she would have spread out the work of weeding over twenty-five years. Instead, she waited until a crisis was at hand, and she had to do twenty-five years' worth of work in two months—while pregnant with twins to boot! Keeping up with your systems keeps you from having a huge, overwhelming, time-consuming task to do during a stressful life transition. It allows you to keep a series of molehills from turning into mountains. Who benefits from keeping things in balance? You and the people you love.

The second reason to look at the Nine Strategies, even if you're not facing a major life event at the moment, is that you *could* be facing one tomorrow. In that case, wouldn't you want to be able to devote your time, attention, and energy to the issue at hand without having to worry about unfinished business? A life-changing event causes enough stress. Why compound it with obstacles and distractions?

Fortunately, most people only need to fine-tune their systems to run at optimum performance. Others, like Madeline, reach a point where life events bring a problem (caused by a missing strategy) into sharp focus. For them, the task of getting things operating smoothly involves some catch-up work. Once things are back in balance, they can put the strategies in place and go forward. Finally, there is a group of people, like Leo, who have undergone such immense transformations that their systems have broken down entirely. In these cases, all nine strategies are missing, and the result is chaos. The job of getting back on track takes a lot of time and work, but it is an essential step toward regaining a sense of balance and control. Once a new system is installed using the Nine Strategies, it is possible to turn toward the future and resume living.

No matter where you fit into this spectrum, the most difficult step in getting your organizing system to fit your life is the first one: figuring out what is really going on. If you want to solve your organizing problems effectively, you have to identify them correctly. The next section shows you how to look at your situation objectively in order to pinpoint the real source of your messes.

Looking Through the Eyes of a Stranger

Before you begin to apply the Nine Strategies of Reasonably Organized People, you need to ask yourself, "What is really happening in my life?" The reason for this is simple. The foundation for a reasonably organized life is laid by matching your systems to your life *as you're living it right now*. Whether you're using this book to help you recover from the fallout of life transitions (large and small), or because your systems are working smoothly and you want them to stay that way, you need to figure out exactly where you are *today* in order to build a reasonably organized future.

Doing this by yourself is harder than it sounds. When you're immersed in the details of daily living, it's difficult to step back and see the big picture. Yet you need to see the big picture to keep the details moving in the right direction. This is where an additional pair of eyes can be helpful. So together, you and I are going to do a quick appraisal of your life to figure out exactly where you're starting from. No pencil and paper are required for this exercise. The only organizing tool you'll need (besides this book) is your most important one—your mind.

Note: You can do this exercise in your imagination, or you can do it in real life, whichever feels most comfortable. It works equally well

Figure I.2 Eyes of a Stranger

in offices, cubicles, bedrooms, dorm rooms, businesses, trailers, second homes—wherever you spend your time and keep your stuff. Remember, this process is for you alone. No one else is involved. So be honest, and be kind to yourself.

Step 1: The Eyes of a Stranger

Imagine yourself standing in front of your home, gazing at the outside of the building. You are wearing a pair of Groucho Marx glasses, without the fake nose and eyebrows (see Figure I.2). These magical glasses give you the power to enter your home as if you've never been there before, as if you're looking at it for the first time. Through these Eyes of a Stranger, you'll see your life from an outsider's point of view, clearly and without distortion.

Now, moving slowly, walk up to and through your front door. Stroll through each room, looking around carefully, checking in the corners, opening every drawer, peeking into all the closets. Don't forget the cupboards, storage areas, basement, attic, garage, and yard. Scrutinize everything with your objective eyes. Take your time.

Remember—as a stranger, you have no attachment to this home, these things, this life. Your detachment allows you simply to see things as they are, without expectations and without judgment. It is important to silence the critical voices inside your head. After all, as an outsider, you don't know what life events have affected the occupant(s) of this home. You're just interested in the facts.

What Do You See?

Every person who does this exercise will have a different answer to this question. There will be a mix of things that do and don't work in every home. You may run across one of those messes we mentioned on page 18, the ones that keep coming back every time you clean them up. Some of these are:

- a mound of miscellany on the kitchen counter that changes every day but never goes away;
- a desk covered with papers, sitting next to a file cabinet jam-packed with old files;
- closets crammed with clothes no longer worn but in perfectly good condition;
- several junk drawers in the kitchen instead of one;
- kids' rooms perpetually littered with toys, books, clothes, and papers;
- a dining room table that's never dined on because it takes too long to clear it off;
- a spare room, garage, basement, or attic full of unused things too good to get rid of;
- piles of bills and unopened mail scattered here, there, and everywhere.

If you find something like this, make a mental note of it and move on. You don't need to write it down—that might be daunting. You just need to be consciously aware of it.

Once you're satisfied you've seen everything, get comfortable again, take off the Eyes of a Stranger, and relax. It's time for us to take the second step in your appraisal process.

Step 2: Looking for Trouble Spots

Now that you've looked objectively and honestly at your home through the Eyes of a Stranger, you know a great deal about how your life is going. After all, your home is the vessel that contains your life, the place where all the threads of your life converge. The way it's set up, the people and things that flow through it, the information it holds, the way you use it—all these bits of data offer revealing insights into your values, priorities, interests, and history.

Now it's time to analyze the data and figure out where there's room for improvement. Think back on everything you saw through the Eyes of a Stranger, then answer this question:

Among all the things you observed, what *one* thing bothers you the most?

As with the previous question, your answer will be different from anyone else's. It might be something no one has ever experienced before. Or it might be one of the messes from the list on the previous page. Everyone selects something unique to their own situation:

- "I haven't been able to put my car in the garage for ten years," or
- "I'm moving across the country, and I don't want to bring most of these clothes," or
- "I haven't filed a tax return for the last three years and I need help finding my receipts," or
- "There are stacks of mail stashed all over the house, and more comes in every day," or
- . . . just about anything else you can think of.

The one thing you've selected is your own personal #1 Challenge. It's the first thing you need to change if you want your life to work better. After you fix it, you can come back and select the next most bothersome issue to address, then the next, until you work through your mental list. Picking out your unique #1 Challenge is the second step in your appraisal process.

Step 3: Tackling Your #1 Challenge

Once you've decided *what* you want to change, the next step is to figure out *how* to change it. Traditionally, this is where people get into trouble. Remember the scenario about the mess that comes back no matter how many times you clean it up? That's because the pile is the symptom, not the cause, of the real problem. And a single symptom can have multiple possible causes. In order to figure out the right one, you need to look deep into the heart of the thing that's bothering you and ask why.

Why *Is This Bothering Me?*
If you've ever had a conversation with a three-year-old, you know the power of this short question. As soon as you offer your best answer to something like, "Why is the sky blue?" the child asks again, "Why?" Each succeeding answer gets the same response: "Why?" A child can drive you crazy with this tactic! Yet it's the best and only way to get to the real problem behind an organizing mess. If you ask "Why?" not just once, but over and over again, you'll finally get down to the crux of the matter. When you do, you'll hear yourself thinking, "Aha!" The thing that elicits the "Aha!" is the *real* issue (see Figure I.3). When you solve it, you will make the pile go away and stay away.

Let's use a common mess as an example. When I asked three different clients the question, "What one thing bothers you the most?" all three gave me the same answer: a dining room table that's always covered with papers. Same problem, right? No! Same *symptom*, but different problems. Listen to Tess's answers to my "Why?" questions:

Figure 1.3 Aha! Lightbulb

Q: What bothers you the most?

A: My dining room table drives me crazy. We can't eat on it anymore.

Q: Why?

A: I pay my bills on it, it's always covered with piles of stuff, and it takes too long to clear it.

Q: Why do you pay your bills there?

A: I don't have anywhere else to do them.

Q: Why don't you do them at your desk?

A: I don't have a desk.

Q: Why don't you have a desk?

A: I'm staying home with my kids, and since I'm not working, I didn't think I needed one. Oh! You mean, I need a desk even though I don't have an outside job anymore?

Aha! The crux of the matter for Tess is that she didn't have the proper equipment to support the job of bill-paying and managing her household (*#4, Use the Right Containers and Tools*). We solved her problem by getting her a desk and putting it in the family room where she could pay the bills and still interact with her husband and children.

Now here's Pam with the same symptom, but a completely different cause:

Q: What bothers you the most?

A: My dining room table. We don't need it for dining, but it's always covered with papers and it looks so awful.

Q: Why is it covered with papers?

A: I do all my work in here instead of in the office down the hall.

Q: Why don't you work in your office?

A: That's where my file cabinets and my reference materials are, but I like working in the room next to the kitchen.

Q: Why don't you put your file cabinets in here so you have a place to put the papers away?

A: But it's the dining room! Oh! You mean it's okay to keep my file cabinets in here?

Aha! The bottom line for Pam was a problem with labeling (#5, *Label Everything*). Because she thought of the room as "the dining room," it had never occurred to her to equip it as an office. As soon as she started calling it "the office," she was able to furnish it with office equipment and put all her papers away neatly.

The final example to illustrate how a single symptom can have multiple causes is Jeanne:

Q: What bothers you the most?

A: My dining room table. It's such an eyesore because it's always heaped with mail and papers and files.

Q: Why are all these papers here?

A: I pay the bills and manage my investments here instead of at my desk.

Q: Why don't you use your desk?

A: I just finished renovating the downstairs and I have a wonderful new office down there, but I haven't been able to use it because it's full of boxes from my aunt's estate.

Q: Why did you put your aunt's things in your new office?

A: Because the garage is full of stuff I've been meaning to give away, but haven't gotten to yet. Oh! You mean, if I get the give-away stuff out of the garage, I can move my aunt's boxes in there, and then I can do the paperwork in my office?

Aha! For Jeanne, the real issue was that her storage space was overflowing into the rest of the house. She had been moving things into the garage to give them away, but she hadn't actually gotten them out of the house. Once she cleaned out the garage (*#7, Decide to Decide*), all the other stuff could be stored properly, and she could move her papers from the dining room into her new office.

With these examples in mind, let's turn our attention back to you. Think about your #1 Challenge. Why does *this one thing* bother you the most? What is the heart of the matter? Why haven't you been able to solve this problem? If you're like Tess and Pam and Jeanne, the answer to these questions may be buried several layers beneath the surface. After all, if your #1 Challenge were easy to address, you would have taken care of it by now, wouldn't you? So let's apply the toddler's tactic.

First, ask yourself *why* this issue upsets you. Then listen carefully to the answer that comes back. If you want to, write it down. This answer is the first layer of your #1 Challenge. Now repeat the process again, asking "Why?" about the answer you just gave. Does another response come back? Write it down, too. It's the second layer of your #1 Challenge. Look carefully at this short list. If you addressed the issues in these two answers, would your #1 Challenge be solved? Probably not. It's not at the top of your problem list for nothing! So repeat the process. Ask another "Why?" about the second item on your list, write down the answer, and take a hard look at it. Keep asking questions until you have nothing more to ask and every answer is written down.

Take a moment to study the list you've just created. It shows, in detail, the layered issues that have fused together to create your top organizing dilemma. If you address each item on this list, you will make your #1 Challenge go away. This is your "To Solve" list (see Tess's "To Solve" List on page 30 for an example).

Now, even if you don't feel quite ready, it's time to dive headfirst into the Nine Strategies of Reasonably Organized People. The book will build on your objective appraisal, help you figure out which strategy will fix each item on your "To Solve" list, and give you the tools and information you need to clear up your #1 Challenge.

Each of the next nine chapters focuses on a single strategy. Every chapter starts with a brief *overview* of the concept, then gives you a *symptom* list describing the kinds of messes that grow when this strategy is not being followed. If one of the symptoms resembles an item on your "To Solve" list, you'll know this strategy is an important one for you. Remember, the same symptom can be caused by several different strategies, so don't be surprised to see some of them on more than one list.

The second section of each chapter illustrates the strategy using *real-life stories* taken from my experience as a professional organizer. Wearing the Eyes of a Stranger, we'll peek into other people's lives to see how the strategy affects them. The stories run the gamut from simple applications of the concept to a *full-blown crisis* in which the absence of the strategy has created major chaos. As you read them, you may encounter situations similar to the ones you saw in your own home during the appraisal process. You'll see how people's systems got out of sync with their lives and what they did to solve their problems. You may even stumble across an "Aha!" for yourself.

The final section in the chapter includes *specific tips* to help you apply the strategy to your overall organizing system. The tips reinforce the points highlighted in the real-life stories and offer additional ideas to help you put the strategy to work for you. This section is designed to stand alone so you can refer back to it as an ongoing resource. Along with the *self-evaluation questions* found in Appendix A, the tips will help you keep your system running smoothly.

Tess's "To Solve" List

Tess was doing all her family's paperwork on the dining room table. The questions and answers on her "To Solve" list looked like this:

Q: #1 Problem?
A: My dining room table is a mess.

Q: Why?
A: I do all my family's paperwork on it.

Q: Why?
A: I don't have a desk.

Q: Why?
A: I didn't think I needed one because I don't work outside my home.

Q: You need one. Where should it go?
A: I like to pay bills in the family room, where my husband and kids are.

Q: Is that the best place?
A: As long as I can keep the papers put away neatly, that's the best place.

By the time you finish reading this book, you'll see your situation with the crystal clarity of the Eyes of a Stranger, and you'll know just how to put the Nine Strategies of Reasonably Organized People to work *for you*. Then you can make some headway with your #1 Challenge and start to bring your organizing system back in line with your life.

Remember—the whole point of this book and the Nine Strategies of Reasonably Organized People is to give you the tools to get and stay *organized enough* to handle all the changes, major and minor, that life is going to throw your way.

CHAPTER 1 | **STRATEGY #1**

Make Your Systems Fit You and Your Life

The elements that make up your overall organizing system must be designed to fit the way you actually live, or they won't work. Getting them to function smoothly for you is the foremost consideration. Other values, such as aesthetics, expense, sentiment, or fashion, need to come after utility.

Overview of Strategy #1

Whenever you find yourself struggling with a tangible, physical organizing problem, your first challenge is to figure out what part of your system has broken down. Perhaps your closet is full of clothes you never wear. Maybe you're drowning in a sea of miscellaneous papers. Or it could be you've just moved and you can't find an essential item. No matter what the exact dilemma is, any mess that's causing you a problem is a sure sign that your organizing system and your life are no longer on the same track. The presence of a pile lets you know one or more of the Nine Strategies of Reasonably Organized People is missing from your system.

Strategy #1, Make Your Systems Fit You and Your Life, is the first step toward figuring out what isn't working. It helps you design a new framework for your organizing system. By putting on the Eyes of a Stranger and looking objectively at your life (see pages 21 to 23), you've already started applying it. The appraisal tour told you what your current life looks like. Now you need to find the gaps in your organizing system, then determine which of the Nine Strategies will fill them in. As you identify the missing strategies and take steps to reinstate them, you'll bring your systems back into line with your life. The result is a freshly designed organizing system that fits the way you're living right now.

Symptoms That Your System Doesn't Fit You or Your Life

The most obvious mismatch between a person and his or her system happens when life progresses but the system stays the same. If you, like the people described in the Introduction, have experienced major life changes and your system hasn't kept up, *Strategy #1* is an issue for you. The symptoms of a mismatch caused by life-changing events look like this:

- You've stopped doing things you used to do, but you still have the stuff for those activities and your space is set up as if they're still important to you.
- You've started doing new activities, but the things that go with them are piled up in corners and on flat surfaces because they don't have their own space yet.
- You feel nostalgic about activities or relationships you enjoyed in the past. Even though they're over or gone, you find yourself hanging on to every tangible memento of those experiences and people.
- You're anticipating a major life event in the future, and you don't want to commit to any organizing projects until after that. Your current life is on hold.

A second type of person-to-system mismatch occurs when the organizing system is set up to function in one way, and the person who uses it actually operates in a different way. Every individual has a unique set of skills, habits, learning patterns, and natural tendencies. If your organizing system requires a different skill set than you actually have, it won't fit you well enough to work smoothly. (For help in figuring out your personal skill set, see Appendix B: "What's Your Organizing Style?") Here are the symptoms to look for if you think your organizing system requires a different skill set than you actually have:

- You have a perfectly good dresser, but your clothes are draped on chairs and doors instead of put away in the drawers.
- You have a perfectly good file cabinet, but there are piles of paper on every flat surface in your office.
- You have a perfectly good planner, but you don't write all your appointments in it and you never use some of the sections.
- You have a perfectly good _____ (choose any common organizing tool), but you don't like to use it.

A third common mismatch occurs when someone designs a system to support one set of activities, then tries to use it to do something completely different. If you've ever worked hard to get things a certain way, then figured out later that your carefully planned setup wasn't what you really needed after all, this type of mismatch applies to you. When your system is designed to support one set of activities but you're using it to do something completely different, you'll find these symptoms:

- You have beautifully designed rooms in your house that you never use.
- Your furniture looks great, but it's either uncomfortable (if it's

upholstered) or it doesn't hold the things you need it to hold
(if it's wood).

- There's no place in your home that's set up for activities you
  must take care of, so you try to get them done in places designed for other functions.
- You have a hobby you love, but there's no permanent place for
  it in your home, so you have to put your projects away as soon
  as you're through working on them (which means you rarely
  get them out in the first place).

The final type of mismatch between person and system is more
subtle than the first three, but just as powerful. It happens when
there's something about your setup that you intensely dislike. Even
though we're not conscious of it all the time, our five senses are constantly sending us messages and letting us know when something is
amiss in our environment. If you're getting subconscious warning
signals from your surroundings, they will keep you off balance and
prevent you from operating efficiently. Here are the symptoms to
look out for:

- You concentrate all your activity into two or three rooms because the rest of them somehow make you feel uncomfortable
  or unsettled or nervous.
- It's much easier for you to function in your home and get
  things done during the day than at night.
- You've set up a reasonably designed space for a specific activity,
  but you actually do that activity somewhere else.
- You don't invite people over because your house feels crowded
  and confining rather than expansive and welcoming.

If you encountered any of these symptoms during your appraisal,
it's time to redesign your organizing system using *Strategy #1*. The

real-life stories in the next section will help you answer two key questions:

1. Where are the gaps between your system and your life?
2. What can you do to get things back in line?

Put on your Eyes of a Stranger, get yourself comfortable, and take a look at how other people have applied *Strategy #1*.

Real-Life Lessons:
Strategy #1 Missing in Action

As a performance artist, Maya books engagements months in advance. She sets aside blocks of time in two- or three-day chunks for each gig. Because she is a visual person who understands her calendar best in several-month chunks, Maya created a handmade folding insert for her planner that showed the next six months on a single long page. Each separate engagement was color coded on the calendar, allowing her to see clearly which days were booked and which were still free. For Maya, this format worked quite well. Yet she asked me if I knew some easy way to get the information off the fold-out calendar and into the week-at-a-glance boxes in her planner. When I asked her why she wanted to do this, she replied, "My planner is set up with each day as a box, so I thought I needed to fill them in."

Because Maya's planner divided the calendar into a different grid than the one in her head, Maya had been making work for herself by recording the same schedule of engagements in two different formats. I encouraged her to give the planner up entirely and stick with the visual calendar that matched her personal sense of time. She also created a computerized version of her pen-and-ink grid so it would be easy to print out new fold-out pages.

Don't try to tailor yourself to fit your system. This just creates extra work and is enormously frustrating and nonproductive. Instead, tailor your systems to fit you. Design them so they support the ways you think and work. (See Appendix B: "What's Your Organizing Style?")

Shannon, in preparation for the birth of her second child, called for help getting her spare bedroom cleared out and cleaned up. She had no trouble making decisions to give away any of the household items accumulating on the beds, but the closet was a different story. It was full of formal work clothes Shannon had worn in her preparenting life as a full-time accountant. Since her son's birth four years before, Shannon had changed to part-time work in a much less formal setting, so she no longer needed this wardrobe (not to mention that the clothes no longer fit). Standing side-by-side and staring into the closet, we discussed why it was so difficult for Shannon to let go of clothes she wasn't using, even though they were getting in her family's way. It became clear that Shannon's real issue was her nostalgia, not for the clothes themselves, but for what they represented—her life as a young, single, successful professional with no parental responsibilities. In giving up her old work clothes, she was grieving for the permanent loss of that period of her life.

Ultimately, she decided to pick one or two nice pieces of clothing to keep as a sentimental reminder of her young, carefree days and to give the rest of the clothes away so someone else might be able to enjoy them as she had. This way, she could evoke her nostalgia without having her mementos take up space her growing family needed.

Don't let sentimental collections take up space needed by people. Cull the collection to a few cherished items so you can evoke the nostalgia without using up a lot of room. Allow yourself to grieve, then let go.

Brad is a clothing salesman who owns a much larger wardrobe than his wife has. In the master bedroom, all but two of the drawers in the matching dresser and dressing table are filled with Brad's underclothes and T-shirts. In a small room down the hall, he keeps the remainder of his clothes: sweaters in neatly folded stacks, slacks and dress shirts on portable clothing racks, and suits in the closet. Every morning, Brad walks the equivalent of a mile just to get dressed. He makes multiple trips between his dressers, the bathroom, and his private dressing room to assemble an outfit suitable for a man in the business of selling clothes. When Brad and his wife asked me for some help figuring out how to make this morning task less onerous, I suggested they move the larger dresser from the master bedroom into the room down the hall so all his clothes were in one place. Brad's wife objected in a shocked tone, saying, "But the dresser matches the bed!"

In this example, the factor governing the placement of the dresser was *not* Brad's need for a suitable container for his clothes. Instead, Brad was being noticeably inconvenienced *every day* in order to satisfy the decorating assumption that a suite of bedroom furniture belonged in the same room. Aesthetics were getting in the way of the person. We solved the problem by referring to the two rooms, master bedroom and adjacent dressing room, as the "master suite." This meant the furniture could be spread between the two rooms but still be considered a functional unit, and Brad could get dressed in the morning without walking a mile.

The needs of the people in your life are more important than the aesthetics of the furniture or the decor. If the design is getting in the way of the people, it needs to be changed. Create your design to support the people, then make it beautiful—not the other way around. Make the form follow the function.

Emma is an active mother of two young children who volunteers at her children's schools and participates in a lively mothers' club. Since she and her husband began a trial separation, she's been working as a part-time consultant. The income from her consulting work more than replaces the money she previously earned selling cosmetics and Tupperware from her home. Yet Emma's dining room, file cabinet, and garage are still devoted to the remaining inventory from these past businesses.

Even though Emma and her husband haven't decided whether they will reconcile or divorce, it is clear she has moved beyond the home-based businesses that used to be a source of income and entertainment for her. We set up a plan for clearing out her leftover inventory and freeing the space in her dining room, file cabinet, and garage for the expanding activities of her growing, active children.

When you're finished with a job, a project, or an activity, it's important to allow yourself the time you need to clear away the things (paper, equipment, furniture) that go with it. Otherwise, those things will get in your way as your life moves on. Don't let the debris from past activities clog up your space so there's no room for the things you're doing now.

Gordon's large wraparound desk was covered with piles of paper even though his well-equipped office had multiple file cabinets with room for more file folders. After we weeded through everything, discarded all the obsolete or unnecessary papers, and filed things in the proper file drawers, he still had a collection of eight stacks spaced neatly across his large work surface. When I asked him why he hadn't put these papers into folders in his cabinet, he said, "They're for projects I'm actively working on. If I put them away, I won't remember that I need to do things with them. But if I leave them spread out like this, they're always in my way."

In Gordon's mind, file cabinets were workable containers for archival items, but not for things he was currently using. He needed visual cues to keep his projects moving forward. The design of his office storage did not match his skill set. We solved the problem by putting each of the remaining paper piles into a boldly labeled file folder and standing them up in an open steel desktop file next to the central work surface. That way, the papers were still on the desktop and easy to see, but they took up much less space and left the desktop clear for work in progress.

If you're a visual person who needs to see something to remember that it exists, set up your systems so you can keep things orderly and visible at the same time. Don't fool yourself into thinking that you'll be able to function with closed containers. Find the right containers for you and use them. (See *Strategy #4, Use the Right Containers and Tools*, for ideas.)

Robin is recovering from a painful divorce that forced her to move from her lovely suburban home into a townhouse. A full-time professional who spends most of her time at the office, Robin actively avoids going home. She eats out every night, takes her newspaper to a local coffee shop each morning, and meets friends at restaurants instead of inviting them to her house. Her living space is furnished, but it feels cold, sterile, and unlived-in.

When Robin is ready, she will begin to take the steps required to transform the townhouse from a mere shell of a dwelling into a home. In the meantime, it's been hard for her to manage routine tasks like paying bills and doing laundry because these are at-home functions. We set up a portable file container with a space for office supplies so she could pay her bills at the coffee shop, and I encouraged her to send her clothing out for laundering as well as dry cleaning.

Sometimes it just takes time to work through the emotions that go with life-changing events. It's okay to set up a temporary system to handle must-do chores like paying bills, as long as you acknowledge that it's a stop-gap measure and won't hold up well in the long run.

Angie is a consultant who runs her business from her home. She wasn't getting any work done because she hated working in her home office. When she hired me, we went straight into her office to figure out what was wrong. At first glance, no major problem was apparent. The desk was set at right angles to the left wall and faced the doorway. The light from the single wide window fell invitingly on the work surface. There was a large file cabinet for storage behind the desk, and the far wall was solid bookshelves. However, as soon as Angie sat in her desk chair to show me how she usually used the space, the problem became glaringly obvious.

Angie's file cabinet was a high-quality four-drawer model painted black. It was a vertical file (V), not a horizontal one (H), so it protruded from the wall rather than running along it (see Figure 1.1). When Angie was sitting at her desk, this large, dark, heavy piece of furniture was looming about fifteen inches behind her right ear. Even though Angie didn't consciously perceive her file cabinet as forebod-

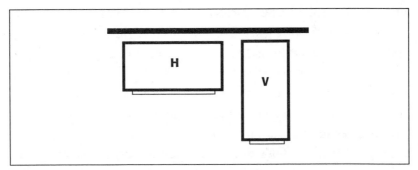

Figure 1.1 File Cabinets

ing or dangerous, her subconscious was telling her it wasn't safe to sit in her office chair. The file cabinet's ominous presence was triggering an ancient flight response and sending Angie away into the comparative safety of her living room.

Fortunately, Angie was able to swap the offending file cabinet for a better one right away. As soon as she installed her new putty-colored four-drawer horizontal cabinet, she was able to use her office quite comfortably. The new unit's light color and orientation along the wall allowed it to blend into the background and kept it from being threatening.

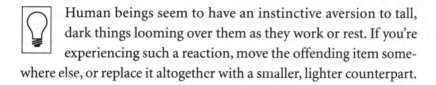

Human beings seem to have an instinctive aversion to tall, dark things looming over them as they work or rest. If you're experiencing such a reaction, move the offending item somewhere else, or replace it altogether with a smaller, lighter counterpart.

Another client who used the words "I hate my office" to describe her biggest organizing dilemma taught me another variation on the same theme. A consultant and writer who did much of her work from home, Barbara had moved from a one-bedroom apartment into a larger one because she wanted to separate her office from her bedroom. Even though her desk, printer, reference books, and files were in her new office, she was actually doing all her work on the kitchen table. When I asked Barbara to talk about her office so we could figure out why she wasn't using it, she said the room felt oppressive and she just didn't want to be in there, especially at night.

In the office itself, Barbara's desk was against one of the side walls. Above it, attached to the wall, was a tiny lamp, the type one might have over a bed for reading at night. When I asked Barbara to show me how she used her desk, she sat down and turned on the tiny wall lamp. The glow from its bulb was so dim it cast a circle of light only about two feet across. The only other artificial light in the room was a central overhead fixture with a long pull-string. Even when it was on, its single bulb did little to brighten the room.

During the day, the two windows kept Barbara's office bright and cheerful. But at night, the windows became black holes and the electric lights were woefully incapable of adequately lighting the room. At night, Barbara's office was so dark it was like a cave. No wonder she didn't want to be in there!

We solved the problem by putting the brightest possible bulb in the ceiling fixture, using a tall floor lamp to bounce bright light off the ceiling and illuminate the entire room, and adding a desk lamp to brighten Barbara's work surface. With shades, she was able to cover the windows at night, adding privacy and coziness. Right away, she moved her work from the kitchen into the office.

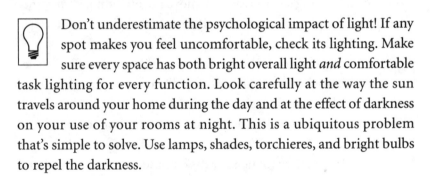

Don't underestimate the psychological impact of light! If any spot makes you feel uncomfortable, check its lighting. Make sure every space has both bright overall light *and* comfortable task lighting for every function. Look carefully at the way the sun travels around your home during the day and at the effect of darkness on your use of your rooms at night. This is a ubiquitous problem that's simple to solve. Use lamps, shades, torchieres, and bright bulbs to repel the darkness.

Anita and Jayne are examples of two people experiencing the same problem from opposite ends of the spectrum. Anita's family is a lively, active bunch with lots of ongoing projects. They use every square inch of their home except the living room. At the front of their house, the living room is set up with comfortable chairs and couches around a large television set. Yet the room seems unused, with none of the clutter and bustle apparent in every other space in the home. When I asked whether the family watched television in the living room, as the setup would indicate, Anita smiled ruefully and replied, "Well, that's what we thought we'd do in here, and this is our biggest television, but we end up watching the small set in the family room instead of coming in here." When I asked her why, she answered, "We like to watch television in the evenings, and it's so much cozier and more private in our family room than in here. This room is too public for us when we're just here by ourselves."

Jayne has the opposite issue. Even though she has a well-appointed office in one corner of her large home, she does all her paperwork and bill-paying at the kitchen table. For her, managing her family's scheduling and financial affairs is a daytime job that she wants to do in the lively center of her house, not at one quiet end. That way, she can simultaneously prepare meals, see anyone who approaches her front door, and get her paperwork done.

For Anita, the task was to rearrange the living room to make it a functional place for some of her family's other activities. By closing the curtains at night, improving the lighting, and incorporating a table with chairs, they could make it into a family space they would regularly use without sacrificing it as the room for entertaining company.

For Jayne, we didn't need to convert the office into space for another function because her family already had room for all its activities. Instead, we bought a rolling file cart for her so she could wheel it from the office into the kitchen when she was paying bills, then wheel it back into the office when she was finished. The permanent file cabinet stayed in the office. This created the proper support for paperwork in the kitchen, but allowed Jayne to cook or entertain without having to operate around her papers.

 A subtle thing that will keep you from using your home to fully support your life occurs when you set up a public space to hold an activity you actually think of as private *or* you try to fit the tools for a public function into a private space. Be aware of your own feelings about public and private activities when you're setting up your organizing systems. Public activities seem to feel most comfortable to people when they're in the front and/or the center of the home. Private functions work best at the back and/or the ends.

Grace lives alone in a small, cozy apartment. She has turned it into her personal haven, using luscious fabrics and carefully chosen knickknacks, candles, flowers, and perfume to create a warm, welcoming environment. Her three rooms—living room, kitchen, and bedroom—all have nooks and gables that invite her to sit, relax, and be comfortable. The only problem with this charming home was that Grace had given herself no place to efficiently manage her paperwork. She called me to help her dig out all the old bills and bank statements she'd been squirreling away into closets and eaves so we could assemble her receipts and file her taxes.

For Grace, the mundane but necessary activities of paying bills and managing her financial affairs seemed jarringly out of place in her cozy rooms. Our challenge was to figure out how she could incorporate the practical tools of effective record-keeping into her lovely surroundings without corrupting the soothing ambiance of her home. For Grace, the key to getting her paperwork under control was a rolling file cart holding her bank statements, bills, receipts, and office supplies. She could keep it in her coat closet, then wheel it out when she needed it. This would give her a way to manage her finances without turning her home into a utilitarian office.

Make sure you have a functional setup for activities you must do, like managing your paperwork. If you don't, you're still going to have stuff that goes with the activity, but it will be floating around cluttering up your space because it can't be put away. Make a place for everything you need so it's at least *possible* to put away.

Sophie lived with her husband and two children in a beautiful home overlooking a lake. She entertained often, was able to afford decorators and cleaners and gardeners, and took great pride in her family and her home. She called me because papers—schoolwork, artwork, photographs, mail, bills, flyers, craft projects, office and art supplies, and financial records—were taking over her kitchen. One six-foot-long counter was devoted to a disheveled row of stuffed folders standing up against the wall and topped by rickety piles of loose papers; the newspaper was spread out over the table; and papers were stuck in every nook and cranny.

The first thing I asked Sophie to do was show me her desk. She led me into her gracious living room and pointed to a beautiful antique with inlaid woods, gracefully carved legs, and three small drawers. Its top was also heaped with papers, including a small army of bulging photograph envelopes. When I suggested that part of the paper problem came from having a desk that didn't have a single file drawer, Sophie said, "But I want to use this one because it's so beautiful." My response was, "It would be even more beautiful if it weren't covered with this ugly pile of papers."

For Sophie, the crux of the matter was that the beautiful antique she thought of as her desk was completely unsuitable for the role she needed her desk to play. She needed a work surface and corresponding storage located in or next to her kitchen if she wanted to really be able to handle the deluge of papers entering her home every day. Instead, she had a desk that was lovely and valuable as an objet d'art, but useless for storing or handling papers, and it was located in a room that was never used for paper processing.

Sophie was about to remodel her kitchen. She incorporated plans for a workable desk with file drawers and storage shelves into her new kitchen's design. Her antique desk could then be cleaned off and admired as part of her living room decor.

If you select elements of your organizing system based on their beauty, without regard to their functionality, their beauty will quickly be obscured by a growing mess. Think about what you want the elements to accomplish, set them up with optimum functionality in mind, then (and only then) make them beautiful. This will work much better for you in the long run.

What a Full-Blown Strategy #1 Crisis Looks Like

In the preceding stories, the main characters were having trouble on a small scale because of a mismatch between their organizing systems and their lives. The solutions to the specific issues were reasonably easy to put in place. But what happens when a person's life and organizing system are so out of sync it affects them in multiple ways instead of just a few? What does a *Strategy #1* crisis look like?

The person whose story best illustrates the chaos that ensues when the life and the organizing system are almost completely out of whack is Leo, the electrical engineer from pages 2 to 4 who was reeling from the combined effects of sudden unemployment, divorce, a move to much smaller quarters, and the death of both his parents.

When Leo's life changed dramatically, it affected every facet of his overall organizing system. The only places where Leo had been able to follow *Strategy #1* and make his systems fit his life were the kitchen, the bedroom, and the bathroom. In those three rooms, he was set up to function efficiently. Everywhere else, chaos ruled. The old systems had been obliterated by the move and the change in Leo's fortunes, and new systems had not yet been put in place. Because the job of getting things sorted out, organized, and back under control was so overwhelming, Leo waited until he was financially and emotionally ready to get started. Then he gathered his courage and called me.

Obviously, getting Leo's life back in order was a major project. It had taken time to create the chaos, and it was going to take time to recover from it. We began by using *Strategy #1* to build the framework for a whole new organizing system. First we did an appraisal, touring the house from top to bottom to get a clear picture of Leo's room layout, furniture, and belongings. I acted as Leo's Eyes of a Stranger by asking him questions in every room. Here's what we found:

Space: Leo had been forced to move from his fourteen-room home, which had a separate carriage house and workshop, into a six-room house with a carport and no workshop space at all. He had enough furniture for his major activities, but it was scattered in a fairly haphazard way throughout the house. His bedroom was the only room in the house with a functional furniture arrangement.

Things: Leo's collection of tools and materials, which he needed in order to work and support himself, was spread out among the two spare bedrooms in his new house, a spacious but unheated warehouse space four miles away, and a rented storage area. The house was stuffed with things he had inherited from both his parents, along with the piles of personal belongings he'd brought from his old home. He didn't have room to put everything away even if he wanted to, so it was almost impossible to find anything easily.

Information: In his previous employment as an engineering executive, Leo had a secretary who maintained his collections of scientific information. He had set up his extensive files in one spare bedroom's closet, but they were hard to get to because the door was blocked by piles of boxes. If he climbed over things to get out a file, it was so hard to return it that he just left it out, where it melted into the general mess. Because he didn't have a steady source of income, Leo couldn't afford a new computer, and the hard drive on his old one was small and almost full. He hadn't filed a tax return for several years because the receipts were scattered everywhere (and there wasn't much income to report, either).

Time: Without a job, Leo had time on his hands, but a lot of it was wasted just trying to find things in the mess. He was able to get part-time work, which allowed him to pay his most pressing bills, but it also kept him out of the house and made it even harder to tackle the enormous and overwhelming task of getting his home sorted out and organized.

Relationships: Even though Leo was blessed with many good friends and a large support network, he had trouble keeping track of all his appointments because, again, they were swallowed up by the general mess in his house. Only a few friends were invited over, and he would clean his living room madly before they arrived, sweeping things into the spare bedrooms and throwing them on the piles. Fortunately, Leo is charming, well educated, a good conversationalist, and a thoughtful friend, so this element did not suffer as much as the other four.

At the end of the tour, Leo knew exactly *what* his physical environment contained. Our next task was to figure out *how* to make it work better. We sat down together and listed Leo's everyday activities, responsibilities, and priorities. Then we compared the list to his actual setup to identify the gaping holes in his organizing system.

Leo needed four crucial functions supported right away: working, keeping track of his finances, living, and storing things. As soon as he was set up to handle these activities, he could operate at a functional level while the long-term organizing project went slowly forward. We applied *Strategy #1* by mapping out where he was going to do each activity.

Leo needed a *functional work space* to make a living. We designated the spare room at the opposite end of the house from Leo's bedroom as his workshop. This separated the public function (work) from the private one (sleeping). Any heavy work requiring large tools would be done at the unheated off-site workshop if it wasn't cold outside.

Leo needed a *functional desk* to handle paperwork. We designated the dining table at one end of the large central living/dining area as the paperwork center. Leo preferred to do paperwork here, in the center of the house, instead of in the spare rooms at either end. On the desktop, we set up a box to catch the mail until it could be opened, a box to catch receipts, and a visible desktop file to hold bills to pay.

Leo needed a *functional storage room* to store unused items. We designated the spare room next to Leo's bedroom as the site for all items not currently being used. All extra shelving units went in here, as well as a tabletop on sawhorses to use for sorting and weeding.

Leo needed a *functional living space* in which to relax and entertain friends. The remainder of the living/dining area was designated as a place for sitting, reading the paper, playing or listening to music, and entertaining guests.

With the map we created firmly in hand, Leo and I spent several sessions moving the furniture so it supported the new design. The resulting setup gave him designated places to put things and allowed him to begin taking charge of his environment and his time. It also laid the groundwork for the sorting (*Strategy #2*) and weeding (*Strategy #3*) that were next on Leo's "To Solve" list. By designing the layout of Leo's home around his actual activities, we used *Strategy #1, Make Your Systems Fit You and Your Life*, to begin turning Leo's life around.

If your life is going through major upheaval, figure out what your must-do tasks are and make sure you have the setup you need to get those things done. When you're ready to get organized again, use the Eyes of a Stranger to see how far your systems have diverged from your life, then design your new structures around the way your life works now.

How to Put Strategy #1 Back in Place

If you recognize that elements from the past are cluttering up your organizing system, or parts of your system don't fit you comfortably, you've identified gaps between your system and your life. To close them, you need to apply *Strategy #1, Make Your Systems Fit You and Your Life*, and create a new organizing plan for yourself.

Use the activities and interests you're actively pursuing today as your guide. The purpose of getting organized is to arrange your life so you can do what you *have to do* and what you *want to do* without wasting time and effort. What space, things, information, and time do you need to support your current activities? Are any of these resources missing? Is anything extra getting in your way? How are your relationships affecting your activities, and vice versa? Think about what you want the five elements of your organizing system to do for you. List your thoughts on paper. This is the beginning of your new design.

Now compare the list to the system you already have. What do you need to change? Which of the Nine Strategies do you need to apply to close the gaps between the old system and the new one? The tips in this section offer concrete ideas to help you answer these questions.

Make Your Space Fit You and Your Life

- Design each space so it supports the things you're actually doing in it.
- Set up the furniture and decor in each space based on how you're using the room.
- Make sure you have a functional setup for all your activities.
- Make a space feel good by adding design elements that appeal to all your senses.

- If a space makes you uncomfortable or uneasy, figure out why and solve the problem.
- Pay attention to the flow of people and things through each space; make it easy.
- Make every space comfortable for the people using it.
- Incorporate the needs of each person who uses a space into its design.
- Don't underestimate the psychological and practical role played by light! Make sure every space is brightly and invitingly lit so you can use it.
- Put public activities in the front and/or the center of your home.
- Move private functions to the back and/or the periphery of your living space.
- Remove or replace tall, dark items that loom over you in places you might like to sit. These include furniture, artwork, drapes, dark paint on surfaces, cupboards, and so forth.
- When you're finished with a project or activity, clear away the things that go with it. Don't let it sit around and get in your way.

Make Your Things Fit You and Your Life

- Don't keep lots of things you aren't using (but keep in mind that having a strong attachment to something is a way of using it).
- Make a place for everything you need so it's at least *possible* to put it away.
- Store things in containers that complement your skill set (i.e., clear containers if you're a visual person).
- If a pile of "stuff" is getting in your way, figure out what's in it

and either contain it in a functional container or move it to a more useful location.

- Store things next to the place where you use them.
- Keep in mind that a major function of your furniture is to store things. Make sure your furniture adequately contains your things. Also, make sure your seating is comfortable for family and guests.
- Don't let sentimental collections take up space needed by people. If a collection is overflowing into your living space, weed it out, store it elsewhere, or let it go.

Make Your Information Fit You and Your Life

- Set up data storage and retrieval systems that match your skills. If you're visual, keep the papers you need in a container that allows you to see them.
- If, in all honesty, you know you aren't going to need a piece of paper again after you've read it, don't put it in a pile—recycle it or throw it out.
- Have one place—a folder, box, file, or large envelope—to collect all your tax information for the year. It doesn't need to be sorted as you go; it just needs to be stored.
- If piles of paper are getting in your way, figure out whether you *really* need them. If you don't, get rid of them. If you do, file them so you can retrieve them later.
- If you don't like your desk, try turning it so its short side is against the wall and you can see the door of the room from the desk chair.
- If you find yourself in the throes of a major life event, set up minimal systems to handle must-do chores like paying bills. Just do the basics until things calm down.

Make Your Time Fit You and Your Life

- Select a calendar that represents time in the way you think of it, then use it every day.
- Make sure your calendar is portable, so you don't neglect to write down all your appointments.
- Schedule your time to meet your priorities. Make sure you aren't neglecting to spend time on things that are important to you.
- Know how long it really takes you to do things, get to often-visited places, and finish important tasks. This allows you to schedule your time accurately.
- Make time for yourself every day, even if it's just ten minutes. Time spent relaxing is *not* time wasted.

Make Your Relationships Fit You and Your Life

- Incorporate the needs of your loved ones into your organizing plan.
- Make time for your most important relationships.
- Spend more time on the people you love than on your space, your things, or your data.
- Don't waste time with people you don't care about or who don't care about you.
- Have regular discussions with your family to talk about how things are working and what needs to be improved.
- Pay attention to the needs of the other people you live with, as well as your own needs.

These suggestions are specifically designed to help you figure out how your organizing system can best support you and the life you're living today. The goals you set for your system using *Strategy #1, Make Your Systems Fit You and Your Life* underlie the remaining Strategies of Reasonably Organized People. As you read about them in the next eight chapters, you'll see how each one helps you shape your organizing system to support your current life.

Now that you've thought about what you want and set down your goals, the next task is to physically move things around to put your new design in place. It's time to go on to *Strategy #2, Sort Everything by How You Use It.*

Sort Everything by How You Use It

Sorting is a basic mechanism for creating order. Effective sorting is based on how each item is used. Things that are used together belong together. Store the items in a collection in one place so you know what you have. Keeping like with like is more functional in every regard than a jumble.

Overview of Strategy #2

If the main idea behind *Strategy #1, Make Your Systems Fit You and Your Life*, is to come up with an organizing design that matches your current life, *Strategy #2, Sort Everything*, is the first step toward putting your new structure in place. By sorting everything to fit the way you're actually using it, you can physically rearrange the elements of your system so they support your activities. Once things that are used together are grouped in the same places, your organizing system will start to work better for you.

Sorting things into categories is a basic human developmental task. It allows us to bring order from chaos. When you divide things into logical groups, it is easier for you to use them, put them away, retrieve them, and share them with others. Conversely, when things are spread out or scattered around or jumbled together, you'll find yourself wasting time just trying to find the items you need. Every task will take longer to accomplish because it will include the time you have to spend searching for your tools and materials.

Sorting is also important in helping you know how much of something you have. If you collect anything—clothes, knickknacks, photographs, magazines, tools, books—it will be hard to keep track of your collection if it's stored in multiple places. Duplicates and overflows can result when a collection is kept spread out instead of in one place. A constantly growing collection can put a real strain on your storage spaces (see What Are *You* Collecting? on page 57).

You might think of sorting as a principle that applies only to things and to data. In my experience, however, it can also be applied to space and time. If things are scattered or jumbled in your space or on your calendar, it will be hard for you to operate efficiently, and you'll always feel as if you're out of control.

Symptoms That Your System Needs Sorting

Let's look at some specific ways the elements of your overall organizing system might be suffering because things you're using together are not kept together.

- Some spaces in your home are holding lots of different activities, while other spaces are left unused.
- You spend most of your time in one or two rooms, and the furniture, data, and supplies that go with multiple activities are spread in messy layers around those spaces.
- Things are jumbled together haphazardly in piles, drawers, closets, and containers around the house.
- Things that you use together are stored in different rooms.

What Are *You* Collecting?

People collect all sorts of things. Almost everyone has a group of special items that could be called a collection. Here are some collectibles I've run across:

Antiques
Baby clothes
Barbies
Batteries
Beanie Babies
Bottles of holy water
Cameras
Catalogs
Change
College term papers
Computer equipment
Cookbooks
Cosmetics
Craft materials
Crow feathers
Depression glass
Empty boxes
Furniture
Gadgets
Greeting cards
Hats
Holiday decorations
Hotel soaps
House plants
Kids' artwork
Kitchen utensils
Leather jackets
Linens
Lingerie
Lionel trains
LPs and/or CDs
Magazines
Mortars and pestles

Mugs
National Geographic magazines
Never-used wedding presents
Newspapers
Odd-sized envelopes
Old letters
Old broken furniture
Old suitcases
Pens and pencils
Pets
Photographs
Pieces of lumber
Pins
Plastic storage containers
Rocks
Rubber bands
Screws and nails
Sets of china
Sewing material
Shaped figurines (all sorts)
Shoes
Souvenir glassware
Sports equipment
Sweaters
Toiletries
Tools
Trading cards
Travel souvenirs
Used file folders
Watches
Wine
Wrapping paper
You name it!

- You constantly find yourself spending precious time looking for things.
- You don't put things away when you're through using them because it's too far or inconvenient.
- Once you put something away, you can't find it again.
- You don't know how much of something you have because the collection is stored in multiple locations around your home.
- You never do an activity you enjoy because gathering the supplies and equipment for it is too time-consuming and difficult.
- Your desk is covered with miscellaneous piles of paper.
- Your kids can't put their toys away themselves.
- Your kids can't find their toys once they're put away.
- You find yourself with lots of little chunks of available time, but no big blocks.
- You spend time duplicating errands because you get home and realize you've forgotten to do something.
- Your furniture and rooms are set up to fit *you*, but they aren't functional for other members of your family.
- You never get to spend time with people who are important to you.

If you recognize any of these symptoms, then your efficiency would improve with an application of *Strategy #2, Sort Everything by How You Use It*. Here are some stories to show you how *Strategy #2* applies in real life.

Real-Life Lessons:
Strategy #2 Missing in Action

 Dana led me right to her stereo when I asked her which pile in her house was bothering her most. The top of its tall narrow stand in one corner of her living room was heaped with loose CDs, audiotapes, empty CD cases, and cassette boxes. A few cassettes and discs had overflowed onto the adjacent sofa and the floor. All of this was clearly visible from the apartment's entry, making it an eyesore to anyone coming in the door.

To figure out why this mess had sprung up, I asked Dana to get a tape and show me how she used the stereo. She turned around, crossed from the living room into the dining room, walked to a bookcase on the far wall, and got a cassette from the collection of tapes on the shelf. Then she returned to the living room, took out the new tape, and put the empty cassette box on top of the pile on the stereo. Pushing the eject button, Dana removed the previous tape from the player and inserted the new one. The old tape went on top of the pile, too, and promptly slithered to the floor as music filled the room.

During this process, Dana's attention was focused on getting the new tape playing. It would have taken extra time to find the empty box for the old tape, put the tape in the box, return across the dining room to put the tape away, then go back to the living room to listen to the music. Tapes, CDs, and empty cases were piled on the stereo because they were stored too far away from where they were being used. The task of putting away the old tape got in the way of listening to the new music, so it just didn't happen.

We solved this problem with a simple solution. We moved the bookcase from the dining room into the living room and stood it right next to the stereo rack. Then the old tape and its empty cassette could be matched up and put away without Dana having to walk a single step, all while the new music was already playing. This made it easy to keep the stereo area neat.

 Store things in the room where you use them. If possible, store them right next to their point of use so it takes no extra motion to put them away. This will prevent piles from growing.

Karen's dining room was a multipurpose area for her family. They primarily used it for homework, art projects, and crafting. Occasionally, they ate there as well. The formal dining table, covered with a thick mat to protect it from paint and glue, took up the entire center of the room. Other furniture lined the walls, leaving fairly narrow walkways even though the room was an active passageway between the kitchen and the living room. All of it—buffet, dish cabinet, and extra chairs—was layered with piles of craft supplies. Two window alcoves were filled with large, opaque plastic bins stacked haphazardly to waist height and overflowing with cloth, beads, ribbons, bric-a-brac, wrapping paper, and so forth. Karen asked for ideas to help her with the crafting materials. She said the bins never seemed to get put away once they were taken out, and the remains of old projects were littering every flat surface in the room, making it cluttered and hard to work in.

When I asked her where the bins were kept when the family wasn't using them, Karen led me to the unheated glassed-in front porch outside her front door. Against the wall of the house, tall shelves held numerous other bins like the ones in the dining room. Every time family members needed craft supplies, they would have to leave the dining room, walk through the living room, go out the front door, get the proper bin, and bring it back through the house to the dining room. This was an especially daunting proposition in the winter, when the temperature dropped below freezing.

Clearly, the distance between the crafting activities and the supplies that went with them was turning the dining room into a jumbled mess. But moving the activities closer to the supplies was not the answer for Karen's family. For them, the dining room worked well as the center of activity. Instead, we focused on moving the supplies closer to the place where they were being used. We discovered that the storage shelves would fit into an alcove in the living room, just around the corner from the crafting table. This alcove could be closed off from the living room with a curtain if company was expected, but would allow the family easy access to the crafting materials they were using all the time. The overall result was to fully support the family's activities by changing the storage system to fit them.

When your system isn't adequately supporting your activities, bringing them physically closer together can solve the problem. Figure out which works best for you—moving the system or moving the activity. Then rearrange things to bring the function and the systems that support it into the same space.

Ginny likes to peruse the stack of catalogs from the day's mail while watching television in the family room every evening. She pages through each one, looking at the tantalizing pictures of things she doesn't need but can imagine having. When she finishes with the stack, she puts it on the coffee table in front of her, intending to take it to the kitchen later for recycling. But by the time her TV show is over, Ginny is usually tired. She often goes straight to bed without taking time to recycle. This leaves a pile of catalogs perpetually teetering on the coffee table, creating an eyesore and getting in her family's way. She asked me for ideas.

What Ginny needs is a recycling bin or basket next to her family room sofa, in addition to the one in the kitchen. This would make it possible to discard the catalogs instantly, without having to go somewhere else to do it.

If you often find yourself getting up from your chair to use something in another room, consider putting a second one of those items next to you. This applies to things like wastebaskets, pens, scissors, tape, and so on. Put the tools you need in the places you need them. Get one for every spot where you use it. Don't make yourself get up over and over again for commonly used items.

Nikita is a four-year-old girl with lots of toys. Her father built her a beautiful toy box in his woodworking shop, and at the end of a hard day of playing, her mother helps her pile her toys back into it. The problem arises when Nikita wants to find a specific toy. She can easily locate larger toys, but if she's looking for a smaller toy, or one she uses less frequently, or something with lots of little pieces, the only way to find what she wants is to tip the whole box on its side and dump its entire contents onto the floor. Then Nikita can spread everything out with her hands, locate the specific thing she's looking for, and take it out to play. This might have the desired result from Nikita's point of view—she found her toy and can play with it—but her parents have to deal with the resulting mess. They consulted with me about better ways to handle Nikita's playthings.

Several problems arise when you try to keep a varied collection of things—in this case, toys—in a single large container. First, all the small things trickle down through the container until they land in a mingled layer on the bottom. The larger items stay at the top of the container, effectively blocking your view of everything underneath. Even when you can see the bottom, it's hard to pick the one small thing you want out of the scramble. Finally, the only way to retrieve anything from the lower layers in the mix is to root through the whole mess until you find what you're looking for. Sometimes, as with Nikita's toys, this requires you to dump out the entire contents of the box. By the time you finally find the object of your search, you've made a big mess. The only good thing about a jumble in a large container is that at least it's easy to put things back in.

To make it possible for Nikita to find a specific toy without totally trashing her room, we started by sorting her toys into groups that made sense to her. In one pile, we put the little plastic figures. Her dishes and kitchen utensils went into another group. A third category held her dress-up jewelry. Gradually, we transformed the toy box jumble into a set of orderly piles. Then, based on the size of each pile, we selected an appropriately sized clear bin to contain it. Finally, we labeled the open bins and put them on low shelves. The end result? Nikita could see each collection of toys, neatly retrieve the single toy or group of toys she wanted to play with, and put toys away in the proper containers by herself. The new system also allowed Nikita to begin to control her own belongings, even at the tender age of four.

Don't keep things jumbled together in large containers. Instead, separate them into logical categories according to how you use them and store them in appropriately sized smaller containers. This makes it much easier to find things, retrieve them, and put them away.

Olivia and Quinn had just moved into a three-bedroom apartment. Both had demanding full-time jobs, with little time to spend setting up their new home. Because the new apartment was bigger than the old one, they didn't have quite enough furniture to adequately equip the space. And this apartment was so different in layout and configuration from their previous one that Olivia was feeling at a loss about how to organize it. So their boxes, furniture, and equipment were placed randomly among the six rooms, and their clothes, papers, books, and portable belongings were haphazardly strewn everywhere. Olivia consulted me for professional advice on how to turn this hodgepodge into a comfortable, workable home.

Even though the apartment *looked* like a big problem, the solution was simple and quick. First, Olivia and I sat down together and listed the activities she and Quinn were doing in their home. Then we looked at the available space and decided which functions would work best in each room. The next step was to sort the furniture and equipment for each activity into its designated room and set them up. The last step was to unpack the boxes and put away all the portable items as close to their point of use as possible.

At the end of two days, the two of us had turned the apartment from a disaster zone into a home. The living room was set up for entertaining, listening to music, and watching television. Next to it, the dining room held the formal table, chairs, and dish cabinet on one side, and a roomy desk, the computer, and a file cabinet on the other. In the kitchen, food, utensils, dishes, small appliances, and pots and pans were stored in the cupboards next to where Olivia was using them. Seldom-used items were placed on shelves in the back hallway just outside the kitchen. A small table gave Quinn and Olivia a spot for casual meals. In the master bedroom, the closets and dressers held all the couple's clothing, neatly sorted onto hangers and into drawers. The second bedroom was set up for guests, and spare coats hung in its closet. The third bedroom, off the dining room, had been transformed into a music room where Quinn could play his keyboards and guitars. Off-season clothes filled its generous closet. Even the basement, formerly a riotous mess of boxes and books, was cleared up and organized. Throughout Quinn and Olivia's home, sorting had created order from chaos.

Sort your furniture, equipment, and things into rooms according to the way you use your space. When a space contains everything you need to support all the activities you're doing there, it will work well for you.

Besides managing her own part-time business, Faith is in charge of a very busy family. Her three school-age children are involved in all kinds of activities, from sports to music to dance, on top of their homework and school responsibilities. Faith is their chauffeur, purchasing agent, chaperone, and cheerleader. She and her husband entertain regularly, support local political causes, and volunteer their time at not-for-profit community organizations. Faith called me because her schedule was overwhelming her, and she wanted some time management ideas.

The problem with Faith's schedule was obvious to both of us. She was trying to cram more activity into each day than she could reasonably handle. And no matter what she did, she couldn't buy herself any extra time. She had the same twenty-four hours as everyone else. So Faith knew the solution to her crazy schedule was to *weed* it out and stop *doing* some of the things currently on her plate. We used sorting to help her figure out which activities to keep doing and which to discontinue.

If you take a close look at your daily activities, you can sort them by whether or not you *have* to do them. Another way to sort the same activities is to decide whether or not you *want* to do them. But the most powerful way for dividing your time is to combine these two categories into a single chart I call the Require/Desire Grid (see Figure 2.1).

Faith and I made a list of all her activities, from time-consuming items, like making meals and driving kids around, to mundane tasks, like dropping shirts at the cleaners and calling doctors to make appointments. Then we started plugging each activity into the grid. The hardest part for Faith was to acknowledge that some of the things she thought of as "had-to-do" were really "want-to-do" activities. For instance, she didn't *have* to sew a new Halloween costume for each child, even though she wanted to. By the time we had everything sorted, it was clear Faith's "Don't Want To/Don't Have To" box had too many things in it. This gave her the information she needed to extricate herself from some of her activities, thus allowing her to ease up on her schedule and build in a little down time (see Figure 2.2 for an example of a filled-in grid).

If you find yourself with too many activities to handle effectively, make time to sort what you're doing into your own Require/Desire Grid. Anything that falls into your "Don't Have To/Don't Want To" box is something to stop doing. Sorting your activities gives you information with which you can make good decisions.

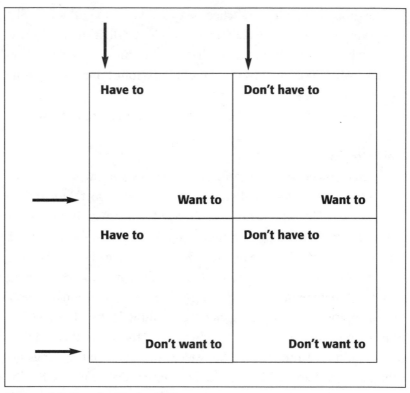

Figure. 2.1 Require/Desire Grid

Claire was about to move across the country for a year to work on an exciting but temporary project. She wanted to take some of her belongings with her and leave the rest in storage until she returned. She asked me for help sorting through her things in preparation for the move. As Claire showed me around her house, opening closets and drawers so I could see what she had, we discovered clothes stashed in every nook and cranny. The rest of Claire's belongings—furniture, papers, kitchen supplies, office equipment, books—seemed to be present in reasonable quantities for a single person. But she had many more articles of clothing than any one per-

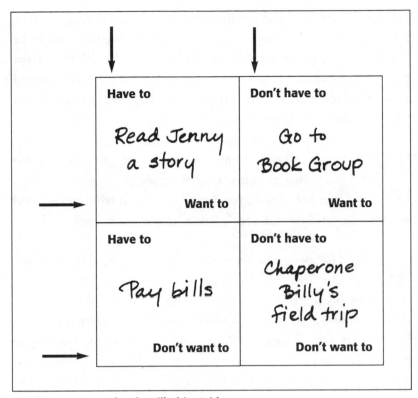

Figure. 2.2 Example of a Filled-in Grid

son could possibly need, and they were spread all around her house.

The first thing Claire and I had to do to make it *possible* to sort the clothes was get them all in one place so we could see exactly what she had. If she knew she had six black sweaters, it would be easier for her to give four of them away and only keep her favorite two. But if she didn't know what the entire collection contained, it would be hard for her to decide to give anything away. So we turned Claire's spare bedroom into a giant closet, set up temporary clothing racks, and went searching for every article of clothing we could find. Once they were all in the same room, we began sorting and weeding. Claire gave away dozens of garbage bags full of sweaters, dresses, jackets, skirts, lingerie, and accessories. By the time she moved, her wardrobe had been culled down to a reasonable collection of lovely things that not only fit her, but made her look great. She didn't have to spend money to move a bunch of things she couldn't or wouldn't wear, and she didn't have to pay to store them either.

Sorting is not only a mechanism for bringing order, it also helps lay the groundwork for weeding out a collection. It is much easier to make good decisions about what to keep and what to discard if you can see the entire collection at once.

After twenty-two years of marriage, Celeste decided to separate from her husband. She moved with her two young sons into a tiny apartment designed for one person. It had one regular-sized bedroom, another small bedroom without a door, a minuscule kitchen, and a living room. In the expensive San Francisco real estate market, this apartment was all Celeste could afford on her teacher's salary. Celeste asked me for help keeping the clutter under control and making their lives function smoothly in such constrained surroundings.

In Celeste's apartment, the room that presented the biggest challenge was the living room. It was the center of the family's activities: playing, reading, watching television, listening to music, eating, doing paperwork, and just generally being. It was also the entry into the apartment. Because the only outside door opened right into the room, everything that came in or out of the house came through the living room. Given that the room was small—a rectangle sixteen feet by fourteen feet—keeping it comfortable and functional despite all this activity was a perpetual challenge.

In any small space, you can effectively juggle multiple activities if you use the furniture and rugs to divide the room into separate areas. Then each area can support a different function. Do you remember your

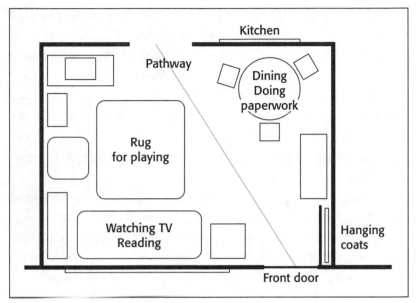

Figure 2.3 Celeste's Living Room

kindergarten classroom? It probably had a spot for naps, an area with tables, a play kitchen, some easels for painting on, a place to play with blocks, some open space for jumping around, and so on. When you wanted to do a particular activity, you would go to the place set up for it. We sorted Celeste's living room in a similar way (see Figure 2.3).

The most important thing to work around was the pathway from Celeste's front door to the other rooms in the apartment. It dissected the room diagonally, creating two separate spaces big enough to hold furniture. We designated the smaller one as the Dining/Paperwork Area. Since it included a cutout to the kitchen in one wall, it was a good place for Celeste's round table and three chairs. The family ate at the table, and Celeste did her paperwork on it in the evenings. To separate the table from the front door, we put the tall antique hutch against the right-hand wall. This gave Celeste a place to store her active files and her table linens.

Then we designated the other side of the room as the Relaxing Area. The sofa under the front window became the reading spot. Across from it, in the far corner, we put Celeste's TV on a swivel stand so it could be seen from any part of the room. A tall bookshelf anchored the front left corner next to the sofa, and a rocking chair between the bookshelf and the TV provided more seating. We used the living room rug to define the center of this side of the room. It became the children's play area, where they could spread out their toys without blocking the pathway.

The final function for which Celeste needed a designated spot was Entry/Exit. Otherwise, there was nothing to do with jackets, backpacks, and mail except dump them on the sofa. A small table next to the door became Celeste's drop-spot, where she put her purse and the mail as she entered. Everyone hung their backpacks and jackets on a peg rack behind the front door.

These three functional areas allowed the family to use their main room effectively and keep it relatively free from clutter.

Even in a very small space, multiple activities can be effectively managed by dividing the room so there's a specific area for each function. Use furniture and rugs to define each activity area, then put the tools and supplies for that activity inside it. Move the people to the activity. Don't let the tools and supplies wander away from the activity area.

Rose used to make a hobby of printing silk-screen designs on T-shirts and giving them to her family and friends as gifts. Then she took some of her creations to a craft fair and suddenly found herself inundated with customer orders. The more people saw her work, the more successful she became, until a bona fide home-based business was born. The trouble was, Rose needed a lot more space to support the business than she had needed to work on her hobby, but her house was still the same size it had always been. It was a two-story dwelling with the family's main living space upstairs and a large recreation room, storage room, and garage downstairs. Rose called me to see if I could help her incorporate her business into her home.

When I got there, I discovered that the rapid growth of Rose's company had been under way for some time. With each successive expansion, she had been tucking different business-related functions into unused corners of the house. Her desk and computer were in the family room. A spare bedroom held files and computer supplies. The main workroom had been set up in the recreation room downstairs, with several large tables on which to spread out the work. And the garage held boxes and boxes of plain T-shirts awaiting silkscreening. All the pieces of the business were there, but they were so spread out that efficiency and productivity (and maximum profitability, too) were impossible.

This is where sorting makes all the difference. Rose needed to separate the functions of her business from the activities of her family and create a workable setup for both. Fortunately, her house was well suited as a container for these two distinct functions. The upstairs, with the kitchen, family and living rooms, bedrooms, and front entry, could be the family space. The downstairs, with the large open rec room and garage, could be allocated to the needs of the business. Rose's two part-time employees could come and go through the back of the house without disturbing the family. The only overlap between the two function zones would be the storage room (reserved for the family's use) and the laundry room (shared by the business and the family).

To make the transformation happen, we had to move all of the business-related furniture, papers, and equipment that were upstairs into the lower level. Then we needed to clear the garage to make space for the business by moving still-used items into the storage room and giving away some miscellaneous furniture the family was no longer using. Once things were located on the proper level, each separate space was rearranged to support the activities being done there. The family was able to spread its activities throughout the upper level. And the business was properly assembled downstairs in the rec room and the garage, making it possible for Rose to operate efficiently and start to build up her profits.

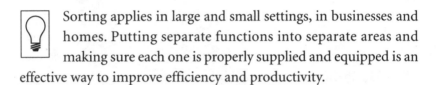 Sorting applies in large and small settings, in businesses and homes. Putting separate functions into separate areas and making sure each one is properly supplied and equipped is an effective way to improve efficiency and productivity.

Gwen runs her therapy practice from a small apartment in the lower level of her house. She sees patients in the apartment, then brings files upstairs to her home office because she is compiling case studies and data for a book she's writing. Because she is sole proprietor of her practice, Gwen must keep her business and personal financial receipts separated. She asked me to help her set up a file system to keep track of all her papers.

Gwen had two distinct challenges: to maintain her patients' privacy by keeping their records safely locked away when she wasn't actually using them; and to collect the financial information she needed in order to file her personal and business tax returns. These tasks were complicated by the close proximity between her office and her home. Because she was actively moving records from one place to another, it was hard to keep track of everything appropriately.

For Gwen, the key to a functional file system was making it easy to keep her personal and business files sorted and separated. We set this up using mirror-image locking file cabinets in both her offices. In each one, the four drawers were allocated to the same four categories: Personal Finances, Business Finances, Personal Files, Client Files. If she took a file from one office to the other, she could keep it in the drawer that matched the one it came from. And when she needed to retrieve a file, there were only two possible places it could be. Because her categories were basic and uncomplicated, it was also easy for Gwen to decide which drawer to file something in. She didn't need to decide among a host of detailed headings to put something away or to find it again.

When you're sorting paper, the most effective systems have simple categories with broad subcategories. The drawers in your file cabinet allow you to segregate different categories physically as well as logically. This makes both storage and retrieval easier. Don't let your paper storage get too complicated, or it will be too hard to use.

Kate is a busy person with a packed schedule. Not only is she responsible for handling her own affairs, she manages her children's lives, takes care of her home and the family pets, sees clients while her children are in school, and volunteers in her community. She takes care of bill-paying and keeps track of the family's finances. Like Faith, she asked me to give her some ideas so she could stay on top of her schedule.

Kate's dilemma sprang from the fact that most of the tasks she was responsible for didn't take much time. The nature of her work—consulting with clients in two- and three-hour increments—and her role as mother and homemaker—chauffeur, shopper, homework helper, cook, bookkeeper—caused her calendar for a regular day to look like one long chain of short appointments. In an effort to be punctual, Kate was allowing herself more time between appointments than she actually needed. She arrived at each destination ten or fifteen minutes early. This was enough time to relax briefly in her car, but not enough time to get anything useful done. Kate was frustrated that she never had a big enough block of time to work on a few cherished, longer-term projects that required concentration.

For Kate, the key was to set up her appointments so they were closer together. If she could eliminate the sitting-and-waiting time, she could take care of the same number of tasks in fewer hours. This would give her bigger blocks of time each day, which she could use for her projects. Together, we made a list of all the places Kate found herself sitting with time on her hands. Then we figured out how much time it really took to get from her house to each of these locations. Kate started to actively manage her schedule so her appointments were closer together, with intervals between them that matched the amount of time it actually took her to get from one place to another. By sorting her time this way, she was able to mix some fun things into her daily life.

Don't schedule yourself so you have lots of little chunks of time between activities but no big blocks for your longer-term projects. Figure out how long it really takes you to get from one place to another and allow only that much time between appointments. Make your schedule serve you, rather than making you serve your schedule.

What a Full-Blown Strategy #2 Crisis Looks Like

So far, you've seen a variety of sorting challenges affecting only one or two elements of the main character's overall organizing system. As with *Strategy #1*, solving simple issues is fairly straightforward, but when a person has allowed functions, equipment, space, and information to overlap haphazardly for a long time, the consequence is a tangled mess that takes time to unravel. Here's what such a scenario looks like.

 Pete's story dramatically illustrates the chaos that ensues when everything has been thrown together willy-nilly, without an underlying design. He's an expert in the workings of the stock market, a very bright man with a profound understanding of the minutiae of specific kinds of trading. Pete runs his business from a new, sophisticated computer room attached to his garage, which is across the yard from his large old house. Several other people work part-time for Pete, either in his home or in his office. Yet despite the presence of excellent equipment and multiple helpers, Pete's operation was struggling along. He called me for ideas about how to make his business function more efficiently.

As with Leo's situation in the previous chapter, the way to unravel a complicated organizing problem is to begin with an appraisal of the entire system, then sit down and map out a plan for fixing it. Pete and I started with a tour of most of the property (he was too embarrassed by two of the rooms to show them to me) to identify the underlying problem. By asking him questions, I helped Pete look at his organizing system with the Eyes of a Stranger. Here's what we found:

Space: Pete lives in a three-story house on the side of a hill. He operates a computer-driven brokerage business in a large computer room attached to the new garage he's just built forty yards from his house. During business hours, Pete spends his time in five separate spaces: the living room of his house, where he opens the mail and talks on the telephone; the garage, where he makes trades at the bank of computers in the workroom; a furniture-less room in the lower level of his house, which contains his file cabinets and books; the kitchen, where he gives things to his administrative assistant and eats lunch; and the upper story of the house, where he retreats to play music and relax.

Things: Because his activities are spread out across his property, Pete's things are also scattered. He has no real desk. Pete has to walk back and forth between the house and the computer room to accomplish just about anything. In the computer room, components and cables litter the floor all around the edges of the room. Large pieces of exercise equipment take up the corners, and bookshelves line the walls. There are no cupboards or drawers, so supplies are tossed around on flat surfaces or spread out across the shelves. In the house, some rooms are stuffed with things, while others are completely empty. In one room, we couldn't see a thing even in broad daylight because there were no light bulbs in any of the sockets. Pete's musical instruments—guitars and keyboards—are scattered randomly throughout the living space.

Information: When the mail comes, Pete carries it around with him as he crosses back and forth between the house and the computer room. Since he doesn't have a desk, he processes some papers in the living room, some in the kitchen, and some at his computer. He has hired a woman named Helen to handle his bills and paperwork, but she doesn't have a desk, either. Instead, she sits at the counter in the kitchen to do her work. When it's time for lunch, Helen has to clear the papers to the side so she and Pete can eat. The files she uses are in the basement, and she can never be sure that all the bills she's supposed to pay are in her kitchen in-box.

Because Pete's business relies heavily on his knowledge of a wide variety of topics, he collects articles, magazines, and essays on all of them. Some of these are stored in the house's lower level, jumbled in boxes on the floor rather than in the (mostly empty) file cabinets. Other articles are sitting on the shelves in the computer room in numerous, unlabeled stacks. Pete can't tell which pile contains what unless he gets each one down and looks through it, so he just creates another stack when he gets something new.

Time: Since there's no designated place for anything, Pete is constantly looking for things. Although he concentrates fully when he's working at his computer, the rest of his time is scattered. He spends a major portion of every day trying to locate one thing or another.

Relationships: Three different people work for Pete part-time and are in and out of the house and computer room every day. There is only one desk in the computer room for the two interns who work there, so they can't work simultaneously. One of their responsibilities is to answer the office phone, which is always for Pete. But since Pete is often somewhere else, they have to get up and go across the yard to the house to find him when he gets a call. Helen, the woman who pays Pete's bills from the kitchen counter, has to go to the lower level to file anything and also has to run around trying to find Pete when the home telephone is for him. Needless to say, working for Pete is a challenge.

By the time Pete and I finished the tour and sat down to map out an organizing plan, the underlying problem was crystal clear. Pete had been operating for years with no sorting strategy. Even though the equipment and supplies he needed for his activities were somewhere on the property, they weren't grouped together according to use. To turn things around, we applied *Strategy #2, Sort Everything by How You Use It*, by selecting a location for Pete's major activities, then sorting the furniture, equipment, things, and information for each activity into its designated spot.

Pete's first priority was to support his *trading activity*. This function belonged in the garage where his computers were already set up. The supplies scattered around the room would go into the cabinet in one corner, and a folding work table would be set up next to it for the extra components currently spread out on the floor. All the reference materials currently stored in the lower level of the house would be moved onto the computer room shelves. This would put them in the spot where they were being used and give Pete ready access to them. The exercise equipment, which Pete intended to use to help him relax during breaks in intense trading, we planned to put in one corner, out of the way of the other activity taking place in the room. Finally, we figured out how to create desk space for both interns so they could work simultaneously.

The *paperwork handling* function needed to be set up, not for Pete, but for Helen. If she had an actual desk, with a file cabinet, a telephone, and her own work surface, she would not only be able to do her job efficiently, but Pete would have a good spot to put the mail when it came in. After a discussion among the three of us, we decided Helen's work area should be assembled in the brightest, most cheerful spot in the house. This was a quadrant of the living room which already had the kind of hanging light fixture commonly found over dining tables. Located between the staircase going up and the stairs down to the basement, and only about six feet from the kitchen, this was a good central location for Helen's crucial work.

To transform this sunny spot into Helen's office, we first had to clear out several old, broken chairs, a five-foot-tall cat scratching post/tree house, several stockpiled cartons of toilet paper and tissue, and a number of paper bags full of cleaning supplies. Then we found an unused desk in one of the downstairs storage rooms, moved a file cabinet up from the lower level, and purchased a chair. Helen moved her in-box from the kitchen to the desk, so Pete could easily drop the mail in it as he entered the house, and she was all set to start operating efficiently.

The solution for *handling telephone calls* involved technology. First, both telephone lines—home and business—needed to be wired into the house *and* the computer room. Then, two-line portable phones could be used so any phone could receive any call. Finally, everyone had to acknowledge that Pete's natural tendency to move around throughout the day was not going to change. They planned to purchase a beeper for him so all his employees could track him down when they needed him without having to get up from their desks.

Our last task was to set up the upper level of the house as a *music room* to support Pete's hobby. We picked a large, bright room at the top of the stairs for this function. All the instruments spread out around the house were brought up here—keyboards, guitars, and computers for music composition. This transformed an almost empty room into a lovely, functional space Pete could use and enjoy.

By sorting his belongings—furniture, things, information, and technology—to support his major activities, Pete started to bring order to the environment he was sharing with his employees. Once everyone got set up using *Strategy #2, Sort Everything by How You Use*

It, their ability to use time efficiently made it possible for each person to accomplish more in the same amount of time. Thus they were able to take care of some of the long-term weeding and organizing that had been neglected because of the chaos. Lots of things improved right away, and everyone's stress level decreased dramatically.

When you sort your furniture, supplies, tools, and equipment into groups that support all your major activities, it has the effect of unstopping a bottleneck. The increased efficiency created by sorting frees time for other tasks that have been neglected.

How to Put Strategy #2 Back in Place

The stories in this chapter highlighted some of the ways people have applied *Strategy #2, Sort Everything by How You Use It*. First, they figured out what their activities were (*Strategy #1*), then they designated a specific place for each one and physically rearranged their furniture, supplies, and/or equipment to support it. The goal of *Strategy #2* is to keep things you *use* together *grouped* together. When things are kept as close to their point of use as possible, you don't waste time and energy finding them, retrieving them, and using them.

Here are some tried-and-true ways to sort your space, your things, your information, and your time so they support your life. There are also a few ideas to improve your relationships using sorting strategies.

Sort Your Space by How You Use It

- Sort your furniture, equipment, and things into rooms according to the way you're using your space.
- Put the setup for each activity in the room where you most enjoy doing it.

- Put things that are used together in the same space.
- In multifunction rooms, segregate activities into separate areas. Use rugs and/or furniture to separate each function from the others.
- Once you've set up workable space for each major activity, encourage people to do that activity in that space. Bring the people to the activity, not the other way around.
- When your system isn't adequately supporting your activities, rearrange things to bring the function and the furniture/supplies/equipment that support it into the same space.

Sort Your Things by How You Use Them

- Keep things as close to their point of use as possible.
- Don't keep things jumbled together in large containers. Separate them into categories by how you use them and store them in appropriately sized smaller containers. This makes it easier to find things, retrieve them, and put them away.
- Use clear, open containers on shelves to store small collections (such as children's toys) and keep them sorted.
- Do *not* mix different items in a single container. (This is how you get "junk drawers.")
- If a collection grows beyond its container, either get a larger container or weed the collection down. *Don't* separate the collection into multiple containers.
- To weed out a collection, bring it all into one space so you can see everything at once. This will help you make good decisions about what to keep and what to discard.
- If you only have one of an item you use in multiple places—pens, scissors, tape, notepads, wastebaskets, recycling bins,

coasters, and so forth—get more of them. Put one in every spot where you might use it.

- Store videotapes, DVDs, CDs, and audiotapes on shallow shelves right next to their players.
- If you have lots of sports equipment, sort it into a different-colored duffel bag for each sport. Keep the bags on shelves so it's easy to see and retrieve the equipment you need.

Sort Your Information by How You Use It

- For sorting your papers, set up simple categories with broad subheadings. Don't let your paper storage get too complicated, or it will be too hard to use.
- Usc your file cabinet's drawers to segregate major categories.
- Figure out a few broad categories that encompass all the little pieces of paper on your desk. Put a folder for each category in a stand-up file so you can see it. Drop those pieces of papers into the folders instead of onto your desktop.
- Use cardboard stationery sorters (boxes with multiple slots for 8½-by-11-inch paper) to hold different kinds of stationery or multiple forms, with a separate type of paper in each slot.
- Keep the owner's manual for each piece of electronic equipment right next to or under it. When you need to reset the clock, the directions will be right there.

Sort Your Time by How You Use It

- Set up your schedule so activities follow one another closely without overlapping. Leave yourself some big blocks so you can accomplish longer-term goals.

- Actively manage your schedule. As much as possible, make appointments so they're convenient for *you*.
- Wait until you have several errands to do before you go out. Do them in a big circle.
- Sort your activities into a Require/Desire Grid (see page 66). Stop doing anything that falls into your "Don't Have To/Don't Want To" square.
- If you *have* to do something, whether you want to or not, set aside enough time to finish it and do it quickly and efficiently.
- If you don't *have* to do something, but you want to do it, set aside time for it and commit to doing it.
- If you don't want to do something, but you think you *have* to do it, figure out why you think you have to do it, try to get over it, and then don't do it.
- If you really *have* to do something you don't want to do, figure out the easiest way to accomplish it and get it done as quickly as possible.
- If you find yourself doing something you neither have to nor want to do, state your reasons graciously to whoever needs to be informed and stop doing it.
- Schedule some free time for yourself every day, even if it's only fifteen minutes. This will make you a happier, calmer person who's more fun to be with.

Sort Your Relationships by How You Use Them

- Make sure everyone you live with has the setups they need for all their activities.
- Set up your children's rooms so it's possible for them to manage their things by themselves.

These suggestions will help you keep things sorted so they're easy to find, use, and put away. Sort your space, things, information, and time so they support your life as you're living it right now. By practicing *Strategy #2, Sort Everything by How You Use It,* you increase your efficiency and give yourself more time for the activities that are important to you. Sorting also gives you the information you need if you're getting ready to implement *Strategy #3, Weed Constantly.* Read on to see how *Strategy #3* works.

Weed Constantly

Aside from the personal reasons people hang on to things, our materialistic culture pressures us to have more than we need. Every day, we're barraged with paper, news, advertising, and information. When you keep things you're not actively using, they get in your way and create work for you. It requires constant vigilance to prevent yourself from being overwhelmed by the onslaught. Keep everything weeded down so you can retain a semblance of control over your life.

Overview of Strategy #3

Once you've sorted everything using *Strategy #2*, you may find yourself standing in the midst of an enormous pile. You're not the only one. If you asked a hundred people what their biggest organizing problem is, most of them would answer, "I have too much stuff." It's easier for human beings to acquire things than it is to give up something when it's no longer useful. People keep things they no longer need for a wide variety of reasons. These range from "It was my father's," to "I paid good money for it," to "I don't need it now but I might need it someday," all the way to "Oh! I didn't know I still had that!"

Aside from the personal and emotional reasons people have for hanging onto more than they can handle, there are cultural influences constantly pushing us to get more and more stuff. Every day, bills, catalogs, and credit card solicitations arrive in the mail; TV commercials convince us to buy things we might want but don't need; our children come home from school loaded with artwork and papers; newspapers and E-mails show up daily; and magazines entice us with the clothes or cars or homes of our dreams. As products of an affluent society, we are afforded the means to transform many of those dreams into reality.

Because of all these personal and cultural pressures, we are loaded down with more information and goods than we can reasonably manage. The piles of paper and things fill up our space, get in our way, and create work for us to do. Then we have to spend time taking care of stuff and moving it around, which takes time away from the relationships and activities we care about. If we let this cycle go unchecked, it can quickly cause our systems to get out of whack with the life we *want* to be living.

So what can you do to counter this onslaught? How do you keep from disappearing under a huge pile of stuff? The key to staying on top of the pile instead of drowning underneath it is *Strategy #3, Weed Constantly*. By paying attention to what's coming in and making a corresponding amount of stuff go out, it's possible to maintain a reasonable balance in your environment and your life.

Another effect of weeding constantly is that it teaches you something about yourself. If you've let things pile up for a while, then you start to cull through them, you can instantly see which kinds of items you've been hanging onto way past their usefulness. The next time one of those items presents itself and tries to get in your door, it will be easier to say, "I don't need another one of those."

Keep in mind: The goal of *Strategy #3* is *not* to make you give away everything that means something to you just because you haven't used it in the last six months. If you have a strong emotional attachment to something, you *are* using it. (On the other hand, if something you think you're attached to has been sitting inside the bottom box in a stack in your garage for five years, you might want to examine the strength of your feelings for it.)

Symptoms That Your System
Needs Weeding

Here are some of the indicators that your organizing system isn't supporting your life because it's overloaded with stuff. See if you need to do a little weeding.

- You have more stuff than actually fits into your space.
- You can't do things you want to do without moving piles of stuff out of the way.
- You can't put away stuff you're using because your storage spaces are full of things you rarely or never use.
- You don't like to have people over because the place is so cluttered.
- It's hard to squeeze another thing into your clothes closets.
- Items you really should put in a storage room are overflowing into your living space.
- You've inherited a pile of things from someone you loved, and you're keeping them even though they're of no use to you.
- Every time you go out, you come home with something new.
- You need a certain item, and you know you have it somewhere, but you can't find it, so you go out and get another one.
- One (or more) of your collections is getting out of hand.
- When you get new stuff, it piles up because there's no place to put it.
- You pay good money every month to rent a storage locker.
- You're keeping a bunch of things you never use because they're too good to give away.
- You're keeping a bunch of things you never use because you might need them someday.
- You have piles of paper on flat surfaces because your file cabinet is so full, you can't stuff another piece of paper into it.

- When someone drops in unexpectedly, you run around tossing things into closets and behind furniture before you open the door for them.
- You spend more time managing your stuff than with the people you love.
- You resent doing something because it takes time away from the people and activities you care about.

If any of these symptoms apply to you, chances are your organizing system needs to be lightened up a bit using *Strategy #3, Weed Constantly*. Here are some of the ways other people have put *Strategy #3* into practice.

Real-Life Lessons:
Strategy #3 Missing in Action

June and Larry had a lot going on in their home. Both active participants in their community, they also volunteered their time as coaches and Scout troop leaders for the children in the neighborhood. Their three kids were always inviting friends over, and the house had become a drop-in center for local youth. Along with all this activity, lots of things constantly moved in and out of the house—sports equipment, arts and crafts supplies, school papers, camping equipment, and so forth. Fortunately, both June and Larry are high-energy people who enjoyed the lively life they were living. But June was starting to notice a rising level of clutter that was threatening to get in the family's way. She called me for some ideas.

Throughout her house, June pointed out the piles that were bothering her. There were papers on the desk because the file cabinet was full of old tax files. The closets in the master bedroom were stuffed, and camping clothes had overflowed onto the chairs. The kids' rooms had storage for their small toys, but the big items were taking up noticeable floor space. The living room, where the TV and stereo were located, had more furniture than it needed. And the kitchen was overflowing with craft supplies and material, along with the usual clutter of utensils and plastic containers. Then I started to notice a common theme in June's remarks. In our discussion about each pile of stuff, the word "basement" kept coming up. Every pile had something in it that really belonged in the basement. So I said, "Let's go look in the basement!"

Down the stairs we went, with June protesting at every step that the basement was a mess. She was only half right. On the one hand, everything was neatly arranged and stored. All the items were reasonably contained—in bins, on shelves, stacked in piles, on hanging racks, and enclosed in file cabinets. The room was obviously well cared for.

On the other hand, there was no place left to put anything except for the few paths connecting the stairs, the bulkhead door, and the laundry area. Every square inch of space was taken up, which is why all the upstairs piles contained items that belonged in the basement. For fourteen years, June and Larry had been putting stuff they weren't actively using into the basement because it was too good to give away. Gradually, the shelves along the walls filled up, and new stuff got piled on the floor in front of them. The farther something was from the path, the longer it had been sitting there. When the family ran out of basement storage space, they started piling things in the house. They were experiencing a serious storage overflow.

To solve Larry and June's problem, the first job was to clear out the basement. Because a lot of the stuff had been sitting there for a long time, they no longer had any attachment to it. Also, some of the things had suffered from a long stay in storage. If they had been valuable before they went in, they had lost their value over time. This made the basement easy to weed out, thus creating storage space for some of the stuff that had crept upward into the house. Finally, as they sorted through the piles, Larry and June started to recognize that some types of things they'd been in the habit of saving weren't worth storing. They were just taking up space. So some of the items in the house which fell into those same categories—such as old, unwanted furniture—went straight to a charity instead of going into the basement.

 Weed your storage areas first. It's easier to make decisions about things you haven't used for a while. This creates space for items you're actually using. Don't let your storage areas get so full they overflow into your living space.

Ingrid has three children, two preschoolers and a kinder-gartner. When her second child arrived, she quit her full-time job to stay home with her kids. She's the kind of mother who bakes with her children, gets down on the floor and plays with them, and uses the kitchen table as a center for crafts, artwork, and color-ing. She also likes her home to be well decorated, orderly, and com-fortable for grown-ups. She called me because the child-centered activity taking place in her kitchen was starting to tip her organiza-tional balance toward messiness. She wanted some ideas about kitchen storage.

The setup in Ingrid's kitchen was well designed, with numerous cupboards, a floor-to-ceiling pantry, and space for a table and chairs. But one side of the room opened straight into the family room. If the kitchen was cluttered, it couldn't be closed off from the view of anyone sitting on the sofa or watching television. Ingrid pointed to her kitchen counter and the top of her refrigerator as the biggest problem spots. In one corner, papers and phone lists and coupons were piled haphazardly on the counter by the telephone. The pile was creeping toward the stove, which was flanked by small appliances, utensils in two stand-up jars, and a bread bin. The sink had a drainer full of children's bowls and cups on one side, and a very small open work surface on the other. There was little room for preparing food. On the opposite side of the room, a big pile loomed on the refrigerator. The top of it was loaded with placemats, pads of paper, bags of paper plates and cups, and snack boxes. Every time someone opened the refrigerator door, the items on top of it teetered ominously.

With all these things lying around in full view, my first question was, "So what's *in* all these cupboards?" When we went from cupboard to drawer to pantry, opening each one and doing a quick scan of its contents, we discovered the real problem. Ingrid's kitchen cupboards—prime real estate—were loaded with things she never used. We found two sets of cookware because one was too heavy to cook with, but too good to give away; a collection of mismatched brandy snifters and cocktail glasses collected before Ingrid and her husband got married; three shelves of miscellaneous coffee mugs; more plastic storage containers than could possibly fit in her refrigerator, even if there was nothing else in it; twice as many plastic tops as there were containers; and an assortment of single-use wedding presents still in their original wrapping. Things were sitting out on Ingrid's counters and refrigerator because there wasn't any other storage available. Her kitchen was full and overflowing.

In four hours, we went through every drawer and cupboard in the room. First, we took everything out so Ingrid could see what she had. Then she made decisions about each item, based on how much she used it. She weeded through the pots and pans, mugs, utensils, plastic containers, glassware, dishes, food, wedding presents, and specialty tools. The only things she put back were items her family was using. The rest she gave away, including the whole set of expensive cookware that was too heavy for her to use. The things she had stored for sentimental reasons—the souvenir glassware and unused wedding presents—no longer had meaning to her and were just getting in her way. They went, too. Then, we cleared off the refrigerator and the counter, put everything away, and the kitchen looked beautiful.

When a storage space gets full, especially if it's in a high-use area like the kitchen or office, weed it out right away. Some of the things you put in there for sentimental reasons may no longer hold value to you, and you can let go of them. Even though *you* are not using them, someone else might if you give them away.

Kendall has been a high school teacher for fifteen years. She shares a tiny, narrow office with a colleague, whose desk can only be reached by squeezing between Kendall's chair and her bookshelves. In the corner next to her desk, she has a tall four-drawer file cabinet. The top of the cabinet holds binders and boxes of educational materials. The bookshelves are chock-full, with three-foot piles of additional books and videotapes stacked on the floor in front of them. The tops of the shelves hold papers and forms for students, who also have to squeeze in behind Kendall's chair to retrieve their paperwork. Kendall needed to make some space, so she called me for help.

In such close quarters, we weren't going to be able to add furniture or containers to create additional storage, because there simply wasn't room. It was *not possible* to expand the storage so it matched the stuff. Instead, we were going to have to shrink the stuff to fit the available storage.

We started with the file cabinet. It turned out all four drawers were filled with fifteen years' worth of student handouts. Each handout was filed in a separate folder, and each folder held forty or fifty copies of the worksheet. Kendall explained that the copy machine was far enough away to be inconvenient, so she always made lots of extra copies whenever she used it. Although this habit saved her time in the short run, over fifteen years it contributed heavily to her office storage crisis. Her tiny office didn't allow her the luxury of maintaining an inventory of extra papers.

Once we recycled all the obsolete forms and culled the ones she was using down to a few copies each, Kendall had enough room in the file cabinet for all the papers she'd been keeping on her bookshelves. In turn, this made enough room in the bookshelves for all the books on the floor, and then some. The crisis was addressed, and Kendall promised to stop making more copies than she needed.

 When you have limited storage space, it is especially important to keep your collections small enough to put away. Weed as you go so your storage spaces don't overflow.

Becky and Dan had recently bought their first house from the estate of an elderly woman. It had become available suddenly, and they snapped it up, which enabled them to move in right away. Because they were coming from an apartment in the same town, they had friends help them move their things instead of hiring a moving company. They were thrilled to own a place of their own, even though the house was a bit small. When I met them, they had already started adding a room to one end of the house. Becky asked me for help setting up the other rooms to support her family's life during construction. Her first goal was to find safe play space for her three small children.

When Becky gave me the official tour of her home, we started at the top and worked our way down. The rooms were all cozy, but small. No obvious extra space for a play area presented itself in the main body of the house. Our last stop was the basement. This was a large, open space under the whole body of the house, with concrete walls and several windows. Against one wall stood the washer and drier, with an 8-by-10-foot rug on the floor next to them. The rug was covered with toys, and Becky explained that her children liked to play here while she did the family's laundry (a time-consuming task with three small children). It struck me right away that this would be a great play space for her children if it were set up properly. There was only one problem.

Except for the walkway from the stairs to the washer/drier, and the rug where the children played, the entire floor of the basement was taken up by furniture, boxes, and miscellaneous household goods piled five feet deep throughout the room. The piles were covered with canvas tarps and coated with dust that had accumulated over a very long time. Becky explained that the whole pile belonged to the previous owner of the house, and her heirs had left it there as part of the deal when they sold their mother's property. Becky and Dan had been so rushed between the day they purchased the home and the date of their move that there had been no time to clear out all the junk cluttering up the basement. So they moved in, leaving the basement cleanup for later. Then, once they'd gotten settled, the task of getting rid of all this bulky stuff was so daunting they continued to put it off. The stuff was still there, and it was in their way.

Of course, the obvious thing for Dan and Becky to do was to get this stuff out of their house as soon as possible. They rented a dumpster, invited the same friends who helped them with their move to a cleanup-and-pizza party, and spent a day transforming their basement from a junk pile into a safe, warm playroom for their children.

When a pile is in your way, don't put off dealing with it. This will just make the pile spread, or cause other things to pile up elsewhere. Set aside a day for a big project, get someone to help you, and a few hours of weeding will transform your space right away.

Nina dresses up for her downtown job, then comes home and relaxes in casual clothes. She enjoys several sports—skiing, tennis, running—and exercises regularly at a local gym. Nina lives in an old house with small, deep closets, but she has no problem hanging up her clothes because she uses the closet in a spare bedroom for off-season garments. The issue is Nina's shoes. The closet in her bedroom has shoes stacked in boxes on the single shelf, jumbled in a huge pile on the floor, and overflowing into her room. The spare bedroom closet holds additional pairs of dress shoes and boots. There are shoes under her bed, at the front door, and in the living room. In the course of a general consultation, Nina asked me for specific ideas to help her manage her footwear.

The first task was to get all the shoes in one place so we could see them. We gathered every pair we could find from every corner of the house, and put them all in her bedroom. Then we grouped them according to use—work shoes, sports shoes, casual shoes, dress shoes—and color (*Strategy #2, Sort Everything*). Finally, Nina stood back, contemplated the entire collection, and started laughing. "I guess I have more shoes than I need!" Indeed.

Because her shoes were so spread out, Nina hadn't realized how many pairs she owned. Once we got them all in one place, she could see she didn't really need five pairs of black leather pumps with one-inch heels. Then she had to decide how many she *did* need, figure out which ones she should keep, and decide where to put them. Nina elected to keep only as many shoes as would reasonably fit in her bedroom closet and the spare room closet. Old or worn-out shoes went right into the giveaway pile. Then Nina picked out her favorite pairs to save and a few specialty shoes for unusual occasions. The ones she used all the time went in her bedroom; the seldom-used pairs got put away in the other room. Because she knew she had kept all the shoes she needed to support her life, Nina was able to give the rest away. She also knew she didn't need to shop for any more shoes in the foreseeable future.

Keep your collections weeded so they don't take over your storage. Check your inventory before you purchase new items so you don't get duplicates. Figure out how many you really need, then make an old item go out every time a new item comes in. Practice the FIFO inventory system: First In, First Out.

Pat represents the millions of people who struggle every day with one of the most insidious weeding dilemmas we all grapple with—the daily mail.

Every day, a dedicated employee of the federal government visits Pat's home and leaves a pile of items for Pat to sort through and deal with. Usually, the pile contains:

- 4 envelopes, each containing 1 bill, 2 inserts, and 1 smaller envelope;
- 3 envelopes, each containing 1 solicitation letter, 2 inserts, and 1 postage-paid envelope;
- 3 catalogs, each approximately 36 pages long;
- 1 magazine, with 40 pages of articles and 60 pages of advertising, plus 4 postcard inserts;
- 1 newsletter, 12 pages long, with 1 donation request letter and 1 envelope inserted; and
- 5 grocery store fliers and a 20-page coupon ad, all wrapped in 1 newsprint folder.

If you do the math (20 + 15 + 108 + 104 + 14 + 26), this means Pat receives 287 new pieces of paper every single day (except Sundays and federal holidays), most of which are unsolicited advertising. During the holiday season, which now begins in mid-September, the catalog mailings bring in an additional 108 pages per day. In a single year, Pat has to process approximately 95,709 individual pieces of paper. If you spread that number out over an average adult lifespan of 54 years, Pat will have to deal with 5,168,286 papers before dying. And this is a conservative estimate that doesn't include the newspaper or the latest information onslaught—E-mail. What a nightmare!

If Pat is a ruthless person, the task of managing all this paper is time-consuming but not difficult. Ruthless Pat just rips every unsolicited piece of mail in half and tosses it directly into the recycle bin.

The bills and their return envelopes get put right in Pat's "To Pay" folder, but outside envelopes and inside inserts are immediately discarded, too. Pat might scan through each catalog, keeping a page or two in the "To Order" folder if there's an interesting product on display, but most (if not all) of the pages go straight into the bin. Finally, Ruthless Pat might sit down and read the newsletter and the magazine. If there are interesting articles, Pat will pay close attention to them. However, once they've been read, Pat knows they have no further use and recycles the whole document. The only pieces of paper left over after this process are bills to pay, which are important. The rest of the pile is gone before it has a chance to get in the door.

The real problems arise when Pat is too nice or too busy or too tired to be ruthless. Then the mail goes into a pile called "To Deal With Later" instead of into the recycle bin. Sometimes, this pile is already pretty tall because the same thing happened yesterday and the day before. Before you know it, Nice Pat's mail pile is so big, it starts to spread out around the flat surfaces and make its way into paper bags in the closets. Then Nice Pat starts to worry because there might be something important in all that mail. This means it's too risky to just recycle it without looking at every piece first. And before you know it, a giant weeding dilemma is born.

The problem with collections of paper is that you can fit a whole lot of them into any given storage container. Imagine a large plastic bin. How many sweaters would fit in it? Not that many. Then imagine the same bin filled with papers. How many would fit? Thousands. But you'd still have to look at each one to weed it out. This is why keeping them from entering in the first place is the right tactic to use with all types of paper, especially the mail.

 With paper, an ounce of prevention is worth a *ton* of cure. Be ruthless. As soon as you've read something, recycle it. Don't keep any piece of paper unless you absolutely, positively need it.

Jim is a computer junkie. Long ago, when he started his career as a statistician, he used slide rules and calculators and adding machines to make calculations. Then PCs became available, and instantly the computer became his most useful tool. Jim was hooked. In the decades since the first desktop models came out, Jim has traded up from machine to machine, always adding power and peripherals as he upgraded. In his home office, his chair is surrounded by equipment: a huge monitor, two desktop computers, two printers, a scanner, and several extra hard drives. Two laptops sit on the floor, ready to hit the road. The nearby closet holds several other laptops, and the basement is a veritable component graveyard. You may think Jim called me to help him weed out his equipment, but that was not his main problem. The real issue at Jim's house was the empty boxes.

Every carton containing electronic equipment has a label that says, "Keep the original packaging for this equipment in case you need to return it." This short phrase was Jim's downfall. Over the years, he'd given away or thrown out all kinds of obsolete computer equipment, but he still had the box for every component he had ever bought. Twenty years' worth of empty equipment boxes take up a *lot* of space. Even though Jim lived in a large house with abundant storage, the boxes had filled it all up, and things were overflowing into his living space and office. He needed help.

In twenty years, despite the cryptic warning on all those labels, Jim had rarely had to send anything back. I suggested this meant he didn't really need any of the boxes. He wasn't ready to get rid of all of them, so we compromised by putting a few of the most recent ones in the garage. My next advice to Jim, phrased delicately, was that a dumpster would be very helpful if he wanted to get rid of all these boxes quickly. He was reluctant to get one, thinking we'd never fill it up, so we compromised again and ordered a small one. Then we went on a box hunt.

We found empty cardboard containers piled in every closet and storage space in the house. Small cupboards contained small boxes.

Big closets held big boxes. In the garage, we found one that might have once held a refrigerator. There were so many of them, our dumpster was quickly overwhelmed. To get them all to fit, we had to flatten each box so it took up the minimum amount of space. When we were finished, all the closets in the house had plenty of room to spare, and you couldn't have squeezed a playing card into that dumpster.

Despite the warning label on each piece of equipment, it had been a waste of Jim's storage space to keep the boxes for more than thirty days. If Jim had needed to send back something whose box had already been discarded, he would have been able to get another one that would do.

If you're not using something, but you're worried that you'll find a use for it as soon as you give it away, apply this question: "If I get rid of this, and I need it again, can I get another one?" Most items are replaceable. Don't turn your house into a junk shop by keeping things you're unlikely ever to use again.

Molly is an accountant. Several years ago, she and her husband moved from their city apartment to a nearby suburb after their first child was born. When their second child turned out to be twins, Molly stopped working full time and began a consulting practice out of her house. She asked me to help her get her papers under control.

Molly's home "office" is a desk in a corner of the family room. In another corner nearby, she has an old four-drawer file cabinet, and the desk has two deep file drawers. None of these drawers are useful because they're all chock-full. So Molly's papers are spread out on the desktop and the top of the file cabinet and on the nearby air hockey table and ironing board. There are also piles of papers on the floor under the air hockey table and on the counter that runs along one wall of the family room.

Because the file cabinet presented the best possibility as a useful container for Molly's papers, we looked there first. When Molly opened the drawers, she revealed a set of papers so tightly packed, it would be hard to get something out, much less put something in. I asked her what was in the folders. She peered closely at the headings and said, "These are my papers from college." We went through the remaining three drawers and discovered a similar scenario. In each drawer, all the space was being taken up by documents from five, ten, or fifteen years ago. The papers were relevant when they were initially put in the cabinet, but they had nothing to do with the life Molly and her husband were currently living. This was not a problem in itself, except that the old papers were taking up space needed by today's important documents.

So Molly and I got to work and went through the file cabinet folder by folder. We recycled everything that didn't fit Molly's life today, shredded financial documents that might hold important numbers, and cleared out the old to make space for the new. At the end of the project, she had plenty of room for all her papers, and her file cabinet was a reflection of her current life. The family room looked much better, too.

Don't keep papers unless you know you'll need to retrieve them. Put sentimental papers in a single box, then weed it down when it gets full. Documents that mattered to you in the past need to be archived or recycled. Don't allow them to clutter up your active files.

Several years ago, my husband's company decided to move its base of operations from one side of the country to the other. After discussing our options, we decided to move along with the company. As soon as we made our decision, I immediately called the coordinator of a volunteer program I'd been participating in for several years and told her I would no longer be able to work in the program. She thanked me for my work over the years and wished me the best of luck in my new location. Even though she needed someone to cover the job I'd been doing, she didn't try to get me to change my mind. Both of us knew perfectly well I couldn't continue to volunteer from the other coast.

After I made this telephone call, I thought about the impulse that prompted it. I hadn't even waited a *single day* before I used my family's impending move to extricate myself from that particular obligation. Then I realized something: Even though I didn't like doing that particular job, and I resented the time it took away from my family, I'd been doing it for a long time because I knew they needed someone to do it, and I knew I was capable of getting it done. I'd been wanting to get out of it for some time, but I had felt too guilty about possibly leaving the organization in the lurch to say, "No, thank you." The hassle-free excuse of moving across the country had been an opportunity, and I'd seized it.

In essence, the volunteer job belonged in the "Don't Have To/Don't Want To" square in my Require/Desire Grid. It should have been weeded out of my schedule as soon as I realized how much I disliked doing it. All I needed to say was, "This is valuable work, and it should be done by someone who can give it the time and attention it deserves. My family obligations prevent me from being that person." This is not an excuse—it is a *good reason* to say no. The needs of my family come before the needs of an outside group.

Weed your time by getting rid of any activities that fall into the "Don't Have To/Don't Want To" square of your Require/ Desire Grid. Decide which activities these are by filling in this blank: "If I found out I was moving across the country, I'd stop doing _____ as fast as possible."

Madeline, the woman described in the introduction who was expecting twins and had more clothes than she could reasonably use, taught me an important lesson about weeding. When she called me for a consultation, Madeline said she needed advice on how to prepare for her babies. She didn't mention anything about clothes. In her mind, the pending arrival of the babies had absolutely nothing to do with her wardrobe. Finding space for the children was a challenge; storing the clothes was a given.

It was only after we'd toured her apartment and sat down to talk that the clothes came up as an issue. I recommended she weed through her wardrobe and give most of it away. Madeline was taken aback: "Why should I give my clothes away? There's nothing wrong with them!" When I pointed out how much space they were taking up—space needed for the babies—the light dawned in her face. "I see! The problem isn't the clothes themselves, it's that they're getting in the way of the people!" Exactly. The people needed the space currently occupied by inanimate objects.

An item doesn't have to have something intrinsically wrong with it before you can let it go. It can be perfectly good or useful or functional, but still need to be given away because it isn't good or useful or functional *for you*. The opposite is also true. When you make a decision to let something go, it does not suddenly become worthless. Your decision to pass it on doesn't rob it of its intrinsic value. Someone else will be thrilled to make good use of it, even though it is no longer benefiting you.

Once Madeline could see that weeding out her clothes was an act of caring for the people in her life instead of a disservice to her clothes, she was ready and willing to let them go. She chose to give her people higher priority than her things.

 Don't let your systems become so cluttered they get in the way of the people who matter to you. Put people before things.

When the stuff is getting in the people's way, weed it out. Let someone else use it if you no longer find it useful.

 Vera and Ron live frugally in a comfortable suburban home. Their teenage daughter is the focal point of their lives. Between trips to school, sports activities, and dance class, they like to work on projects in their home. But they were having trouble keeping the clutter from piling up, especially in the garage. They asked me for advice on how to keep everything flowing smoothly.

One of the things I noticed as they showed me around their home was a substantial collection of household goods bought in bulk. The garage, which was crowded and hard to maneuver through, had cartons of toilet paper and detergent and dishwasher soap sprinkled liberally among the piles. Later, when we were starting to work on a kitchen weeding project, I noticed a new box of dishwasher soap in a grocery bag Ron had just brought in. When I asked him why he had bought a new carton when there were already boxes of the stuff in the garage, he said he hadn't been able to find one when he needed it, so he'd just gone out and bought one.

Vera and Ron had been buying items in bulk to save money and to increase convenience. But because they couldn't easily reach their stockpiled supplies, they ended up spending more money *and* taking up more space than if they had just bought the item from the grocery store in the first place. In this case, the family had two choices. Either they could clean up the garage and get the bulk items stored in plain sight on shelves, or they could give up buying in bulk and just purchase things when they needed them.

Don't stockpile things unless you can retrieve them easily. If you can't find them when you need them, buying bulk goods wastes your money and your space, and just creates clutter.

What a Full-Blown
Strategy #3 Crisis Looks Like

Everyone I've ever met has at least one pile of stuff that could benefit from weeding. When it grows big enough to get in the way, it gets weeded. In the preceding stories, you've seen some examples of collections that have gotten a bit out of hand, but all were small enough to handle in two days or less. What happens when nothing ever gets weeded? When there are too many collections to count, or stuff is coming in fast and furious but nothing is going out, or there's never a good enough reason to let something go? The next story is just such a scenario.

Natalie's story best illustrates the chaos that ensues when every single item is part of a collection and nothing is ever thrown out. She is a stay-at-home mom with two sons, ages eight and six. Her husband is a successful doctor, and Natalie manages their home. She called me for help dealing with clutter.

Before we went on a tour of her home, Natalie talked about her family. She is devoted to her children and spends much of her time chauffeuring them from one activity to another. The boys keep busy with year-round sports and have all the latest toys and equipment. The whole family takes lavish vacations to exotic places several times a year. Natalie and her husband also have many interests—gourmet cooking, exercise, outdoor sports, genealogy, computer games, arts and crafts, and so on.

To support all these activities, Natalie has been bringing things into the house for eight years but never sending anything out again. The clutter was starting to overwhelm the house. Here's what we saw on our tour.

Space: Natalie's family lives in a thirteen-room home in a gated community. The rooms in the house are spacious, with high ceilings and arched windows. Upstairs, the master suite includes a small den, two walk-in closets, and a generous bath with a Jacuzzi and separate shower. One bedroom is reserved for Natalie's stepdaughter, who lives there for part of every summer. Two other bedrooms round out the layout on the second floor.

On the main floor, a curving staircase sweeps upward from the two-story entrance hall, which is flanked by the formal living and dining rooms. The spacious kitchen is well equipped with cabinets, counters, an island, and a large eating alcove. A den holds the TV and gives the family access to the backyard and swimming pool. Two rooms serve as playroom and family room respectively. The smallest bedroom in the house is set up for guests. The three-car garage completes the picture. Throughout the house, generous closets and pantries provide ample storage for a family.

In almost every room, the beauty and graciousness of the space is marred by the piles of stuff choking every nook and cranny. Toys crowd the sides of the curving staircase and line the walls on either side of the entryway. The large family room, which holds a grand piano and four computer desks, is so full that pathways provide the only open space. In the small playroom, a universal gym dominates the space. The children's toys fill every inch of the floor except a spot in front of the TV, which is hooked up to a play station. To actually play, they bring their toys into the den. Maneuvering around the hanging racks filled with outgrown children's clothing, the boys do their homework there, too. Meals are eaten sitting on the sofa because the kitchen dining table is heaped with papers, books, magazines, and mail. The formal dining area is also unavailable for dining. Instead, it is the repository for brand-new items that are unopened or are waiting to be given as gifts. In the garage, two of the three bays are taken up with toys, bikes, climbing structures, sports equipment, and three drivable toy cars. The kitchen and the small guest room are functionally designed and relatively uncluttered.

Upstairs, three of the bedrooms appear virtually unused. The step-daughter's is comfortable and inviting. The other two are adequately furnished, but spare in their decor. However, piles of linens and racks holding more children's clothing line the hallway. The bedrooms seem unlived-in because the boys actually sleep in the den off the master suite. Not only that, most of the master bedroom is taken up by a huge wooden climbing structure that the boys have outgrown, so it has become a storage unit for clothes, linens, and laundry. The bed Natalie shares with her husband is shoved into one corner of the room, across from a huge TV equipped with theater sound.

Things: Most of the obvious collections in Natalie's home revolve around the children. There were sets of toys, clothes, bikes, blankets and sheets, sports equipment, and climbing structures stored all over the house. The two boys had enough tiny matchbox-sized toy cars (hundreds and hundreds) to fill a plastic bin commonly used to store quilts. And this was only one *type* of toy. In every category, the boys owned a staggering number of individual items. Obviously, there were so many toys they couldn't possibly use them all. It was hard enough just to find a place to play among the piles.

Information: Natalie kept track of her family's information in her kitchen, the most organized room in the house. She was good at storing things such as telephone lists and school fliers so she could retrieve them again. The family finances were maintained by her husband, so the only area needing tweaking was mail. Natalie needed a specific spot to put the bills so her husband could take care of them. We set that up right next to the phone in the kitchen. The rest of the mail she faithfully processed and recycled every day. The piles in the house were *not* filled with random papers.

Time: All this stuff was affecting the schedule of every occupant of this home. The children struggled to keep track of their favorite things among the piles. Natalie's husband also had to maneuver through the maelstrom to find the things he was using. But the person whose time was most affected by all this stuff was Natalie. Not only did she spend hours and hours shopping, she also filled her calendar with tasks related to maintaining all her things: finding places for them, keeping them clean, operating around them, and moving them out of her way. Such a crowded, cluttered environment was stressful for every family member.

Relationships: Obviously, the child-centered nature of the clutter revealed Natalie's desire to care for her children. Natalie also put some of her purchasing energy to work for her husband. She bought the universal gym and much of the sports equipment for him. But the clutter and stress were having a deleterious effect on him. After a hard day at work, he wanted to come home and relax, and there wasn't any place for him to do that. The den, where most of the family's activities took place, was crowded with toys and clothes. The climbing structure took up the lion's share of the bedroom. All the other possible havens were crowded, so he usually ended up eating his dinner in the den, then going up to the bedroom and watching TV by himself. During the week, there was little family interaction that included him. When Natalie and I talked about what she wanted help with, the first item on her list was clearing out space for her husband so he could relax.

Natalie and her family were obviously suffering from too many possessions. Two powerful forces fueled the overload. First, Natalie's ambition was to meet all her children's needs and expose them to a wide variety of activities and experiences. Second, the family's affluence enabled her to satisfy each family member's every material whim. Even though her purchases could not guarantee happiness, she used the power of her purse to show her love and concern for her family. The net result of these two factors—ambition and affluence—was unmanageable clutter. And once something got in the door, it never left.

The daunting but necessary solution for Natalie's family was a large-scale infusion of *Strategy #3, Weed Constantly*. They needed to pare down their belongings until everything fit comfortably into the house, then create and maintain a balance between incoming and outgoing in order to lessen the stress and make life more pleasant.

The first task was to *stop things from coming in*. Except for food, they already had everything they needed to survive. If Natalie was still out buying things while simultaneously trying to clear the extra stuff out of her house, she would be working at cross purposes with herself. So she needed to put her credit cards in a drawer for a while and resist the impulse to buy anything else.

Second, because sorting is a necessary preliminary step to weeding, Natalie needed to *sort the collections* and gather each one into a single spot. Until she could really see how many items she had in each category, it was going to be hard for Natalie to give up anything. But once she had all the items in a collection in one place, it would be quite clear to her that she didn't need to keep all of them.

Third, she needed to *weed every collection* down to a reasonable level. This might require renting a dumpster or calling the Salvation Army, but it was essential if Natalie wanted to regain control over her house. I recommended she break up the project into manageable chunks by going through the house one room at a time. It had taken years to build up the mess; it was going to take a while to pare it down.

The final step in the weeding process is to *put away everything that remains*. Once she reached this step, Natalie would be ready to apply the rest of the Strategies of a Reasonably Organized Person. Without all the clutter obscuring her view, it would finally be *possible* for her to create a functional design for her organizing system and put it into place (*Strategy #1, Make Your Systems Fit You and Your Life*). A functional system would then allow the family to relax and use their things instead of being overwhelmed by them.

 Having too many things is stressful. Even if you *can* buy anything you want, ask yourself whether you *should*. Purchase things to use, not just to have. Weed constantly to keep the pile from taking over your home and your life.

How to Put Strategy #3 Back in Place

If you recognized yourself in any of these stories, your organizing system is out of sync with your life because it has too much stuff in it. Things you don't need and aren't using are getting in your way and bogging you down. Use *Strategy #3, Weed Constantly*, to trim your system so it supports only your current activities. When you're no longer encumbered by all that extra stuff, your life will work better. Then you can use *Strategy #3* to keep things from piling up again. Don't let outside pressures coerce you into wasting your precious time and energy (not to mention money) on anything you don't really need.

The tips in this section give you practical ways to decide what you want to keep and what you're ready to let go of. Here are some ways to *Weed Constantly*.

Weed Your Space Constantly

- If your space is set up for activities you used to do, remove the furniture, supplies, and equipment left over from those activities if you're no longer using them.
- Pay attention to the corners and flat surfaces in each room. Piles tend to collect in these spots first. Every time you see a pile developing, go through it and weed it out.
- Every time you finish working on something or playing with something, put it away so it doesn't clutter up your space.
- When a storage space gets full, weed it out right away. Let go of

things that no longer have value for you. Give them away so someone else can use them.

- If you have a big weeding project to tackle, start with your storage areas, then move into your living space. It's easier to let go of things you haven't used in a long time.
- When you have limited storage space, keep your collections small so they don't overflow into your living areas.
- Don't keep artwork or knickknacks you don't like. It clutters up your visual space.

Weed Your Things Constantly

- Even if you *can* buy anything you want, ask yourself whether you *should*. Purchase things to use, not just to have.
- When you notice a cupboard/closet/storage area getting full, check it for items you don't need. Give them away or throw them out to make room for things you're using.
- When a collection outgrows its container, weed it down so it still fits. If it's still too big for the container, get a bigger container. Do *not* divide the collection.
- Check your inventory before you purchase new items. Figure out how many you really need, then practice the First In, First Out (FIFO) inventory system.
- Don't keep clothes that don't fit you, or that you don't like. They'll just take up space you need for the clothes you're actually wearing.
- If your closet contains a lot of clothes that are too small for you, remember that if you lose the weight, you'll want to get new things instead of wearing that dusty old stuff.
- Don't overload your children with toys. When they don't have

a specific play item, they improvise, which fosters their creativity. Encourage them to use their imaginations.

- Give away your children's clothes as soon as they outgrow them, unless you *know* you're going to have another baby in the near future. Pass them down to someone you know. It's fun to see smaller children wearing clothes your children enjoyed.
- Help your children weed out their toys periodically. Invite them to pass no-longer-used items along so another child can enjoy them. Don't allow them to hoard things.
- Keep a giveaway box in your house. Encourage everyone to put things they no longer need in the box. Take it to your local church or charity periodically.
- Don't stockpile things unless you can retrieve them easily. Otherwise, bulk items are a waste of space and money.
- For food storage, use clear plastic containers with matching tops. Keep enough to fit on two shelves in your refrigerator, and no more. Discard every top and container with no mate. Toss *all* opaque containers (food just rots in them).
- Weed out your medicines frequently, using expiration dates as a guide. Don't keep your medicine cabinet cluttered with expired pills and potions. They are a health hazard.

Weed Your Information Constantly

- Be ruthless with papers. Don't keep any piece of paper unless you absolutely, positively need it. Consult your accountant or attorney to figure out what papers you really need. Recycle or shred the rest.
- Go through the mail and your kids' backpacks every day. Don't let mail and school papers pile up.

- When kids bring home work from school, crow over it the day it shows up. Recycle all worksheets immediately. Display artwork until the next creation comes in, then recycle it. Only keep outstanding work that shows your child's special creativity.
- Store your child's special creations in a cardboard file box. Keep *one* for each child. When the box gets full, weed it down to make more room.
- Don't file papers unless you need to retrieve them.
- Don't allow documents from the past to clutter up your active files. Recycle them or put them in storage.
- If you must file something, don't keep any extra pages. Flatten the document and staple it together. Never use paper clips in your file cabinet.
- Every time you open a file folder, scribble the date on the outside of it. Go through your files periodically and let go of folders with no dates on them.
- Be honest with yourself about reading material. When you don't read a magazine or newspaper or article right away, admit you'll never read it, and recycle it.

Weed Your Time Constantly

- Don't do anything you dislike doing unless you absolutely have to. If you must, then do it as quickly and efficiently as possible.
- Don't go shopping unless you need something specific. Try not to make impulse buys.
- Spend your time on people and activities you care about.
- Follow the Nine Strategies of Reasonably Organized People so you don't waste time.

What Treasures Are You Hiding?

Here are some of the things I've found while helping clients weed through some big messes:

- The Ferrari keys, which had been missing for a month
- Five years' worth of unopened Christmas cards
- Two uncashed checks for $92,000 each
- Twelve sets of clothes for a small statue (the clothes were in the attic, and the naked statue was on the porch)
- Four full vacuum cleaner bags, sitting in a dusty heap on the floor in the corner of the living room
- Six gold-and-gemstone rings from the Home Shopping Network, still in their original boxes, buried at the bottom of a closet
- The carcass of a mole, the client's first attempt at taxidermy when he was eight years old (he is now fifty-eight)
- A strand of pearls, a pair of gold earrings, and two gold pins in a box otherwise full of costume jewelry
- Hundreds of dollars in cash and savings bonds

Weed Your Relationships Constantly

- Don't waste time with people you don't like. If you have to spend time with them, make it the minimum possible amount.
- Weed out your mailing lists periodically.
- Stop doing any activities that fall in the "Don't Have To/Don't Want To" square of your Require/Desire Grid. Use the "If I were moving across the country . . ." test.
- If the clutter in your environment is so bad that it is straining

your relationships with people you care about, weed out the clutter. Show people you care about them by putting them first.

These suggestions will help you cull out all the extra baggage that's been cluttering up your life. Another useful resource is Appendix C: "Two Aids for Sorting and Weeding." When you're finished clearing out the things you don't need, you'll discover everything that's left is important for the way you're living right now. It's either serving a practical function, or it's emotionally important to you.

The next step in getting your life to work smoothly is finding the right tools and containers to store and use all the things you've decided to keep. It's time for *Strategy #4, Use the Right Containers and Tools.*

CHAPTER 4 | **STRATEGY #4**

Use the Right Containers and Tools

Effective containers allow you to keep track of things and use them easily. Bad containers make things hard to manage. The right tools help you accomplish necessary tasks quickly and efficiently. The wrong tool can keep you from accomplishing anything.

Overview of Strategy #4

After you've devoted some time and energy to designing your systems so they fit you and your life (#1), sorting everything according to the way you're using it (#2), and weeding everything down so it supports you instead of getting in your way (#3), you're ready to look at storage. *Strategy #4, Use the Right Containers and Tools*, focuses on ways to contain the things you've decided to keep. The containers you select comprise the physical, tangible structure of your organizing system. Your tools help you use and manipulate the elements of your system to support your activities.

In this concept, it's important to define the key words, *container* and *tool*, precisely. The first one—container—is a common word, generally understood to be something big enough to put things in and small enough to carry around. In a word association exercise, the word *container* might prompt you to respond with *box* or *bin* or *basket*. My clients think of containers as items that can be purchased at stores like Target and Wal-Mart. And when I began working as a professional organizer, that's what I thought, too.

Over time, however, I've discovered that the concept of a container is much broader than this limited definition conveys. In an organizing system, a container is anything that holds something else. This expanded definition includes the bins and boxes one normally thinks of, as well as chairs and sofas (containers for people), wood furniture (containers for things), closets (containers for clothes and things), rooms (containers for activities), and buildings (for instance, your house is the container for your family's life). You could even call your calendar a container, because it holds a record of the way you spend your time. As you apply *Strategy #4*, you'll see how this broader definition helps you recognize the role of effective containers in all the layers of your organizing system.

The second key word—tool— also benefits from an expanded definition. Even though the word might conjure up the image of a hammer or a screwdriver, organizing tools are not limited to handheld mechanical implements alone. Instead, in *Strategy #4*, a tool is any instrument that helps you accomplish a specific task. The word *tool* encompasses a wide variety of instruments. Containers are just one type. A tool can range from something as simple as a box top to a complicated piece of equipment like a computer, as long as it does the job you want it to do. If you ever tried to drive a nail with a screwdriver because you couldn't find your hammer, you know the difference the right tool can make.

In your overall organizing system, containers and tools play essential roles. Each one of them has a job to do to support you and your activities. The right ones are the ones that help you live your life today and are flexible enough to support you if your life changes tomorrow. The trick is deciding which one is best for the organizing task you need help with. If you want to store dishes, for instance, a dresser won't do. By the same token, a kitchen cupboard isn't a good container for sweaters. Sometimes, selecting the correct tool or container for a specific job is a tricky proposition.

When I started my business, I had no idea how hard it was for people to select containers and tools that actually solved their organizing problems. It turns out that in the last decade, marketers have discovered "Helps You Get Organized!" is as good a sales pitch as "Fat Free!" in our "more is better" culture. As a result, stores are flooded with hundreds of horrible products that actually *hinder* organization instead of promoting it. For any given organizing dilemma, there are a plethora of products billing themselves as the solution. But only a few of them really work. In this chapter, you'll get some concrete guidelines on how to make tool and container choices that support you and your activities.

Symptoms That Your System Needs Better Containers and Tools

Let's look at some of the ways you can tell you haven't had good luck *Using the Right Containers and Tools.*

- You have boxes stacked on top of each other in all your storage spaces.
- You've got years' worth of photographs stashed in numerous drawers and closets, sitting next to empty photograph albums.
- There's never a pen or notepad by the telephone when you need it.
- There are food and drink stains on the carpet around the chairs in your family room.

- Your office doesn't have a single functioning file drawer.
- You have lots of nice jewelry, but you wear the same three pieces day in and day out.
- You miss appointments because they aren't recorded in your calendar.
- There's a pile of books and/or magazines on the floor next to every bed.
- Everyone in the family throws their dirty clothes on the floor.
- There are always wet towels sitting in a soggy lump on the bathroom floor.
- You can never find tape, scissors, or a stapler when you need one.
- Family members are always fighting over who gets to sit in the comfy chair.
- Shoes are in a jumble at the bottom of all the closets.
- Your desk doesn't have any file drawers.
- You don't like to sit at your desk.
- You don't have a desk.
- You're always cleaning up water drips from the kitchen and bathroom floors.
- You don't like to put things away in your drawers because then you can't see them.
- When you want to throw something away, you have to get up to do it.
- There are videotapes and game cartridges sitting in piles on the floor next to the TV.
- Your children drop their backpacks and jackets on the floor when they get home from school.
- There's a pile of bills in the kitchen or family room because you pay them there instead of in your office.
- Your preschooler's books are always spread out all over the floor.

Do any of these sound like you? Then you could be suffering from the insidious effects of bad tools and containers. In the following stories, you'll get some great ideas from watching other people apply *Strategy #4* to some of the most common container and tool problems.

Real-Life Lessons:
Strategy #4 Missing in Action

Hillary complained to me about how difficult it was to get her holiday decorations out of the attic. Since many attics are hard to get in and out of, I wasn't surprised. But it turned out that Hillary's attic was a walk-in room at the top of her house. No ladders or trap doors had to be negotiated, so getting in and out of the room wasn't the problem. Then we went inside, and the real issue became crystal clear. In Hillary's attic, boxes were piled on top of each other all around the room. Each pile was four to five feet tall. Although it was possible to approach every pile, only the top boxes were accessible. To retrieve a lower-down item, she had to move everything on top of it first. Since Hillary's holiday decorations were buried under other, more recently stored items, she practically had to rearrange the attic to retrieve them.

A *shelving unit* is a simple, commonly available tool that allows you to pile items up and get any single one out without moving the others. When boxes, books, or bins are stored on shelves, it's easy to get them out and put them back again. Tall shelving units around the edges of any room—attic, garage, storage room, basement, and throughout your living space—are an essential organizing tool. Make sure you have enough shelving units for your belongings, and get units with adjustable shelves whenever possible.

In Cynthia's refrigerator, a mixed batch of plastic containers holds leftovers and cooking ingredients. Some of them are clear, allowing Cynthia to see what's inside. Others are opaque. When Cynthia looks into her refrigerator, trying to find something to cook or eat, she always chooses among the clear containers. Periodically, at refrigerator-cleaning time, she takes the opaque containers out and dumps their fuzzy blue contents down the garbage disposal. This is a waste of food *and* storage space.

Clear containers are infinitely more functional than opaque ones. When you can't see into a container, you tend to ignore its contents. For toys, craft materials, clothes, food, and all kinds of stored items, clear works best. Don't use opaque containers unless you're prepared to label them in detail.

Scott's problem was trash. Throughout his living space, plastic wrap from packaging, old catalogs, junk mail, small broken items, and plastic bags littered the surfaces. The problem was especially noticeable around Scott's favorite chair, in which he watched television and opened his daily mail. When I asked Scott where the wastebasket was, he got up, walked into the kitchen, and opened the cupboard door under the sink. The kitchen garbage can and a small decorator can in the bathroom were the only wastebaskets in his roomy apartment. He needed a lot more of them.

To keep trash from piling up on your surfaces, have a *roomy wastebasket* in every room (including children's rooms). Make it easy to discard something. If a wastebasket is too far away when you make the decision to throw something out, you'll just put it on the nearest table instead of making the trip. In places where paper trash accumulates, install a recycling bin or basket. I've never seen a home with too many wastebaskets or recycling bins.

Terri worked full-time from her home. Even though her second bedroom was set up as an office, she was doing most of her work at the kitchen table because she preferred it to her desk. It turned out Terri's real problem was her office chair. A sturdy, straight-backed oak chair, it was exceedingly uncomfortable. It also lacked wheels, making it hard to maneuver when she needed to turn and reach something. Terri needed a comfortable, ergonomic, rolling chair to sit comfortably at her desk and do her work effectively.

A chair or sofa is a container for a person. If it's uncomfortable, it won't get used unless it's the only one available. Make sure you have *comfortable seating* if you want people to stick around and relax (including you). Replace uncomfortable chairs and sofas with comfortable counterparts. If you need any of your seating to embody other qualities—for instance, to swivel or roll—make sure your furniture fits the bill.

Pauline had trouble finding a pen or pencil whenever she needed something to write with. On her desk, writing implements were scattered randomly among the papers. In the rest of the house, they seemed to travel from the kitchen whenever she wasn't looking. The only things left to write with in the drawer by the telephone were leadless pencils, a few crayons, and five pens that didn't work.

A great use for your extra mugs is as *pen- and pencil-holders*. Put one in every single spot in the house where you might need something to write with—next to each telephone, in the family room, by your dining table, on all the desks, next to every bed, and even in the living room if that's where you do the cross-word puzzle. It's a good idea to have a pair of scissors in each of these places, too. Mugs and small vases are useful, functional holders for pens, pencils, letter openers, scissors, X-acto knives (blade down), markers, rulers, highlighters, and so on. They make all these tools easy to see, get out, and put away.

In Janice's family room, the carpet around the sofa and two chairs is dotted with food and drink stains. Even though people try to be careful with their plates and glasses, there is no place to put them except on the floor. That's how accidents happen, leaving behind a hard-to-clean mess.

Next to every seat in your home, especially in heavily used areas like the family room, there needs to be a hard surface where people can safely put things when they sit down. If you have no *end tables* or *coffee tables* within easy reach, you are guaranteed to have spills. The same principle applies to beds as well. Make sure there's a place to put a book and a glass of water next to each person's bed.

Every day after Johnny takes a shower, he walks around as he dries himself off. His wife finds damp towels randomly draped over doorknobs, the backs of chairs, and on the floor. She has asked him a thousand times to hang his towel up on the bar when he's finished, but her requests fall on deaf ears.

A *hook* is a much easier place to hang a towel than the towel bars found in most bathrooms. It takes fewer steps and still gets the job done. If his wife installs hooks on the walls or the backs of the bathroom and bedroom doors, Johnny is much more likely to hang up his damp towel every time.

Elena was about to go back to school, and she knew she'd be spending much more time doing desk work than she was used to. When she was employed full-time, it had been okay to do her paperwork at the tiny dining table in her sunny kitchen. But she was worried that her current setup, which required her to move the papers aside at mealtimes, would be inadequate to support her life as a graduate student.

Elena was right to assume that her kitchen was not the *right room for the activity* she was planning to do. For schoolwork and studying, Elena needed a larger work area dedicated solely to those tasks. We rearranged the furniture in her living room to set up a spacious desk next to the front window, then moved all Elena's paperwork functions there. The living room was a better container than the kitchen for Elena's new activities.

The rooms in your home are the containers for your activities. If you avoid doing a task because you don't like being in that room, consider moving the activity to a better location.

Sandy's closet was a modular one, with hanging space for clothes of varying lengths and a bank of wooden drawers for such things as underwear and socks. When we finished sorting and weeding Sandy's clothes and put them back into the closet, we discovered a problem. Sandy's wardrobe needed less hanging storage than the closet contained, and she had more shirts, sweaters, pants, and shoes than fit in the sections designed for them. The built-in design of the closet was not a good fit for Sandy's clothing storage needs.

To solve this mismatch between collection and container, we bought ten *extra shelves* for Sandy's closet. We installed them into the closet, putting them close enough together so no space went to waste. Then the clothes went onto the new shelves. This was especially effective for Sandy, who is a visual person and likes to be able to see everything.

In many shelving units, particularly the ones available for custom closets, the basic setup doesn't give you enough shelves. If possible, get at least one extra shelf every time you buy wooden shelving units. Set them up so there are no big gaps above the items you're shelving.

Allison's three school-age children get dressed and undressed in their bedrooms. Every evening when she goes to tuck them in, she trips over the clothes perpetually strewn across each bedroom floor. On wash day, Allison's back suffers from the bending and stooping she has to do to retrieve all the dirty laundry from her children's rooms. She asked for suggestions to solve these problems.

Every person in a household needs his or her own *hamper* for dirty laundry. If there is no place to put soiled clothes, they usually end up on the floor in a messy heap. A hamper is not only a good catch-all for laundry, it can also be used to carry dirty wash to the washing machine, then bring clean clothes back to the bedroom. If you send some of your clothes out for laundering or dry cleaning, keep a separate hamper for this purpose. Any large open basket or box can be a functional hamper. You don't need to limit yourself to plastic ones.

Lila is a writer who loves to work at her beautiful, well-crafted cherry desk. To handle her files, she purchased a matching cherry cabinet with two drawers. Yet papers are always littering her work surface and getting in her way. The problem is, she can't open her bottom file drawer because it gets stuck on her carpet.

A full-suspension file cabinet is an essential organizing container. Unless your work is particularly paper-intensive, most households need only two drawers. In my experience, metal file cabinets hold up better than wooden ones. I also recommend the horizontal models (long side goes against the wall) over the vertical ones (long side sticks out from the wall) because they fit better into most rooms. One good metal file cabinet is worth its purchase price because it will last forever. Don't waste your money on a cheap one.

In Wendy's new home, the kitchen was a beautiful room graced with custom cabinets, granite counters, a huge island, and high ceilings—it was any cook's dream. The only problem was it lacked a mud room. So every time Wendy's three children and their big dog trekked in from the backyard, Wendy's new wood floors were being marred by the grit and dirt they brought in on their feet.

A simple way to prevent damage to your floors, not to mention all the work involved in cleaning them, is to put *heavy-duty mats* inside every entrance. These will catch the dirt before it has a chance to get farther into the house. If you have a formal front hall, use an attractive but easily cleanable carpet or throw rug to catch and hold incoming grit.

Wendy's kitchen had one additional problem, which again involved the wood floors. When Wendy was cooking meals or cleaning up, every drip made a visible mark on the floor. Since drips are an inevitable by-product of the activity in a family kitchen, keeping them all wiped up was taking a noticeable amount of Wendy's time.

To absorb drips and cushion your feet as you work in your kitchen, a randomly patterned *runner* or *throw rug* (for instance, a rag rug) is quite useful. If such a floor covering fits into your kitchen's decor, it will save you a lot of work in the long run. Bathrooms and laundry rooms also benefit from rugs that absorb drips without any visible trace.

Debbie lives in a five-room apartment with lots of windows. Every room is bright and sunny during the day except the kitchen. Its small window faces north and is partly blocked by the house next door. However, Debbie's pantry has a large, unobstructed window with a small counter below it. Even though the kitchen has plenty of food preparation space, Debbie often finds herself chopping vegetables or mixing ingredients in the pantry instead of the kitchen. This wastes her time and energy because she is constantly moving things around to make space on the pantry's counter.

Debbie was being drawn into her pantry by the *bright light* from the window. For her, it made sense to rearrange her kitchen so the pantry was set up for food preparation. If you find yourself following the light in your home, set up work spaces next to your windows. At night, make sure you have enough *lamps* to brightly light every room. *Torchieres* are good at illuminating a whole room, as long as you keep them away from flammable things like curtains.

William is four years old. He doesn't know how to read yet, but he loves his books. Whenever he wants to find one of his favorite stories, he goes to the bookshelf in his room, pulls down all the books, and spreads them across the floor. When he recognizes the one he wants by the picture on its cover, he grabs it and takes it to his mother so she can read it to him. The rest of the books stay on the floor until bedtime, when he and his mother pick them up and put them back in the bookcase. William's mother asked me if there was any way to keep the books on the shelves.

If you have a preschool child, this is a familiar scenario. The problem is that a pre-reader can't tell one book from another by the words on the spine. A preschooler uses the picture on the cover to identify a book. So a bookshelf that works perfectly well for an older child will not work for a three- or four-year-old. The best container for a small child's books is a common *dishpan*. When books are standing up in a dishpan, facing the child, it's easy for him or her to select one and leave the rest in the bin. Labeled dishpans sitting on shelves are also good containers for collections of small toys.

Children, especially little ones, are naturally disposed to do the easiest thing when they come indoors from outside, which is to drop their stuff on the floor as soon as they enter the house. If you have children and your storage for outdoor gear and footwear is a closed closet, you are guaranteed to have this problem. Either you'll nag your kids endlessly to put away their stuff, or you'll do it for them. There *is* a better way.

Instead of asking kids to hang their jackets on hangers, install a *peg rack* in the garage (if that's where you usually come in) or behind the entrance door. Make sure all your kids can reach it, then remind them to use it. It's almost as easy to hang a jacket on a peg as it is to drop it on the floor, so they'll have no excuse for not hanging up their things. Mittens and hats can go in baskets hung on the end peg, or in reachable bins inside the closet. If you have too many jackets and accessories to store this way, keep off-season ones inside the closet, or weed out the whole collection to make it more manageable. In snowy and wet climates, keep a shallow tray under the peg rack for boots and shoes. Don't let kids track through the house in dirty footwear. Ask them to take off their shoes every time they come inside.

Stashed somewhere in every home, there is a pile of photographs (still in their original envelopes) waiting to be put into albums. Why is this? Because photograph albums are hard to use for storing photographs. They don't hold many pictures; it takes a lot of time to get the photos into the albums; and many of them eventually damage the photographs. Photo albums are only a useful container for preserving the memory of special events like weddings.

I recommend a *photo box* for storing photographs. Similar to a card file box, it allows you to file pictures standing up in groups, with tabbed dividers to separate one set from another. Small envelopes that hold negatives are included with every box, and the tabbed dividers give you plenty of space for recording information about each set of pictures. These boxes are easy to use, easy to store, and easy to retrieve pictures from. If you're worried about preserving your photographs for a long time, you can buy these boxes in acid-free versions. At the very least, if you aren't ready to store your photographs when you bring them home from the developer, scribble the date and a brief description of the contents on the outside of the envelope. This will help you sort them when you're finally ready to deal with them.

Photographs are not the only collection lurking in the closets of every home. Another commonly stashed item is wrapping paper. A number of products are marketed as containers for rolls of paper and bags of ribbons, but most cause more problems than they solve. Never, ever buy a bin that requires you to store the rolls of paper horizontally. In such containers, you have to move the ribbon tray to get at the wrapping paper, and you can't see all the rolls at the same time because only the top ones are visible.

Instead of a bin, use an *upright container* that holds the rolls of paper vertically and has a tray or shelf for ribbons. There are lightweight cardboard boxes like this on the market around the holidays. A tall, round wastebasket will also do, though it doesn't have a place for ribbons.

A third item taking up space in the backs of numerous desk drawers is the unused pages from too-cumbersome time management systems. These highlight how difficult it is to find the right calendar for you.

Every one of my clients has a unique and personal way of keeping track of her or his time. In our computerized world, there are numerous systems on the market to help you manage this essential task. The latest crazes are *personal digital assistants* (PDAs) like Palm Pilots, which are good tools for people who like gadgets and enjoy figuring out how they work. Unless you are such a person, I wouldn't recommend a PDA to you. It takes more steps to do any given task with a PDA than it takes to do the same task with a paper calendar.

In the old-fashioned world of *paper calendars*, the main choice is between a wall calendar and a portable one. Each has advantages and disadvantages. Wall calendars are easy to read, allow all family members to participate in scheduling, and stay put so you always know where they are. But if you make appointments when you're away from home, you have to remember to record them when you get back. Portable calendars, or planners, come with you when you go out, allowing you to write all your appointments in them right away. But they are hard to share with others, and in many of them, the boxes are small.

Among portable calendars, you can purchase products in a wide range of sizes, materials, and weights. Many allow you to choose different kinds of inserts. Some are sold as part of a full-fledged time management system. The number of choices can be overwhelming.

When selecting the right calendar for you, there are two considerations. A *functional calendar must* be easy for you to handle, or you won't use it. Also, it *must* depict time in a way that suits you. For instance, if you think of time in one-week chunks, get a week-at-a-glance model. If you like seeing a whole month at a time, a wall calendar might be best. Figure out what you need your calendar to do, then purchase one that does just that. Discard any sections you never use (don't just stash them in a drawer for posterity).

How many times have you needed to write down something, but you couldn't find a clean piece of paper to write on? Notepads are the most commonly used product for scribbling brief messages or recording telephone calls. They are small, thin, and portable. Another similar product is a note cube, a solid block with 500 sheets. These usually have a design or picture on the sides and are not portable at all.

Because people tend to take notepads with them after they write down a message, I recommend *note cubes* over notepads. They stay in one place, and you'll never waste time trying to find a piece of paper if you keep a note cube next to every telephone. Note cubes also add a nice decorative touch to your desk and phone centers.

Many people have a perfectly good desk and file cabinet somewhere in the house, but still like to pay bills in the family room and/or in front of the television. If you've been carrying piles of papers back and forth between your office and your favorite chair, or if you simply leave a big stack of unpaid bills in the family room all the time, you need a tool to help you keep your papers portable but under control.

For this purpose, a *rolling file cart* is a very useful product. You can use it to store things in your office, then wheel it out to the other room when it's time to pay bills. Most have a rack at the top for hanging files, with two sliding baskets underneath for supplies. Keep the financial files you need for bill-paying in the cart, including a "To Pay" folder. When a bill comes in the mail, put it straight into this folder so you won't have to hunt it down on bill-paying day. Your pens, scissors, letter opener, stapler, and staple remover go in one of the baskets. The other one can hold such items as envelopes and boxes of unused checks. Metal file carts are best. Don't waste money on a flimsy plastic one.

Are you one of the many people trying to manage a home without a proper desk? Running a household is like running a small business. Yet a surprising number of homes are not adequately set up to handle essential administrative tasks like bill-paying. Even if you don't have enough space to designate a room as an office, you need at least one place in your home dedicated to managing your finances.

Every household needs a functional *desk* to support its financial and paperwork activities. If you're in the market for one, here are some things to shop for. First of all, it needs to be *roomy*. This means the surface is big enough to spread out your papers while you work. Get the biggest desk your room's dimensions will allow. Second, make sure your desk is *comfortable* for you. If your legs are cramped, or there's a hutch that looms over you and makes you uneasy, that desk is not the one you want. Third, make sure it has the *storage* you need. If you don't have other places to put your supplies and reference books, the desk needs spots for those things. Finally, you need to *like it*. If you don't like your desk, you won't use it. Keep looking until you locate a desk that fits your specific requirements.

In closets all across the country, especially those old-fashioned ones with a single shelf above a long bar, a jumble of shoes often fills every inch of floor space. The common shoe is a difficult item to contain. To address this problem, every closet shop offers numerous containers supposedly designed for the purpose of holding footwear. Most of them are completely worthless. They are either too flimsy, too small, or too difficult to put shoes in. If you have to wrestle with your shoe container just to put your shoes away, it's no good. Get rid of it immediately.

A *horizontal stacking shelf* works best for storing adults' shoes. Typically made of melamine, these are inexpensive and widely available. If you're tall, you can place one or two of these on the high shelf in your closet. Then you'll be able to see and reach all of your shoes without scrounging under your hanging clothes to find the footwear you want. If you aren't tall, you can stack two or three of these on the closet floor. Put sneakers and boots on the top shelf, or get a stacking unit with a wider gap between shelves for these larger shoes.

For children's shoes, *hanging shoe bags* are the product of choice. These are ten- or twenty-pocket items that attach to your closet rod using Velcro. Usually a bit small for adult footwear, they work wonders in children's closets to clean up the shoe tangle on the floor. With these bags, kids can see their shoes, reach them easily, and put them back.

Hanging shoe bags also work well for storing small things like scarves, evening bags, and visors in your clothes closet, or gloves and hats in your coat closet.

In some homes, sliding closet doors keep people from taking full advantage of their storage spaces. These common building features are a terrible invention. The doors obscure at least half of the closet at any given moment. If you're cursed with a three-door configuration, you can only see one-third of your closet at a time. What a nightmare!

Although new doors can be expensive, sliding closet doors are worth replacing if you're planning to stay in the same home for a few years. *Folding doors*, which allow you to see the entire contents of the closet at once, are infinitely preferable. A curtain could also work, as long as it's easy to slide back and forth.

Many people don't like putting their papers into file cabinets because their organizing style causes them to prefer a more visible paper storage. If you're a visual person, your file cabinet might seem like a black hole into which papers disappear, never to be seen again. For you, a metal desktop file that keeps important folders in plain view works well. Frequently, however, people put off doing their filing because there's something physically wrong with their filing system that makes it difficult to put away important papers.

If this applies to you, see if you're missing any of these essential filing tools: (1) a *file cabinet* with drawers that are easy to open and close; (2) a *rack* inside each drawer for hanging file folders; (3) *hanging file folders* on the rack, each holding one to three manila file folders, so you can easily slide folders back and forth to get papers in and out; (4) *labels* on the hanging and manila folders so you know what's in each one. If any of these tools are missing, it could explain why your file cabinet doesn't work well for you.

A common clutter culprit in the modern family room is a pile of homeless videotapes. There are plenty of pieces of furniture designed to hold them—giant entertainment units, revolving racks, standing cabinets, and so on—but most of them are inadequate. Either they don't have enough space for even a small video collection, or they have slots for the videocassettes that aren't big enough for some video boxes, or their doors are too heavy to shut when they're fully loaded with tapes.

The best storage I've seen for videotapes is a *bookcase* no more than eight inches deep. Videocassettes stored standing up on shelves, just like books, are easy to see, select, and put away. It's even better if the bookcase can be put within five feet of the television. If not, see if it fits behind the nearest door, close yet invisible. And make sure the shelves are adjustable so you can rearrange them when you switch from VHS to DVD.

Somewhere in your dressing area, do you have a tangle of jewelry you don't wear because it's so hard to extricate the pieces you want? There's not room here for a comprehensive discussion of jewelry storage, but one common method, the too-small and jumbled mess usually known as a *jewelry box*, is ineffective at best. Baubles stored in such a container are like toys in a toy box. You can't see what's really there, which means you won't use it. It's a shame to let a bad container keep you from wearing your nice jewelry.

If you have nice jewelry, it needs to be separated and stored in a *container with shallow compartments*. Otherwise, things get tangled. Drawers or trays with low dividers work best. If the dividers are too tall, it's hard to get your fingers into the slots to retrieve the pieces you want.

To find the right jewelry container for your collection, first untangle it, sort it into piles, weed down to things you really like, then look for trays that hold that amount (plus a little room for expansion).

What a Full-Blown Strategy #4 Crisis Looks Like

The stories you've just read focus on specific kinds of containers and tools. Some of them are simple and inexpensive to use—pen cups, note cubes, wastebaskets, lamps, hampers. Others are harder to find

The Worst Container Ever Invented

The worst container I've ever encountered is the one that comes with every large set of Duplo building blocks. (Duplos are the preschool version of Legos.) They have the same basic shape as Legos, and get connected to each other in the same way, but each piece is big enough for a small child to manipulate. Duplos come in a tall, square bucket made of opaque plastic. It has a carrying handle and a top shaped like a Duplo brick. Inside, it holds sixty or so Duplo pieces in varying shapes, sizes, and colors.

Imagine, for a moment, that the four-year-old owner of these building blocks wants to retrieve the green alligator from the bucket. First, the child looks at the outside of the container. It offers no clue as to the whereabouts of the alligator, because it is opaque. Next, the child takes the top off the container, and peers inside. Unless the alligator is one of the six blocks at the very top of the container, it cannot be seen. This means it is somewhere farther down. The child could conceivably stick a hand in and rummage around in hopes of encountering an alligator shape. But the bucket is too narrow to do this easily. So what does the child do to find the alligator? The child *must* dump all the Duplo blocks on the floor to retrieve a single block.

Here's the reason this is the worst container ever. *It isn't really a container at all, it is a dumper-outer!* The only way for a child to play with its contents is to de-contain them. And what a mess that makes.

and cost more—desks, file cabinets, rugs and mats, comfortable chairs, shelving units. And if you need to decide which room in your home is the right container for a certain activity, you have a limited number of spaces to choose from. But even though selecting the right containers and tools can take time and money, it's a doable quest when all you're shopping for is one or two items. So what would you do if the container that was causing you the most trouble was the biggest thing you owned, your most valuable asset, and the hardest thing to replace—your home?

To illustrate the chaos that ensues when your home is not a good container for the activities with which you fill your life, we turn again to Leo, the electrical engineer from the introduction. What Leo and I discovered after we'd spent a lot of time sorting his belongings into the rooms in his home, weeding out things he was ready to let go of, emptying his storage locker, and making a dent in the piles of equipment and tools in his off-site workshop was that his house was not well suited to his life. Even though it was in a lovely setting, with a soothing woodland view of a meadow, it was woefully inadequate for the life Leo was trying to live inside it. Let's look at the ways his house was causing him trouble.

Space: Leo is an engineer and inventor. He has an extensive collection of sophisticated tools, some of which are bulky, heavy, oily pieces of machinery that make a mess every time he uses them. This is a man who needs a functional workshop where he can drill holes in metal plates, cut and manipulate large pieces of wood, and use toxic ingredients. He *requires* a workshop to do his specialized work. But his house doesn't have one. All his rooms are set up as living space—carpeted, with white plaster walls and big windows. There isn't a single place on Leo's property for his working and inventing activities. The only way to get such a place would be to build another building specifically for that function.

Things: Precisely because he is an inventor, Leo needs to keep a wide variety of materials, implements, and information on hand. He never knows when an idea will strike him and what supplies he might need in order to act on it. Sitting around in his house are prototypes of various inventions, some the creations of friends, some his own. His house also holds a significant amount of stuff, including several large musical instruments (piano, marimba). Leo inherited a lot of family mementos when his parents died. His house is the repository for much of his entire family's history. Given all that, it's no surprise that Leo's storage-less house causes him trouble. There is no attic, no basement, and no garage to put things into. Again, the only way to get adequate and easily accessible storage for all Leo's belongings is to build it.

Information: This is one element of Leo's overall organizing system that his house would be able to support *if* he had other suitable space for working and storing things. Either one of his spare bedrooms would make a gracious library/home office where he could sit and think and read. However, because these rooms are being used as, respectively, a quasi-workshop and a storage space, neither is available for this function.

Time: Because his work activities are not well supported by his home, Leo keeps some of his tools and materials in the house and some of them down the road in his unheated workshop. This makes efficient use of his work time impossible, because he has to keep jumping in the car to fetch things from one location and bring them back to the other place. Also, inside the house, his lack of storage space means things that might otherwise get put away are sitting around in his living areas. So the lack of adequate built-in storage makes navigating and finding things more difficult.

Relationships: Here's another element where the house fails to support Leo's life. The second spare room would be a nice guest room if it didn't have to act as Leo's sole storage space. Then, when Leo's children come to visit, or he has a guest, he would have comfortable and private accommodations for them. Instead, guests are relegated to the living room sofa. Although this is not a terrible arrangement, it could be improved if the house had better storage.

Of course, changing your house so it actually suits your life and supports your activities requires drastic steps. You'd either have to begin a massive construction project, or move to another house that better fits your requirements. In Leo's case, he bought his home during his divorce, a period when his personal and financial resources were diminished by the circumstances of his life. At that time, things were changing so drastically that it was hard to discern exactly what he was going to be doing after all the life-changing events slowed down. This meant it was difficult to plan out his activities and find a piece of property that supported them.

When his life stabilized and he realized his home was an inadequate container for his life, Leo used his inventor's resourcefulness to attack the problem. He compensated for the limitations of his house by renting storage and work space elsewhere. In the short run, these steps have given him temporary solutions. In the long run, he's saving his money and keeping his eye out for a piece of property that would suit him better.

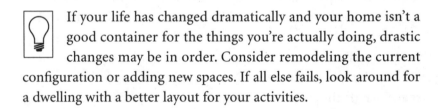 If your life has changed dramatically and your home isn't a good container for the things you're actually doing, drastic changes may be in order. Consider remodeling the current configuration or adding new spaces. If all else fails, look around for a dwelling with a better layout for your activities.

How to Put Strategy #4 Back in Place

Did any of the products described in this chapter resemble the ones causing trouble in your home? It's hard to keep your organizing system working efficiently to support your life if you don't have the right tools and containers for the job. The good ones help you do your routine organizing tasks, large and small, as quickly and efficiently as possible. In the stories you just read, other people solved all kinds of problems by replacing bad products with good ones. Here are some tips to help you select the tools and containers that best fit your unique set of requirements.

Use the Right Containers and Tools for Your Space

- Think about where you've set up the supplies and equipment for each of your current activities. If the location is keeping you from doing an activity effectively, find a better place for it and move everything there.
- Make sure your furniture supports your activities. If you can't store things, select furniture with storage space. If your seating is uncomfortable or inadequate, replace it. Don't let your furniture keep you from functioning efficiently.
- Next to every seat and bed, make sure there's a flat surface that can hold such items as drinks and plates. Have enough end tables and coffee tables for everyone.
- To separate multiple functions in a single room, use low shelves, sofas, and rugs as dividers.
- At your main entrance(s), make sure there's a place to put things that are on their way in or out. Create a "staging area" using a cupboard, bookcase, or basket to prevent this spot from degenerating into a big pile.
- Put heavy-duty mats inside every entrance door to catch dirt and grit.
- Use patterned runners and throw rugs in your kitchen and bathrooms to catch drips.
- Make sure rooms are brightly lit. Purchase more lamps, including torchieres, if your spaces are dim at night.
- Set up important activities next to windows to take advantage of the natural light.
- Make sure your household has a functional desk. This is an essential organizing tool.

Use the Right Containers and Tools for Your Things

- Keep a wastebasket in every room.
- In the spot where you open the mail, put a recycling bin to catch all the junk. Have one in every spot where papers are routinely discarded.
- Make sure children have wastebaskets in their rooms.
- Shelving units are essential organizing tools. Make sure you have enough shelf space in your living space and your storage areas.
- Make sure shelving units have enough shelves for the things you want to store on them. Get extra shelves if you need to.
- Use clear containers whenever possible. They allow you to see the contents readily, which means you're more likely to use the things they contain. Avoid opaque containers.
- Use clear bins on shelves and in cupboards to hold collections. These function like drawers, but are portable.
- Put a pen- and pencil-holder in every spot where you routinely write things down. Keep a pair of scissors in each. Don't make yourself travel to retrieve these basic tools.
- Store videotapes, DVDs, CDs, and audiotapes in shallow bookcases. Stand them up on the shelves like books.
- Put peg racks at your family's main entrance for kids' jackets and backpacks. Use baskets for hats and mittens and a shallow tray for shoes and boots.
- Use the spaces behind your doors for shallow shelves and peg racks. These are good storage spots for all kinds of tall, narrow items.
- If anyone in your household is a visual person who likes to keep clothes out where they can be seen, consider keeping that person's clothing on closet shelves instead of in a dresser.
- Make sure everyone has a hamper. Don't accept excuses if kids still drop dirty clothes on the floor.

- Use hampers to take dirty clothes to the laundry and bring the clean clothes back.
- If you routinely send things out for laundering or dry cleaning, keep a separate hamper for these garments.
- Install hooks in bathrooms and on the backs of bedroom/ bathroom doors. Use hooks for wet towels instead of rods.
- If anyone in your family enjoys crafting, contain their materials on shelves in clear containers.
- In closets, use horizontal stacking shelves for adult shoes. These can go on the upper shelf or on the floor. Throw out shoe storage units that make you work to put your shoes away.
- Use ten- or twenty-pocket hanging shoe bags for children's shoes, hats, and mittens in coat closets and for small accessories in bedroom closets.
- Store photographs in photo boxes instead of albums. Create albums only for pictures of special occasions, but not for everyday snapshots.
- Label photo envelopes with the date as soon as you get them home.
- Keep wrapping paper stored vertically, rather than horizontally. If you have more rolls than fit into a tall, narrow kitchen garbage can, you have more than you need.
- Put a note cube next to every telephone.
- Put your preschooler's books in dishpans instead of on shelves.
- Use dishpans on children's shelves to hold collections of small toys.
- Keep Legos and Duplos in clear, shallow containers such as under-bed sweater boxes. Toss the original containers for these small toys.
- In low kitchen cupboards, use sturdy boxes or bins to function as drawers. You can pull them out, get the thing you want, and put them back again. This keeps you from having to crawl on the floor to retrieve things from the backs of the shelves.

• Don't forget simple, free storage alternatives. Sometimes the best container is a cardboard box. Using a utility knife and hot glue, you can transform a leftover box or box top into the exact container you need. Be creative!

Use the Right Containers and Tools for Your Information

• If you like to pay bills somewhere besides your office, use a rolling file cart to bring your supplies and files with you. Keep them stored by your desk the rest of the time.
• Keep your action files standing up on your desktop in a sturdy metal file holder so you can see them and use them easily.
• Use a heavy-duty full-suspension file cabinet to store your important papers. Most households need only two file drawers.
• Use letter-size file folders, not legal size.
• Use hanging file folders in your file cabinet. These allow you to get in and out of your files easily. The papers themselves go into manila folders inside the hanging folders.
• Consider purchasing a high-quality safe for your home. This will protect your most important documents from theft and fire. A safe is also easier to use than a safe deposit box because it's on-site.
• Use cardboard stationery sorters with multiple slots to store different types of paper.
• Use stand-up cardboard magazine file holders for newsletters, essays, telephone lists, and so on. Keep just one category or logical group of items in each file.
• Keep a heavy-duty shredder in your office, and use it on all recycled documents containing important numbers and personal information.

- If you have a computer and are comfortable using it as a tool, get a money management software program like Quicken to help you manage your financial information. It is a powerful cash management tool and a good program for keeping track of your finances.

Use the Right Containers and Tools for Your Time

- Figure out what kind of calendar works best for you, then shop to get the one you want. Unless you are a high-tech gadget person, choose a paper system rather than a PDA.
- Next to the kitchen phone, keep a folder called "Schedules/ Events" for lists of dates and one-time invitations or fliers. Make it available to all family members.
- Use an answering machine to catch telephone messages and screen your calls when you're busy.
- Examine your system for keeping track of important people— family members, friends, local resources, and contractors. Consider keeping this information in a single binder next to your kitchen telephone. Make sure you can retrieve important numbers quickly and easily when you need them.

Use the Right Containers and Tools for Your Relationships

- Your seating arrangements—chairs and sofas—are the containers for the people in your life. Make sure you have enough of them, and they're comfortable. Replace any that don't fit the bill.

- Make sure your furniture supports the people you care about. Make comfort and ease of use the bottom line in your decor.
- Make sure everyone's activities are supported by the right containers and tools.
- Check with other family members to see how their tools and containers are working. Decide together whether changes need to be made, then make them.

For more ideas about containing things, consult the list of good organizing books in "Recommended Reading." With these tips and your own ingenuity, you can figure out how to *Use the Right Containers and Tools* to get all your tasks done easily. The next step in getting your systems to fit you and your life is to make sure you can retrieve and use everything once you've contained it. It's time to move on to *Strategy #5, Label Everything.*

CHAPTER 5 | **STRATEGY #5**

Label Everything

Labeling is essential to remembering what and where everything is once it's put away. Good labels help you retrieve things and share them with others. Something left unlabeled is likely to just disappear from your radar screen. Something labeled incorrectly is almost guaranteed not to work well.

Overview of Strategy #5

Good labels can make the difference between *having* things and *using* them. In every organizing system, the labels make it possible to retrieve things after you put them away. Once you've stored your things in the right containers (*Strategy #4*), the labels you select provide the visual cues you need to find them again. If you store things without labeling them, they get lost. Imagine, for instance, a whole drawer of file folders, each one filled with papers, but none labeled. Where would you look if you were trying to track down a specific document? You'd have no clue where to start, so you'd have to look in every folder. By the same token, if you had to select a videotape from a bookcase full of unlabeled cassettes, you'd have to play the beginning of each one to locate the one you want. In either case, it would cost you some of your precious time to find what you're looking for.

When you neglect to take a moment to label a storage container or file folder, you make the things inside it invisible. They become simple placeholders—things that take up space but have no name. You can still *use* the contents of unlabeled containers, but not without searching through them first. The harder a stored item is to find, the more time you waste looking for it, and the less likely it is to be used. The longer you leave something in unlabeled storage, the more likely it is you'll forget you even have it. If you frequently store things without labeling them, you invite the question, "Why bother?"

A good label gives you the information you need to use things you've put away. This is easy to recognize when you're talking about boxes and bins and folders. When applied to these kinds of containers, a label is a noun, some kind of "marker indicating contents, ownership, or destination." It is a visual cue that gives you information about your stuff. In *Strategy #5, Label Everything*, however, the word *label* is an action word. It means "to describe or designate." When you label something, you give it a name. This concept extends far beyond the boxes and bins in your organizing system.

Names are powerful. They shape our understanding of things. Do you remember the three people on pages 25 to 28 whose dining room tables were giving them trouble? For one of them, Pam (page 27), the problem was caused by a bad label. Even though her dining room was serving as her office, she wasn't furnishing it for that function because a "dining room" didn't need a file cabinet. As soon as she named the room according to the way she was using it, Pam was able to put together a real office for herself. The name of the room—its label—affected her ability to set it up properly.

Along with their power to shape our understanding, the names of things also give us shared points of reference. For instance, consider the difference between "the white house" and "the White House." One is a generic description. The other conjures up the image of a specific building in a particular place. In your home, when you label things and refer to them by name, you include all the members of the household in a shared understanding. The common names and labels you use throughout your household to refer to different elements become, in effect, your family's personal organizing *language*.

An effective labeling scheme extends beyond boxes and file folders to include pieces of furniture, spaces, rooms, storage areas, and even blocks of time. It includes written labels—such as tags or stickers—and spoken ones—the names you call things when you talk about them. To work *well*, your labels need to name everything according to either its contents (the junk drawer, the games cupboard, the ball bin, the giveaway box) or its use (the dining room, the exercise corner, cleanup time, laundry day). When elements of an organizing system are left unlabeled or have names that don't match their function, the system starts to break down.

Symptoms That Your System Needs Better Labels

Here are some symptoms to look for if you think your labels aren't working well. When labels are missing or inaccurate, one or more of these may apply.

- The name for one or more of the rooms in your house doesn't match the activity that takes place inside it.
- You're not using some of your rooms the way you used to, but you haven't set them up for new activities either.
- You don't know what's inside any of the boxes in your storage areas.
- You can't find parts of your collections because each one is stored in different locations, and you're not sure where they all are.
- Once you've filed a piece of paper, you can't find it again.
- When you want to play a show you've taped, you have to watch the beginning of all the tapes on top of the TV until you find the one you want.

- You keep missing appointments because they aren't recorded in your calendar.
- No one knows what's on the family's schedule except you.
- Your kids' toys are all jumbled together in every container, even though you sorted them out last week.
- Your children can't find their clothes after they've been put away.
- Your kids are always squabbling about things: "That's mine!" "No, it's mine!"
- You're always saying, "Never mind, I'll find it," because it's easier to locate things yourself than it is to explain where they are.
- If something happened to you, no one would be able to find anything.

If these fit your situation, your system could benefit from more labels (or better ones). The following stories illustrate some of the ways other people have used *Strategy #5*, to take advantage of the power in a name.

Real-Life Lessons: Strategy #5 Missing in Action

Elizabeth has lived in her house for decades. Her attic was getting so full, she couldn't squeeze anything else up there. When we climbed the narrow stairs, we were confronted by a sea of boxes. Some of the cartons were labeled, but most of them gave no clue about their contents. Even the labeled ones, it turned out, did not necessarily contain the items listed on the outside of the box.

Elizabeth and I went through box after box, seeing what was inside and weeding out the contents. She remarked time after time, "I had no idea I still had that thing!" It turned out her attic was full of stuff she hadn't seen or used for ten, fifteen, or even twenty years. It had just been taking up space and getting in Elizabeth's way. But at least it was easy to let go of!

When the weeding was finished, there was plenty of room for the things Elizabeth's family was still using. We carefully labeled every box and put it against the wall on shelves. After that, when anyone needed something, they had no trouble finding it.

Don't clutter up your valuable storage space with unlabeled boxes containing who-knows-what. When you put something in storage, make sure you label it so you can tell what's in it without opening it. Then you can find things when you want them and get rid of them when you're ready.

When David was growing up, his mother managed all his clothes for him. She bought them, washed them, ironed them, folded them, and put them away in his closets and drawers. All he had to do was pick an outfit and put it on. So when he grew up and moved out on his own, David had no idea how to take care of his wardrobe. He called me when he moved from an apartment into his own house and asked for help setting up his bedroom.

In David's new home, none of the closets had the shelves and baskets he was accustomed to using for his T-shirts, socks, and underwear. Instead, all the storage spaces were small, with only a hanging rod and a single high shelf for clothes. To hold his nonhanging items, David had purchased a tall dresser with eight drawers. Each drawer held a mishmash of jumbled socks, briefs, receipts, and T-shirts. Our mission was to sort it all out and set it up so he could put things away *and* find them again. My role was to teach him the things he'd never learned from his parents.

First, we got everything out of the dresser and sorted it into piles. Then, we decided which drawer would hold what items. Next, we put everything away. Finally, so David could remember what belonged in which drawer, we put a small label indicating the contents on the outside of each one. I also encouraged David to say the name of the drawer out loud every time he used it, until he was familiar with the setup. The combination of visual and verbal cues made it possible for David to put away all his clothes, find them again when he wanted to, and begin to actively manage his wardrobe.

Teach your children how to take care of their clothes and things. This is a basic life skill and part of your responsibility as a parent. Start by grouping like items together and labeling the containers that hold them. Refer to the "sock drawer" when you ask your child to retrieve or put away socks. If necessary, give children visual labels as well as auditory ones so they can do things themselves.

Ilsa was about to have an empty nest. Our first appointment occurred three weeks before her youngest child departed for college. She invited me over to help her figure out how to rearrange her house so it worked well for one person living alone. She told me the thing she needed most, but had never had space for until now, was a home office.

From our initial phone conversation, I had expected Ilsa to have a small house. But I was surprised to discover she and her daughter lived in a three-bedroom home. Aside from her daughter's space, she already had an extra room that overlooked her gardens. Bright and sunny, it was haphazardly furnished, but could easily be turned into a wonderful home office. Yet Ilsa was trying to do her paperwork in the dining room with a wholly inadequate setup. When I asked her what activities she was doing in her extra room, she said it didn't really have a particular use. In Ilsa's case, the room wasn't registering on her radar screen because it wasn't allocated to a specific function and therefore didn't have a name. So it hadn't occurred to her to consider it as a possible office. As soon as we gave it the label "office," she started to use it.

When something in your overall organizing system has no name, it can be easy to forget it's there. Unlabeled resources become invisible, which means you won't use them to support you and your life. Put on the Eyes of a Stranger and survey your home. Give each separate room or functional space a label according to how you use it. If more rooms are available than you realized, see if the extra ones need better labels so you can incorporate them into your space planning.

Heidi has four children under the age of nine. Like most children these days, each of the four has more toys than Heidi and her six siblings owned altogether when they were children. Fortunately, the house was large, with plenty of storage space. Yet the kids' rooms were in a constant state of chaos. Heidi called for some help getting the toys organized.

When I arrived, I was impressed by the system Heidi had set up in her children's rooms. Each child had shallow shelves for books, deeper shelves for toy bins, and more shelves in the closets for games and larger items. There were even plenty of clear plastic bins of varying sizes sitting on the shelves holding toys. It appeared each room already contained the elements of a good system. So why wasn't the system working?

Glumly, Heidi pulled two bins from a shelf and showed me two jumbled messes. "I sorted these toys the other day and put them away, and now they're all out of order again. The kids never put things back in the right bin." Then I noticed both bins were unlabeled, and the mystery was solved.

Heidi actually had two simultaneous labeling problems. The obvious one was the lack of labels on any of the bins. Heidi's kids couldn't put the toys back in the right bins because they couldn't figure out which one *was* the "right" bin for any given toy. Heidi may have put all the little cars in a certain bin, for instance, but her children couldn't share her understanding because she didn't communicate it with a label.

The second problem is more subtle. *Heidi* was sorting the toys into groups, but her *kids* were the ones playing with them and putting them away. Even if Heidi *had* labeled the bins, it's completely conceivable her kids would refer to the toys differently than she does. It works better if the people *using* the items in the bins are the ones who name them.

Things that are sorted, weeded, and contained but not labeled can descend quickly into a jumble. The label makes the sorting, weeding, and containing worth doing, because it allows the resulting order to be maintained over time. An effective labeling process requires the participation of the people who'll be using the labeled items.

Alex and Amy are sisters who share a bedroom and bathroom. Born two years apart, the girls have many of the same toys, clothes, and equipment. They tend to squabble over who owns what. During play time, the argument goes something like: "This is mine!" "No, it's not, it's mine!" When their mother asks them to put something away, the argument changes: "But that's not mine, it's hers!" "No, it's not, it's hers!" One day their mother, Rachel, begged the other play-group moms for advice on how to end the constant bickering. The resulting words of wisdom demonstrate another facet of good labeling.

The girls were always arguing because there was no obvious way to figure out who was the owner of most of their belongings. Unless Rachel caught one of them in the act, she couldn't tell who had dropped the wet towel on the floor. If both girls had a green stapler, whose was the one that didn't have any staples? A simple tactic solved this problem (and stopped the bickering)—color coding.

The play-group moms advised Rachel to let each girl select her own color, then to buy personal items like hairbrushes, combs, cups, and scissors in both colors, so there would never be any question about which thing belonged to whom. The same idea also worked for larger items like towels and bed linens. Even though the two girls shared a room and bathroom, their linens and towels didn't need to be identical. By allowing the girls to select complementary designs and colors, Rachel prevented turf wars from occurring at all. Finally, to distinguish Alex's toys from Amy's, Rachel adopted a new policy. If someone gave both girls the same item as a gift, they would take one back and exchange it for an equivalent but different model. This way, each girl would have her own things to play with and wouldn't have to tussle with her sister over toys.

A simple color-coding scheme works well to help people distinguish one category of things from another. When the ownership of linens, small tools, and common items can be told just by looking at them, arguments are prevented and serenity reigns. (*Note:* This tactic works just as well for adults as for children.)

Zoe's family calendar hangs on the wall between the kitchen and the family room. It is large, with a big box to represent each day. In a pencil cup that hangs next to the calendar, there are five different-colored markers, one for each family member. Zoe is careful to make sure all the family's activities are written down. Each person's appointments are listed in his or her special color. Anyone who wants to know what's coming up or where they need to be can tell at a glance. And if Zoe is late getting home in the evening, whoever is in charge of the children can figure out where they're going without having to track down Zoe and ask her.

Some people might find a detailed calendar like this hard to maintain. But for Zoe's family, the amount of information it provides makes the time Zoe spends keeping it up-to-date worthwhile. This calendar in itself creates a shared expectation among all family members for how they're going to be using their time. It is a sophisticated labeling system.

Your calendar, like Zoe's, allows you to name the way you're planning to spend your time. When you write down an appointment, you in effect label the time slot with the activity it's going to contain. Someone else can look at your calendar and understand where you'll be in that time slot. This allows the building of a shared understanding.

If your schedule affects people, make sure you write down all your appointments on your calendar. In a family, a visual labeling system like Zoe's can be effective. Another tactic is to adopt a spoken labeling system in which days are referred to by the activities taking place on them—play-group day, laundry day, soccer day, church day, and so forth. Either way, a shared time labeling system enables everyone to know what's coming up.

Sharon sells antiques for a living. To build up inventory, she makes the rounds of estate sales, purchases mixed lots of furniture and household goods, then brings everything home to sort it out and prepare it for sale. Sharon's house is large, but it's also crowded. She has two children, a stepson in college, various pets, and two employees who come in and out of her house every day. So finding storage for her antiques is a challenge. She asked me to come over and help her fit everything in.

On our first tour, Sharon showed me the office space she had set up in her family room and her packing and mailing center in the garage. But it wasn't until my second visit that she felt comfortable enough to take me downstairs and show me the bulk of her inventory. It was stored in a room Sharon referred to as "Joey's room" (Joey is her away-at-college stepson), which turned out to be a cavernous space. In one corner, Joey's bed, dresser, and stereo cabinet explained the label of the room. But the rest of it—a space the size of three big bedrooms rolled into one—was chock-full of old furniture, boxes of books, shelving units crammed with household goods, rolled-up carpets, and so on. Clearly, most of the room had nothing to do with Joey.

This discrepancy between the room's name and its function was causing Sharon problems. Like Pam, whose dining room really needed to be an office, the label for Sharon's inventory storage room was keeping her from furnishing it adequately. However, unlike Pam's problem, a simple name change wasn't going to free the space so Sharon could set it up better. It still needed to be "Joey's room" *as well as* "the inventory room." The solution Sharon and I came up with was a hybrid.

In any large room that encompasses multiple functions, dividing the space into activity areas makes it easier to organize. This is part of *Strategy #2, Sort Everything by How You Use It.* Just as it's necessary to label *things* once they've been sorted, it's important to give names to different *function areas* as well. Once Sharon realized she could call three-quarters of her downstairs room "the inventory room," while still calling Joey's one-quarter of the space "Joey's room," she was ready to use the whole room better. With some of her shelving units erected as room dividers, she transformed Joey's room into a functional multiuse inventory center *and* bedroom.

In multiuse spaces, naming each activity area helps you equip it properly and use it fully. It's okay to have more than one label in a large room, as long as the labels accurately describe the things that take place in the space.

Ingrid's kitchen cupboards were overflowing with glassware, dishes, and appliances she wasn't using. During our kitchen-weeding project, her children happened to be home from school. I was impressed by a clever labeling tactic she used to protect her family room carpet.

In Ingrid's family room, the television was set into a large entertainment center that took up an entire wall. Her small children didn't like sitting on the sofa on the opposite side of the room to watch their videos. Instead, their favorite viewing spot was on the floor in front of the TV. In that spot, a throw rug on top of the wall-to-wall carpet provided additional cushioning.

To keep her children distracted so they didn't interrupt our project, Ingrid started a video for them. Then she fixed popcorn. Giving her oldest daughter the snack bowl, she said, "Take this to the family room and make sure you eat it on the magic carpet." Ingrid had given a catchy label to the throw rug in front of the television. She used the label to entice her children to sit on the throw rug, a safe spot for eating. By using a creative label, the magic carpet, for this mundane household item, Ingrid was shaping her children's behavior to keep her family room clean. The result: Instead of juggling their food over a difficult-to-clean carpet, they were eating it on a portable rug that could be picked up and washed if it got soiled.

 Enticing or clever labels are easy for everyone to remember and fun to use. Be creative in naming things, especially when you want to use a label to encourage desired behavior.

What a Full-Blown Strategy #5 Crisis Looks Like

These stories show the kinds of piles that can cause trouble when one or two elements of an organizing system are misnamed or not named at all. Without good labels, things get jumbled or lost, spaces remain unused, arguments spring up, and people don't know where they're supposed to be at any given time. But each of these problems can be solved quickly with a well-placed and well-thought-out label.

When mislabeling has gone on for a long time, however, it's harder to address the problem. It's human nature to resist change, even a change in label that might seem minor to an outsider. The people whose story best illustrates a long-term labeling issue are Nora and Chuck, an empty-nest couple living in a large, comfortable suburban home. Nora's office was set up in a small, dark room at the front of the house. She didn't like sitting there and found herself carrying her paperwork to other, brighter rooms instead of doing it in her office. She asked me to help her create a better setup.

When we toured the house, Nora took me through all the spacious rooms, including five bedrooms. Chuck and Nora's room was on the second floor, along with three others. The fifth was located on the main floor at the far end of the house. Obviously, Nora and Chuck were getting good use out of the master bedroom, and the first-floor bedroom was set up as a comfortable guest room. But all three other bedrooms on the second floor showed no signs of daily use. So when I asked Nora whether she'd considered setting up one of these as her office, she told me they were reserved for her children: "This is Ellie's room, that one is Tim's room, and here's Cindy's room." Yet it turned out all three of Nora and Chuck's children were married, had children, lived far away, and seldom visited. The last one had departed ten years earlier. Nevertheless, all of the second floor except the master bedroom was set up as if they still lived in the house. Although Nora's nostalgia for her children was understandable, it was keeping her from using her home to support the life she and Chuck were actually living. Here's how.

Space: In an eleven-room home, Nora and Chuck were using only four of the rooms every day—the kitchen, family room, Chuck's office, and their bedroom. Two of their main-floor rooms were used fairly frequently for entertaining—the dining room and living room—and the first-floor guest room also was used regularly. But three rooms were standing unused for all but three or four days per year, while Nora was struggling to find a bright, comfortable place to do her paperwork. She didn't consider the upstairs rooms available, because in her mind they were already allocated to a function that was, in fact, obsolete.

Things: In an effort to stay in good shape, Chuck had purchased several large pieces of exercise equipment. These included a stationary bicycle, a treadmill, and a total gym. Unfortunately, they were set up in a dark basement storage room. Chuck had tried to use the equipment down there, but the surroundings acted as disincentive to him. It was hard enough to get motivated to exercise without having to do it in a dark, low, unfinished room.

Information: Because Nora didn't like doing her paperwork in her office, she found herself trying to take care of the couple's complicated finances and business dealings in other rooms. The kitchen counter held stacks of mail, a long row of file folders, and various office supplies. In the family room, Nora spread her papers around the room to pay the bills in front of the television. Her small office had space for a single file cabinet, which was inadequate to contain all the records she and Chuck needed to store. So papers were piled up and spread out in several other rooms, and additional file cabinets in the basement held some of Nora's active files. If Nora had a larger, brighter room set up as her office, these paper issues could be resolved.

Time: When the things that go with a certain activity are stored far away from where the activity gets done, it's impossible to do anything efficiently. Nora's paper processing was a good example. Because her supplies and storage areas were spread out around the house, getting things out and putting them away again was a time-consuming job. She responded to this by leaving things out in convenient locations instead of putting them back when she was through with them. For

Chuck, the exercising suffered in a similar way. It was so unpleasant to try to stay in shape in a dark room in the basement that he wasn't exercising at all. Also, when he needed an important document from among Nora's piles, he had to spend considerable time just trying to find it.

Relationships: When I asked Chuck why his treadmill and exercise equipment were set up in a dark part of the basement, he sighed and said, "I'm not allowed to keep them upstairs." Because Nora ran the household while the children were growing up, she was accustomed to being in charge of the substantial percentage of the house allocated to family activities. The only room where Chuck got to hold sway was his office. After the children moved away, it didn't occur to Nora to designate any of the newly available space to Chuck. Since she didn't want large pieces of exercise equipment cluttering up "her" rooms, she exerted her long-held authority and insisted he put them in the basement. Chuck decided this battle wasn't worth pursuing vigorously, but a power struggle over space in the house was clearly a potential point of contention between him and Nora.

My recommendation to Nora was that she rename the three upstairs bedrooms and start to include them in her space planning. Since she and Chuck were the only ones who actually lived in the house, their needs for space were more important than the potential needs of anyone else who might visit. If they relabeled two of the bedrooms "the exercise room" and "Nora's office," then set them up for those functions, they would have space for the two major activities currently going homeless. This would give Chuck a comfortable place for his hobby, and when Ellie, Cindy, and Tim came to visit, the third bedroom and the downstairs guest room would still be comfortable places for them and their families to sleep.

In the end, Nora couldn't bring herself to change her labels for the extra bedrooms. Instead of rearranging their space to make better use of it, she and Chuck spent several hundred thousand dollars adding on to their house.

Over time, changes in your life affect the ways you use your space, things, information, and time. These changes can make your names for the elements of your system inaccurate or obsolete. Don't stick with old labels that no longer apply. Select new names that allow you to incorporate all your activities into your overall organizing system.

How to Put Strategy #5 Back in Place

If the stories you just read rang a bell for you, your system isn't working as well as it should because it needs more and/or better labels. Why waste time sorting, weeding, and containing things unless you can find them again when you need them? When everything is labeled properly, it can be retrieved, used, and shared with others.

The point of *Strategy #5, Label Everything*, is to enable you to take advantage of all your resources. First, create descriptive, clever, and enticing labels to identify the things, locations, and processes in your system. Then discuss the label for each element and item with all the people who'll be using it. When old labels no longer apply, change them. By naming every element in your organizing system, you'll keep it up-to-date with your life.

Here are some tips to help you give everything a label so it works well for you.

Label All Your Space

- Give each separate room or functional space a label according to the thing(s) you do in it. Pay particular attention to rooms you don't really use. Give them accurate names so you can start to use them better.

- Base your labels for space on use. Base your labels for storage on contents.
- In multifunction spaces, label each separate area according to the activity it contains.
- Refer to cupboards and closets by the things inside them—"my clothes closet," "the coin collection shelf"—so everyone knows precisely where things go. Then everyone can find things, not just you.

Label All Your Things

- Label all your containers, especially opaque ones (if you have any).
- Make sure every label gives you enough information so you can tell what's in a container just by looking at it.
- Don't put anything into storage without labeling it first.
- Write right on the box when you put a carton into storage. List all the contents. Write the label on the side of the box, not the top, so you can see it once the box is shelved.
- Use a simple color-coding scheme to help people recognize each person's things. Have each person in the family select his or her own color and/or pattern for personal items, including linens and towels.
- Teach your children to keep track of their space, clothes, papers, and things by referring to them using visual and spoken labels.
- With your children's help, decide what to call all their containers and label each one.
- For small children, add a picture of the item to the label. Even a crude drawing is helpful for little kids.
- Create peelable labels by writing on clear Contact paper with

a permanent marker. Then, if you change the contents of a bin, it's easy to change the label.

- Put nametags in every piece of your children's clothing. Then, when they lose them, you have a slight chance of finding them again.
- When two or more kids share a bedroom, give each one his or her own shelf for special belongings. Then refer to it as "Patsy's Special Shelf" so no one else encroaches on it.

Label All Your Information

- Set up your files using hanging *and* manila folders. Make sure the labels on each hanging folder match the labels on the manila folders inside it. Leave the hanging folder in the cabinet when you take out a file, so you know exactly where to put that file back.
- Put often-used items, such as "Bills to Pay," into a colored folder so they're easy to find.
- Go over the labels in your file cabinet with your partner so she or he can find things if something happens to you. This shared understanding is crucial in an emergency.
- If you keep useful papers stored by your kitchen telephone, give the telephone area a name.
- If you keep key information in a particular file holder or binder, give the holder or binder its own label. This allows you to refer to it clearly with other members of the family.
- Name the separate drawers in your file cabinet according to contents. Refer to the drawers by their names.

Midpoint Recap

Now that we're more than halfway through the Nine Strategies of Reasonably Organized People, it's a good time to take a step back and see what we've covered so far. We started with the simple premise that life changes. Given this certainty, it's only possible to stay organized over time if your support systems are simple and flexible enough to change along with your life. Using the Nine Strategies of Reasonably Organized People, you can create a simple, flexible system for yourself.

The blueprint for an effective organizing system is the *design* you put in place with *Strategy #1, Make Your Systems Fit You and Your Life.* By using the Eyes of a Stranger to see your life with clarity, you decide what activities and interests are important to you. Then you plan your organizing system so it supports those activities. The foundation of your new design is your life as you're actually living it.

The next phase is to frame the structure by sorting, weeding, containing, and labeling all the elements of your system so they fit your design. *Strategies #2 (Sort Everything), #3 (Weed Constantly), #4 (Use the Right Containers and Tools),* and *#5 (Label Everything)* are the steps that create the *structure* of your organizing system. With these steps, you get all the elements of your system into shape so you can use them to support you and your activities.

The final phase enables you to keep things moving within your structure. The last four strategies focus on the ways people, things, and information flow through your space and your time. Applying *Strategies #6 (Keep It Simple), #7 (Decide to Decide), #8 (Get Help When You Need It),* and *#9 (Evaluate Honestly and Often)*, prevent common bottlenecks from causing trouble within your structure. These four strategies each address one type of obstruction that can keep your system from operating efficiently and flexibly in support of your life.

Label All Your Time

- Make sure everyone affected by the family's schedule knows what it contains. Keep the whole family informed about what's coming up. Don't let anyone be surprised by unexpected activities.
- Consider using a family wall calendar if your family's schedule is confusingly busy.
- Label your time vocally by referring to blocks of time by their content. For instance, when you want your kids to pick up their toys, establish a "Pickup Time" for that task.
- If you have regularly scheduled appointments or activities, label the time slots they occupy. Then everyone knows what they'll be doing on "Soccer Saturday."
- Make sure your calendar contains all your appointments so you don't forget any, and so others can track you down if they must.

These suggestions will help you give things effective names so you can retrieve them and make full use of them. Creative and enticing labels help you shape your family's behavior, build common frames of reference, share the elements of your organizing system with your loved ones, and keep all the parts of your system in line with your current life.

The next step in getting your life to work smoothly involves taking a look at bottlenecks that obstruct your system because some part of it is too complicated. *Strategy #6, Keep It Simple*, helps you achieve the results you want using the fewest possible steps.

Keep It Simple

Figure out what you want to do, then do it with the fewest possible steps. If you can do something in two steps, why waste time and effort doing it in four? The more steps it takes to do something, the less likely it is to get done. Take on only what you can handle, and no more. Simplicity is the key to efficiency.

Overview of Strategy #6

Strategy #6 is best summed up by a mathematical principle: The shortest distance between two points is a straight line. Some of the biggest messes I've encountered have accumulated because a client is trying to get from point A to point B by a circuitous path. In non-mathematical terms, they're taking many steps to achieve a certain result when fewer steps accomplish the same thing. (See Figure 6.1.) Their systems are too complicated. Let's review some concrete examples from the stories you've already read.

Do you remember Dana from Chapter 2, whose music tapes were kept in a different room from the stereo? To put her tapes away and prevent a mess from growing on top of her music cabinet, she had to walk into and across an adjoining room before she reached the tape shelf. When we moved the tape shelf next to the stereo, she didn't have to take a single step to put a tape away.

How about Ginny from Chapter 2, who was reading magazines on her sofa, but had to get up and go to the kitchen to recycle them when she was through? As soon as she put a recycling bin next to her sofa,

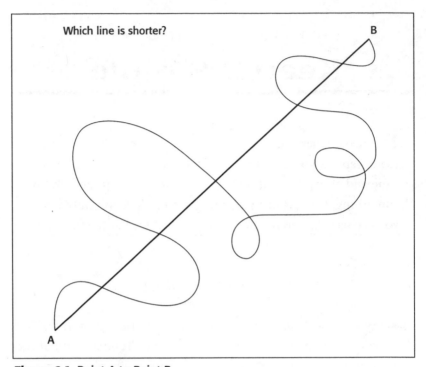

Which line is shorter?

Figure 6.1 Point A to Point B

she no longer had to get up and take a walk to dispose of a magazine when she finished reading it.

Then there's the story of Vera and Ron from Chapter 3, the couple whose bulk goods were hard to retrieve from their garage. When they needed a new box of dishwasher soap, they had to go to the store to buy one because they couldn't find the soap they already had. After they set up shelves in their garage for their bulk goods, the trip to acquire dishwasher soap got much shorter.

In these examples, a too-complicated procedure was causing trouble. Either the task requiring the extra effort just didn't get done and a pile sprouted as a result—tape cassettes on Dana's stereo, magazines in Ginny's family room—or the person had to use much more time and effort than necessary to achieve the desired result—Ron drove to the store to get soap even though he already had some in his garage.

Complicated processes highlight a basic trait of human nature:

The more steps it takes you to do something,
the less likely you are to do it.

When you apply *Strategy #6, Keep It Simple*, you counteract your tendency toward inertia by making things so easy to do, there's no excuse not to do them. In other words, you make it possible to complete any single task using the fewest possible number of steps. If you can achieve the result you want without wasting precious time or expending extra effort, you'll have extra time and energy for things you really want to do. And with your system streamlined, efficient, and ready to turn on a dime, you can keep everything flowing smoothly even if your life takes a sudden turn.

Symptoms That Your System Needs Simplifying

Some warning signs that appear when your processes and procedures are getting more complicated than they need to be are listed below.

- Sometimes you don't do a job or task because it takes too much effort.
- Jobs you do frequently are complicated and take you a long time.
- You don't put things away because their containers are inconvenient or hard to use.
- You've got too many activities on your "To Do" list and not enough time for all of them.

- It's hard for you to put away your clothes, so your closets and drawers are empty, and the stuff that belongs in them is strewn around your living space.
- It's a struggle to get papers into and out of your file cabinet's drawers.
- Things are sitting on top of the containers they belong in, instead of being put away.
- You spend time every day wiping up footprints, stray food, and drips from the floors around your house.
- When it's time to pay the bills, it's hard to find all of them because you don't have a designated spot to put them.
- When it's time to pay your taxes, it takes you days to round up all your receipts because you don't have a designated spot to collect them during the year.
- You have things—books, magazines, papers, boxes—stacked on top of each other all around the house, and it's hard to retrieve every item except the top one.
- Your schedule is overfull because each of your kids participates in multiple activities and each activity requires your participation.
- Sometimes you don't file something because you don't have the right color folder, label, or stand-up tab for it.
- Your planner has sections you never use, but you're carrying them around with you anyway.
- You feel you need a good excuse before you say no to people who call or visit when you're in the middle of something.
- You never actually get around to putting your myriad photographs into photo albums.
- Your kids have lots of toys that are hard to get back into their containers, so they never get put away.

Do any of these ring a bell? It could be a signal that it's time to re-move some of the extra steps built into your current system. In the following stories, you'll see how other people applied *Strategy #6* to save themselves wasted time and effort.

Real-Life Lessons:
Strategy #6 Missing in Action

Maria's office was a large room with an ample L-shaped desk and two four-drawer file cabinets; it was swimming in paper. There were piles all over the desk, paper bags full of unopened mail underneath it, and stacks of who-knows-what documents heaped on all the seats of the nearby sofa bed. Clearly, no filing had been done for a while. So I took a piece of paper off the desktop and asked Maria to file it. If we looked at her filing procedures, we might be able to figure out where the bottleneck was.

Maria took the document and studied it for a moment. Then she pulled her chair in front of her computer and selected a file from the list on the screen. "This is my index," she explained. Using her computer's mouse to scroll through it, she picked out a file category and wrote it on the corner of the document. Then she pulled a clipboard from the shelf above the desk. By the curled edges of the papers it was holding, I could tell she used it frequently. Proudly, Maria showed me a list of approximately three hundred fifty file categories, with a number beside each one. Maria ran her finger down the column, flipping through the pages until she found the category for the document she was holding. After writing its number down, too, she consulted the lower right corner of the clipboard sheet. It had a red stripe drawn across it.

Maria turned to me, showed me the stripe, and told me it meant the document in question belonged in her red file drawer. Standing up and going to that drawer, she opened it. Inside, red folders were labeled in numerical sequence. Consulting the number on the document, Maria pulled out a fat red folder with a red-lined label. Hefting it in her hand, she said, "This one's too fat. I need a second folder for this category." So saying, she went to the closet, rummaged around for a moment and emerged with a red file folder in her hand. Then she returned to the desk, opened a drawer, and peered into it. A worried frown crossed her face, and she turned to me with a sigh. "I don't have a red label, so I can't file this paper until I go to Staples and get some more."

Altogether, this process included at least sixteen separate steps, involved getting up and walking, and took her approximately four minutes—and in the end, *she still hadn't filed the paper*! At this rate, it was going to take Maria a long, long time to file all the papers in her office, because there were literally thousands of them.

When we sat down to talk about how Maria could address her paper backlog, some interesting and pertinent facts came to light. First, she had been using this file system successfully for years. It was only lately that things had started piling up. Second, she enjoyed sorting her papers into categories and having everything color coded, even though this took more work and required a lot more supplies. Keeping her papers in order was almost a hobby for her. Finally, she had recently been diagnosed with multiple sclerosis, and she no longer had the energy to maintain her file system properly. No wonder her papers were piling up.

Our challenge was to figure out a way for Maria to retain the things she liked about her file system—the index, the color coding, her categories—while simultaneously simplifying it so she could use it despite her condition. Although it was hard for her, the first step was for Maria to admit to herself that she *couldn't* do things the way she used to. The next task was to sort and weed out all the papers, including the ones in the file drawers. Then we consolidated her folder categories into a workable set of permanent groupings she really needed. She agreed to use just these categories, instead of creating new ones with each new document. Next we substituted plain manila folders for the colored ones and duplicated the color coding idea by using colored markers to write the category names right on the folders. Finally we moved the drawers closer to the desk and printed out a new, shorter index. The end result: Maria could still use her index and segregate her papers by color, but she could file things quickly without getting up from her chair or making a trip to the store.

Even if you enjoy using a complicated procedure to accomplish a routine task, its complexity can cause you problems if your life changes. Think about ways to subtract steps now, so you don't set yourself up for trouble later.

Lorraine asked me to help her set up a more workable file system for her home-based business. A big part of the job was to purge her existing file cabinet of old bank statements, canceled checks, and other sensitive financial records. Because she wanted to recycle the paper, but didn't want the personal information on these papers out in the world where an unscrupulous person could retrieve them, I suggested Lorraine shred the documents in question. "Good idea!" she said. Then she got up from her chair, opened the door into the adjoining laundry room, and pulled a small shredder from the shelf behind the washing machine. Dragging her roomy wastebasket from the other side of her desk, she put the shredder inside it because it was too small too span the opening. Then she went back into the laundry room, retrieved and unwound an extension cord, plugged it into the laundry socket, and carried the live end back to her desk. Finally, she sat down, plugged in the shredder, and balanced it across her knee. Lorraine was ready to shred.

As she was feeding pages one at a time through her small machine, I asked Lorraine whether she used it routinely for items like receipts. "Yep!" she said. "I use it all the time." In other words, she went through this complicated process every time she wanted to destroy a sensitive document, which was frequently. I suggested she get a much larger, automatic machine with its own wastebasket, plug it in behind her desk, and keep it right next to her. Then she could shred any time. These simple steps saved her a noticeable amount of fuss and bother.

If you notice yourself struggling to take care of tasks you routinely tackle, figure out what the problem is. Get better tools, move things closer to you, and make the task easy to accomplish so you can get it done quickly and efficiently.

April is a successful engineer, and her husband is a CPA. They own their house, have no children, and are financially well off. April works part time, and takes full responsibility for making their home a comfortable, well-organized retreat from the daily grind. She prides herself on her ability to keep everything running smoothly. She even alphabetizes her spices so it's easy to find the one she wants.

April is an acquaintance of mine, not a client. But I learned an important lesson from watching her prepare dinner one night. As she moved back and forth across her kitchen, getting out food and utensils, setting the table, and putting our meal together, I started to think, "There's something wrong with this picture." Finally, I realized that April's supplies for every meal-related activity were stored on the opposite side of her work space from the place she was actually using them. This required her to walk across her kitchen to do any given task (see Figure 6.2).

In April's kitchen, the main food preparation area is the triangle between the sink (S), the stove (C), and the refrigerator (REF). Yet the food she was preparing was stored in the cupboard over the dishwasher (A), and the pots and pans she was cooking with were located in the peninsula separating the work space from the dining table (B). Conversely, the dishes April used to set the table (E) were located

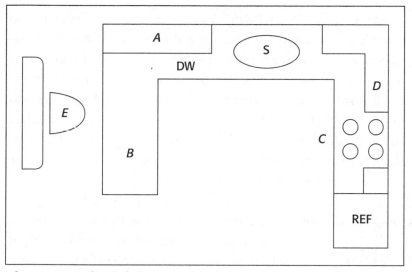

Figure 6.2 April's Kitchen

in the cupboard over the stove (D). Every clean dish April took out of her dishwasher had to be carried across the kitchen to be put away. The placement of things in her kitchen made every food preparation task more difficult than it needed to be. All the extra walking was costing April a noticeable amount of wasted time and energy.

Keeping things stored away from where you use them creates extra work for you. The farther apart things are, the more time and effort you waste. Save time and energy by keeping things where you use them, especially in a center of activity like your kitchen.

Ruby was doing a general cleanup, and I came in to help her. While searching through her bedroom for extra hangers, I noticed that the clothes hamper in Ruby's closet was full to overflowing, with a large clump of items cascading to the floor. Later, Ruby asked me to bring the dirty clothes downstairs so she could wash them. When I went to gather them up, I was surprised to discover that the hamper wasn't overflowing at all. Instead, it was completely empty. The clothes were piling up *on top* of it instead of *inside* it. When Ruby took off her clothes, it was easier for her to just toss them at the hamper from wherever she was standing than it was to walk to the hamper, lift its top, and deposit the dirty item inside. I suggested she simply remove the top and throw it away. This way, she could toss her dirty clothes into the hamper from anywhere in the room, and there wouldn't be a pile.

A hamper with a top becomes a table. Discard the tops of hampers and other often-used containers. Then you can put things away quickly and easily, using only one hand, and keep them from piling up.

Beth was a homemaker who wanted ideas to keep her family's life working smoothly. In the course of our initial tour through her house, she showed me her eight-year-old son's closet. Inside, hanging on wire hangers, were fifteen to twenty neatly pressed cotton T-shirts in different colors and patterns. Curious, I asked whether her son attended a school with a dress code. "No," she said, "he goes to the public elementary school." So I asked why she bothered to iron his T-shirts. She said, "I don't particularly like ironing, but I think it's nice for him to have pressed shirts to play in."

Beth was spending a noticeable amount of time each week doing a task she disliked as a gesture of care and concern for her son. Yet her efforts were being spent on a result—ironed play clothes—he was unlikely to appreciate or even notice. Later in our consultation, when Beth mentioned always feeling pressed for time, I suggested she simply hang his T-shirts on hangers as soon as they came out of the dryer. This way, she could stop wasting her time ironing them, yet they would still be fresh and straight.

If you're feeling pressed for time, take a good look at the activities that fill up your days. See if you're doing any activity or task that isn't worth the time you're spending on it. Subtract those activities and tasks to make time for things that are more important to you.

Gretchen, the devoted mother of two small children, was trying to plan meaningful activities to do with her daughters during the holiday season. One family project that appealed to her was the idea of constructing a gingerbread house. She got out her cookbooks, shopped for ingredients, and gathered her children around her to mix and bake the gingerbread pattern pieces for the house. This turned out to be much more difficult than she anticipated, and her children quickly grew bored and wandered off. She ended up spending hours laboring hard to get the pieces to come out just right. By the time she was ready to put the house together, Gretchen was sick of gingerbread, and her children didn't want anything to do with the project and their grumpy mother. Needless to say, the project was not a success.

Only later did Gretchen discover a gingerbread house kit with prefabricated gingerbread pattern pieces on sale at the grocery story. With the kit, she could have achieved the end result she wanted—a fun time helping her children frost and decorate their gingerbread house—without the hard work of actually rolling out and baking the gingerbread. Instead, she and her children had gotten bogged down in the baking and never got to the fun part. The next year, Gretchen bought the kit, and a good time was had by all.

Sometimes, the traditional way of achieving a certain result involves a great deal of work, effort, and time. If you can achieve the same result using faster, newer methods, you will save yourself a lot of stress. Just because something has always been done one way doesn't mean there's anything wrong with doing it another (more efficient) way. This is especially true around the holidays.

Lillian needed some help organizing her home office. A day trader, she maintained investment accounts with multiple brokerage firms. She also managed several pieces of real estate, and paid all the bills for her family and her home-based business. She used Quicken to keep track of the family's numerous checking, savings, and credit card accounts. Lillian's finances were multileveled and complicated.

On Lillian's desk, the biggest pile of backlogged papers was the stack of already reconciled monthly statements from banks, brokerage houses, and credit card companies. Lillian explained that no matter what she did, this pile never got any smaller. I asked her to show me how she usually dealt with it. So she picked a statement off the pile, swiveled around in her chair to the nearest file drawer, and opened it. Inside, instead of file folders, multiple three-ring binders were hanging on the rack. She pulled out the correct one, opened it on her desk, and popped the rings apart. Then, because the statement was twenty pages long, she removed its staple and divided it into four-page chunks, which she carefully three-hole-punched. The next step was to reassemble the pages in order and place them in the binder. Finally, she closed the binder and dropped it into the file drawer. All told, it took her three minutes to file a single statement.

Lillian's choice of binders might have worked well for a person with two simple bank accounts, but it wasn't a good match for Lillian's complicated financial portfolio. The number of steps involved in preparing the reports for the binders elongated the process and made it so difficult, it just wasn't getting done. We scrapped the binders and set up a hanging file and matching manila folder for each of her accounts. All Lillian had to do to put a statement away was open the file drawer, whip out the folder, drop the packet in, and put the folder back. This shortened the filing process from three to four minutes per piece to fifteen seconds. It also made Lillian's desk much neater.

Don't do something in ten steps if you can do it in two. Examine every task you do all the time and see if there are extra steps you can eliminate from it. If another container or product would help you get the job done faster, incorporate it into your system. Don't let a too-difficult process make things pile up and get in your way.

Henry's home office was in a clutter crisis. He was trying to manage a paper-intensive home-based business, yet he didn't have any file cabinets. Instead, he was using an odd assortment of different-sized small containers—stationery sorters, stand-up magazine files, a metal desktop file holder, empty copy-paper boxes, in- and out-trays—to manage large quantities of documents and records. Each time Henry filled up a container (which was often, given their limited size), he got in his car and went to the local stationery store to get another one. When he wanted to retrieve a particular piece of paper, there were approximately twenty different places it might be.

As soon as we purchased a heavy-duty, full-suspension file cabinet and filed his papers in it, Henry's office became more manageable. Even though he was drawn to the small containers—he liked their shapes and varied materials—they were wholly inadequate for the large filing requirements of his business. They also made filing and retrieving papers a much more complicated task than was necessary.

If you frequently find yourself driving to the store to complete one of your routine tasks, it needs to be simplified. Think about which items you're running out to buy. Keep more of these on hand *or* look for another item that will accomplish the same task more effectively.

Karla, a longtime client, was preparing for a weeklong vacation to the Caribbean. Normally, she would have packed herself. This time, however, she was seven months pregnant with her first child and suffering from high blood pressure. When I arrived, she led me to her bedroom and handed me three sheets of paper she had printed from her computer. One listed different hair and makeup products, one listed a wide variety of medicines and toiletries, and one listed other travel-related items like clothes steamers and eye masks. Then she asked me to retrieve two clear containers from her closet. Inside these big bins, in labeled Ziploc plastic bags, there was at least one of every item on the three lists. Some of the bags held multiple copies of the same item.

Carefully, Karla went down each list and selected the things she thought she would need for this vacation. My job was to locate the item, remove it from the Ziploc bag, and pile it next to her suitcase. As I put it on the pile, Karla checked it off the list. Painstakingly, we worked our way through all three sheets of paper, and I put away the bins when we finished. Then, Karla brought out yet another list for clothes. We went through a similar process to select her vacation wardrobe and lay it out on the bed. Finally we packed everything into her suitcases, a large one she planned to check and a smaller carry-on bag. By the end of this process, which took us two and a half hours, Karla was prepared for *any* eventuality that might arise on her vacation.

Because Karla went on a lot of business trips before she got married, she created the computer lists to help her remember all the little items that made traveling bearable. She bought extra sets of everything so she could keep them on hand and used the bins to contain her inventory. This kept her from having to run out and buy things before each trip. Her system worked well when she was traveling for business, but she was about to give birth. This complicated packing process was going to be too cumbersome with a small child. I encouraged her to simplify it before her baby arrived by shortening her lists and being ruthlessly honest about which travel items she really *needed* to bring with her.

When you know your life is going to change, leaving you with more work to do in less time, prepare by examining your routine procedures and making them as streamlined as possible. If one of them is causing a pile, it's the one to look at first. Remove extra steps *before* the change so you aren't struggling with them afterward.

What a Full-Blown
Strategy #6 Crisis Looks Like

The preceding stories and the "Fast, Faster, Fastest!" game focused on small inefficiencies that only have a big impact when you add them all up. Most of them can be solved by replacing an inconvenient product or subtracting a step or two. But when *every* task has multiple extra steps and takes two or three times as long to accomplish as it needs to, an entire system can be brought to its knees. What does it look like when all five elements of an organizing system have come to a standstill because they're too burdened with time- and space-consuming extra components?

Yvonne's story best illustrates how paralyzing an over-complicated system can be. Yvonne is a psychotherapist who shares a home, a family, and a therapy practice with her husband of eighteen years, Ian. The couple lives in a huge old house; they run their practice from the ground floor and live with their two teenage children on the second and third floors. The office they share is a large room on the second floor.

During our consultation, the first thing I noticed about this big room was its file cabinets. There were sixteen of them. Altogether, the

The Fast, Faster, Fastest! Game

This exercise illustrates how different tools can make a task easier or harder to complete. Your mission is to figure out which tool accomplishes the same result faster. Most of the tasks in question don't take long to complete. But if you *always* choose the slow way to achieve the desired result, the extra effort adds up. If you make each job as quick and efficient as possible, it's possible to save yourself noticeable time and effort every day.

The answers are listed at the end of the game.

Storing Collections of Nonfragile Items

1. Imagine there's a big pile of socks spread out on your bed. Now picture two identical containers sitting, empty, next to your pile. One has a top (a), the other doesn't (b). Which one is easier to put the socks into?

Storing Pens, Pencils, and the Like at Your Desk

2. This time, the pile is on your desk. It contains an assortment of pens and pencils, plus a pair of scissors. If your container choices are (a) your middle desk drawer or (b) a mug on the desktop, which one is easier and faster to put these implements into?

Selecting a Book to Read

3. Pretend you're looking at a bookcase. One shelf has books standing up with their spines facing you (a). The other shelf has books piled in horizontal stacks (b). *The Organizing Sourcebook* is in the middle of each set of books. If you wanted to get it out in the shortest possible time, which shelf would you take it from?

Seeing What's on Today's Schedule

4. On the table in front of you, picture a Palm Pilot with stylus (a) next to a Franklin Planner (b). The owners of these two calendar systems are ready for your signal. When you say "Go!" their mission is to "draw" their tool of choice and get it to show today's calendar. Who will win this contest?

Getting a Document from Your File Drawer

5. This time, you are the one on the spot. In front of you are two file drawers, each containing the exact same labeled manila file folders. In one cabinet, the manila folders are in hanging file folders with matching labels, suspended on a rack (a). In the other cabinet, there is no structure supporting the manila folders (b). Your mission is to get the top sheet of paper out of the "1999 Tax Return" folder. Which setup will allow you to do this more quickly?

Finding Food in the Refrigerator

6. You've just finished eating dinner, and there is enough spaghetti left over for a good lunch tomorrow. You have two choices of container to put it in. One is opaque (a). The other is clear (b). Which container will allow you to find it faster at lunchtime?

Storing Crayons

7. Your five-year-old child has just gotten a new box of Crayola crayons, the big set with its own sharpener. The crayons are spread out all over the bedroom floor. Two storage options are available: the Crayola box they came in (a), or an empty shoebox with no lid (b). Which one will allow your *child* to put the crayons away quickly?

Storing Photographs So You Can Enjoy Them

8. In the middle of your kitchen table, there are two piles of loose photographs. You are holding an empty photo box (a). Your best friend, sitting across from you, has an empty photo album (b). Who will be able to store the photographs faster?

Hanging Up Your Robe

9. If you hang your robe on a hook (a), and your spouse hangs his or her robe on a hanger (b), which one of you can get undressed and into bed faster?

Holding Action Items on Your Desk

10. You have six full file folders, one labeled for each of your ongoing projects. They are lying in your in-box (a). I have six labeled file folders for my

Continued overleaf

projects, but they're stored standing up and facing me in a desktop file (b). Both of us are working on the Farnham Project, and both of us have the Farnham folder at the back of our stack. Which one of us can retrieve it faster?

Storing Spices

11. You've just come home from the grocery store with eight new spices. You have to put them away in either the rack in your drawer, which holds spices in their original containers (a), or a new rack your mother just gave you, which requires you to pour the spices from their original containers into matching white-capped bottles (b). Which spice rack is easier and faster to use?

Storing Barbie Clothes

12. Your seven-year-old daughter has just gotten a new Barbie for her birthday, along with three outfits and a carrying case. The case has a drawer for small accessories like shoes, and a little rack with tiny hangers for the clothes. There is also a narrow slot for the Barbie. Is it easier for your daughter to put the Barbie in the case (a), or in a clear plastic bin with no top (b)?

Answers: 1-b, 2-b, 3-a, 4-b, 5-a, 6-b, 7-b, 8-a, 9-a, 10-b, 11-a, 12-b.

room contained something like forty file drawers. My first question in this room was, "Which file cabinets do you use?" Instantly, Yvonne reached down and pulled out the drawer next to her desk chair. "This one!" she said. Everything in it was impeccably contained. Each manila file folder had a typed label affixed to it, with a matching stand-up label on its hanging file folder. The labels on the folders were staggered so you could read every one. The whole drawer was immaculate.

Then I looked at the contents, and the first three folders caught my attention. Their beautifully printed labels read:

Shell Oil Company   Mobil Oil Company   Standard Oil Company
Acct. #555-123-4560   Acct. #555-789-1011   Acct. #555-121-3147

I asked Yvonne, "Do you use one of these credit cards for business purposes, and one for your household?" "Oh, no," she said. "Every month when the bills come, I go through them with two different highlighters and allocate each charge to either the house or the business. Then I record them in my ledger." So saying, she pulled an accountant-style record book from the closest shelf and showed it to me. It, too, was practically a work of art. Yvonne was clearly proud of it, and I could see why. The amount of work represented in the ledger and the credit card files was staggering. She could have segregated her expenses simply by using one card for the business and one for the household. Instead, she was spending hours every month to achieve the same result. It turned out the whole house was full of similar scenarios.

Space: In the office, the file cabinets held a hefty percentage of all the papers that had ever crossed the threshold into Yvonne and Ian's house, all carefully categorized and labeled. The cabinets themselves took up a large portion of the big room. Yet the only one Yvonne was actively using was the one next to her desk. Thus, the rest of the room was full of well-maintained but essentially useless papers.

The same situation was echoed throughout all the other storage areas in the house. Every cupboard, closet, and container was full (and sometimes overflowing) of stuff, whether or not there was a real use for it. In addition, Ian told me there was a carriage house in the backyard—an entire building—chock-full of things. They didn't want to show it to me because it was so overwhelming to them.

Since the house had the benefit of the extra storage areas in the carriage house, the family's living space was reasonably uncluttered and quite comfortable. So it was not yet affected by the huge quantity of papers and stuff Yvonne was storing.

Things: In the family's closets and storage areas, every shelf was loaded with bins and containers. Each one held multiple versions of common household goods. For instance, one box in the family room closet was full of light bulbs, all different kinds, in lots of shapes. Another one held a wide assortment of batteries. For every household good you could name, there was a full container. Yvonne was maintaining a substantial inventory of numerous items in case anyone ran out of anything. This obviously took time, energy, and attention, as well as space. Again, the carriage house (which every family member, including the children, referred to as "something you don't want to see") was catching the overflow from the closets. Some larger items the family used, like holiday decorations, were stored there.

Information: This is the category where things were starting to overflow into the living space and affecting Yvonne's family. Besides the amount of data taking up space in the office, an entire long room adjoining it was dedicated to processing the mail. Along the far side of two six-foot-long tables, Yvonne had set up box after box, each labeled with a different category. Piles of unsorted mail (including obvious junk) lined the near side, and more mail-filled boxes sat on the floor under the table. There were two paper recycling bins next to the door.

After we finished our tour of the house, Ian asked Yvonne to show me how she processed the mail. She and I went into the long room and stood in front of the table. She picked up a flyer advertising a series of concerts and showed it to me. The first two events had already taken place, but there were three more still coming up. Yvonne unfolded it, glanced at it, and then put it in the "Concerts" box. I asked her whether she was planning to attend any of the performances. She said, "I don't think so, but if I want to go, I'll need the flyer." But she didn't record the upcoming concert dates in her calendar to remind her about the event.

For half an hour, I watched Yvonne give her full attention to each piece of mail she picked up, whether or not it was obvious junk. She hardly made a dent in the pile. Given all the boxes awaiting Yvonne's attention, and the rate at which new mail was arriving, it was obvious she couldn't possibly keep up with it at this pace. Yet it was also clear she wanted to see each item and get it properly categorized and her "failure" to do this was starting to make her feel frantic.

Time: Yvonne was spending more and more of her available time caring for inanimate objects: processing the mail, maintaining her files, and keeping track of the financial affairs of the family and the business, on top of having to maintain the household inventories, find things and put them away, and keep everything neat. The piles of unopened mail were a good indicator that she had reached a critical point—things were coming in too fast for her to keep them under control.

Relationships: The main indicator that Yvonne's time-consuming attention to detail was becoming a burden to her family was the fact that her husband called me in for the consultation. He was clearly concerned, not just about the time Yvonne was spending, but about her growing agitation because she really *couldn't* keep up. Out of concern for his wife, he asked me for suggestions about making things work better. Their children also seemed worried about their mother and her habit of saving and categorizing everything. Everyone except Yvonne recognized that her attention to detail in every facet of life was starting to cause her real trouble.

My recommendations to Yvonne and Ian focused on simplifying their policies and procedures so it was much easier and less time-consuming to maintain order in the house. Yvonne's strong tendency to micromanage every detail, especially those involving papers and things, was a barrier to effective functioning. I suggested specific ways to achieve the same results with much less work, for instance, by using the credit cards to segregate the family and business expenses. Regarding the mail, I asked Yvonne to consider that most of it was, in reality, useless information that the family didn't need. If she could see it that way, it would be easier for her to recycle things instead of categorizing and filing them. I also recommended to Ian that he look for ways to simplify each process, so he and Yvonne could work together to cut out the extra steps (and stuff) clogging up their life. If they could move away from the paralyzing complexity of their current system toward a more reasonable level of control, they would be *organized enough.*

Ian made another appointment, but Yvonne called later and canceled it. She wasn't ready to change the system she had worked so hard to create and maintain.

If you enjoy doing a task beautifully, with every detail lovingly attended to, you may find yourself doing more work to achieve a given result than is necessary. Watch yourself to keep your love of perfection balanced by the demands of your schedule. Don't let detail work bog you down and prevent you from getting all your tasks accomplished.

How to Put
Strategy #6 Back in Place

Did you see yourself in any of the stories you just read? If so, there are gaps between your organizing system and your life because some of your processes and procedures are too complicated. The objective of *Strategy #6, Keep It Simple,* is to trim out all the extra steps clogging your system and transform it into a streamlined, efficient operation. If you can do something in three steps, why waste time and energy doing it in ten? After all, a minute saved is a minute earned. Conserve your resources so they're available for the activities and people you care about most.

The tips in this section list some of the easiest ways to get streamlined, because everything works better when you *Keep It Simple.*

Keep Your Space Simple

- The more stuff you have in your space, the more effort it takes to keep your house clean and get everything done. Figure out what furniture, equipment, and supplies you need to support your activities, then clear out the rest.
- Play around with your furniture arrangements. Select a layout that looks good *and* supports your activities.
- Make sure there are adequate passageways from one space to another.
- Pay attention to piles growing in your space. If they're there because the process for putting them away is too difficult, change the process.
- Save work for yourself by using washable rugs to cushion your kitchen and bathroom floors and collect messy drips.
- Save work for yourself by putting heavy-duty mats at entrances to keep dirt from entering.
- Make your space visually peaceful by removing any jarring or uncomfortable elements.

Keep Your Things Simple

- Pay attention to how long it takes to put things away. Subtract extra steps and make it easy to get things into their proper places so they don't start to pile up.
- Use hooks for frequently used items like jackets and backpacks. It's easier to hang things on hooks than it is to get them onto hangers.
- Discard the tops of hampers and other often-used containers. Then you can put things away quickly and easily and keep them from piling up.

- Use open bins for children's toys. This makes it possible for kids to put things away by tossing them, which is much more fun than other alternatives.
- Make sure your storage space has enough shelves so it's easy to get any one container out and put it back again.
- Keep things you use all the time as close as possible to where you're using them. Things you use less frequently can be stored farther away. "Farther away" includes the high and low shelves in your active work areas.
- Play the "Fast, Faster, Fastest!" game to help you find the most efficient ways to do common tasks. Think of your own categories and competitions. Include your children.
- Avoid containers that require jewel-like precision* to put things in them. The same things can almost always be stored and retrieved more quickly in open containers.

Keep Your Information Simple

- Set up a mail processing center with all the tools you need to handle your mail quickly and efficiently—letter opener, recycling bin, "To Pay" folder, stapler, and so forth. Go through mail as fast as possible and make everything you don't *need* go away instantly.
- Set up one spot to catch your bills as soon as they come in. Put all of them in that spot so you can find them right away when it's time to pay them.
- Set up one spot (the traditional shoebox would work fine) to put all your tax receipts as you get them. Don't worry about sorting them until tax time. Just be sure to catch them.

* This is Leo's clever term for containers that require you to put things into specific shaped slots and are therefore difficult to use.

- Use one credit card for your household and one for your business. Keep your household and business expenses separate by using the correct card. Don't mingle business expenses with household ones.
- If you enjoy working on your computer, use Quicken to pay your bills. It is fast, efficient, and powerful, and it will save you a lot of time and work. Its online banking and bill-pay features are also useful time-savers.
- Use a pen or dark pencil to label file folders and write the label directly onto the tab. Labeling machines and colored labels are fussy, and if you don't have the machine or the right color label, you won't label something. Also, don't use adhesive labels on folders—eventually they fall off.
- Use your computer to store name and address information. All sophisticated word processing programs have quick-and-easy databases for this kind of data. It's much easier to update and retrieve from your computer than by hand.
- Keep file categories broad. Don't complicate filing with lots of small groupings.

Keep Your Time Simple

- Try to do everything as quickly and efficiently as you can. Time is too precious to waste.
- Take a good look at the activities that fill up your days. If you're doing any activity or task that isn't worth the time you're spending on it, subtract it. Make time for more important things.
- Don't clutter up your time by doing things in more steps than they require. Cut out the extra steps in all your processes so you have more time for the people and activities you care about.

- If you frequently find yourself driving to the store for supplies you need to complete one of your routine tasks, keep more supplies on hand *or* look for ways to accomplish the same results more efficiently.
- Use a simple, portable calendar system to keep track of your daily schedule.
- Don't do things you don't like to do unless you have to. Then, do them as quickly and efficiently as possible so you get them over with.

Keep Your Relationships Simple

- Spend as much time as you can with the people you love. Get out of other obligations that keep you away from them.
- Don't waste time by spending it with people you don't care about, or who don't care about you.

These suggestions will help you streamline and simplify your organizing system so you're not clogging it up with extra work. When you *Keep It Simple*, you achieve the results you want using fewer steps. This helps you save time and energy and gives you more time and energy for the people and projects you care about.

It's time now to look at another way to avoid potential clogs in your organizing system. Let's move on to *Strategy #7, Decide to Decide.*

Decide to Decide

Make decisions instead of putting them off and letting them pile up. Sometimes it takes more time to put something on your to-do list than it takes to just do it. Postponing decisions increases the mess and your stress level. Give yourself permission not to do things.

Overview of Strategy #7

The second kind of bottleneck that can throw a wrench into your organizing system is caused by indecision. Imagine a week's worth of mail sitting in a single pile in the middle of your family room floor. Now picture yourself sorting it, piece by piece, into categories. Is there any junk you can toss without even looking at it? Are there bills? What about catalogs or flyers? Go through everything until you've sorted it all. Now step back and ask yourself, "What did I just do?"

The process you used to divide your mail into groups involved a series of small decisions. Each time you put a piece into a particular pile, you were deciding whether or not you needed it in your life. The decisions you made allowed you to throw out all the superfluous items and keep only the things that have value *for you*. When you use *Strategy #7, Decide to Decide,* you exercise your power to hold on to things that matter to you and to let go of things that don't.

Life itself requires every person to make one decision after another. Some of them are mundane, like allocating an envelope to this pile or that pile. Others affect every aspect of your life—for instance, your choice of a life partner. The small decisions are endless and relentless, like a mob of ants. That's why it's best to handle them immediately, before they overwhelm you. The big decisions, while fewer in number, usually take longer to make because you need to consider all the ramifications. Taken all together, your decisions, large and small, keep everything flowing into and out of your life. If something happens to keep you from making them, it can cause your organizing system to falter, or even grind to a complete halt.

In the Introduction, I talked about how most of my clients could trace the disorganized messes in their homes back to specific events. Things were piled up because life changes had left them in limbo for a while—a period in which no decisions were made and no actions took place.

When a major life event occurs—tragic or joyful—it puts people into a state of flux. If you don't know what life is going to look like tomorrow, it's hard to make decisions today—you don't know what you need to keep and what you can discard. During periods of change, it's human nature to keep everything, just in case. Letting go of things becomes a risky proposition. Life events also trigger strong emotions that take time to process. Until you regain your balance, it's natural to forgo decision making. The net result of postponed decisions in either case is that things start to pile up. The longer the limbo period, the bigger the ensuing pile.

If you've been stuck in a groove that has kept you from making decisions, large or small, *Strategy #7* is the cure. As soon as you make up your mind to do something, things will begin to happen. It is the *decision to act* that causes an action to occur. Without the decision, nothing will happen, and nothing will get better.

Symptoms That Decisions Need to Be Made

Read the following symptoms to see if any of them sound familiar. If things have been piling up in your house in any of these ways, it may be time for you to *Decide to Decide*.

- Every day when the mail comes, you pick out the fun things to read and put all the rest in a pile to deal with later.
- Your garage is full of items you're planning to give away.
- Your desk is covered with papers you "should" do something about, but you keep putting off dealing with them.
- You never have time to do the mending or ironing, so it just piles up in your bedroom or laundry room or closet.
- You use Post-it notes as file folder labels.
- You have stacks of things you want to read, but you never get around to reading them.
- You know you need a different setup for one of your activities, but you keep putting off making the necessary changes.
- You've been saving things until you have time to hold a yard sale.
- When you buy new linens/towels/drapes/pieces of furniture, you put all the old ones into your storage areas.
- You can't find time to tackle the one huge project you know would transform your life and make everything else work better.
- You're planning to move, so you don't want to waste time getting your current residence organized.
- Things in your life have changed, but you keep hoping they'll go back to the way they used to be.

Are any of these happening at your house? Then it's time to put *Strategy #7* into action to help you get things moving again. Take your cue from the following stories.

Real-Life Lessons:
Strategy #7 Missing in Action

Paige called me in to help her weed out her desk and office. In the course of our work together, I noticed an interesting pile accumulating. The family used a narrow, uncarpeted back staircase to go up and down between the kitchen and the bedrooms, rather than the formal one in the front hall. At the top of the stairs, a mound of bags, boxes, and large items, such as a rocking horse, were cluttering the hallway. On the steps themselves, miscellaneous bags were taking up a third of the walking space. It was an accident just waiting to happen.

When I asked Paige about this interesting jumble, she showed me the contents of the bags—outgrown children's clothes, old towels and linens, obsolete toys, knickknacks—and the larger items under the quilts. "These are things I'm saving for my yard sale," she said.

Although this might have been a reasonable statement in June, it was November in Massachusetts! The weather was cold, raw, completely unsuitable for yard sales and bound to get much worse before it got better. But Paige was planning to hold the yard sale in the spring. She intended to keep adding things to the pile through the winter so there would be enough items to justify the substantial amount of work a yard sale entails.

One of the reasons Paige had hired me in the first place was that her schedule was too full. We'd been doing a lot of work to trim out extra activities so she had more time to devote to her family. So I pointed out to her that a yard sale was a good way to get her schedule clogged right up again, no matter when she held it. If she just loaded all this stuff into her car and took it to the nearest charity drop-off, it would save her a lot of work. Not only that, she'd get a tax deduction for the same amount the yard sale might have generated, and the stuff would no longer pose a hazard to her children.

Paige had already made the decision to let go of all the items in the pile. But she hadn't made the follow-up decision to actually remove them from the premises. When she decided to decide, the stairs and hallway were safely cleared up, other people got to use the stuff she'd been stockpiling, and she got a nice tax deduction.

Once you decide to let go of things, get them out of your way as soon as possible. The first decision without the second one—to actually remove it—just creates another pile. Take giveaway items to your nearest charity, get a receipt, and deduct the value of the donation from your tax return.

In Chapter 3 (*Strategy #3, Weed Constantly*) you read the story of Becky and Dan. They moved into their first home even though there was a huge pile of the deceased previous owner's old, dusty belongings in the basement. They hadn't had time to take care of this mess before they took possession, so they'd just been letting it sit there, in their way, for months. In the meantime, they were struggling to find indoor space for their small children to play.

Although this story illustrates the value of removing old things when they're in your way, it also reveals the importance of making decisions. Becky was the one most affected by this particular pile of stuff. She had to maneuver around it every day, and she had to keep her children from getting into it when they played on the basement rug. But because it was such a big pile and all the items in it were too large for her to move by herself, it was overwhelming and so she put it off.

As soon as she and Dan decided it was time to clean out their basement, getting it done was easy. They rented a dumpster, bought some pizzas and a few cases of beer, and invited friends and family to help them out. In less than a day, they had a big, empty, clean basement that the whole family could use. As soon as they made up their minds to tackle the problem, they made it disappear.

Sometimes the only thing stopping you from fixing a big problem is indecision. Once you make up your mind to tackle a large project, it'll get done. If you've been putting off a big job even though you know it'll make things work much better, decide to get it done, and just do it.

Tamara's house was comfortable, peaceful, and in good order, except for her office. She called me in despair because she couldn't seem to keep her desk clear of paper piles, and she needed it uncluttered so she could work on the book she was writing. To figure out why the pile of papers kept coming back, no matter what she did, we sat down and took a hard look at what was in it. After an hour of sorting and sifting, we discovered Tamara's desk was the repository for five categories of paperwork: (1) bills to pay, (2) flyers for upcoming events, (3) receipts, (4) financial statements, and (5) work-related notes. These papers were on the desk because she had no designated places for them.

We solved this problem differently for each category. The financial statements, which she needed, were archived in new folders in the bottom drawer of Tamara's file cabinet. The top drawer, because it was easiest to reach and use, was designated the writing drawer. All her work notes went there. Then we created a stand-up file on her desk for two important folders: "Bills to Pay," and "Receipts." It was easy for Tamara to drop those items into the folders as soon as she got them, which kept them off the desktop and helped her find them later. She was thrilled with these changes and assured me she'd have no problem maintaining them.

When we reached the events flyers, however, things went less smoothly. It turned out Tamara had a surprisingly large number of them on her desk. Most of the events had already come and gone, yet Tamara was reluctant to recycle the flyers. No matter what I suggested, she just sat there and stared at the pile, stymied. Clearly, there was more to these flyers than met the eye. So we talked it out.

Whenever Tamara received an announcement for an upcoming event, it sparked her imagination. She would picture herself at the event, enjoying the inspiring work of dancers and musicians, being a patron of the arts. She'd say to herself, "I should go to *that!*" Then real life would intervene. Family obligations, work deadlines, travel distances, and financial limitations would prevent Tamara from attending almost all these enticing events. The only tangible reminder of Tamara's heady dream was the flyer.

Enchanting though this vision might be, it was causing a real-life mess. Tamara decided to eschew the dream for reality and be honest with herself about which events she was really able to attend. When she got a flyer for a doable performance, she called right away to order tickets, recorded the event in her calendar, and saved the flyer in the new "Events" folder we made for her desktop. But when she got a flyer for something she knew, in all honesty, wasn't going to fit into her schedule, she allowed herself to dream for only a moment, then coldheartedly dropped the flyer right into her recycling bin.

A month later, Tamara called to tell me how empowered this new policy made her feel. It had galvanized her to make other decisions she'd been putting off, and her whole life was working better.

 Many postponed decisions have papers and things that go with them. When you put off making a decision about something, you build a pile of these papers and things. Then the postponed decision clutters up your space, as well as your mind. Decide to decide, so you can make these physical and mental roadblocks go away.

 Julia likes to surround herself with nice things. The living spaces in her home are well furnished, well decorated, and very comfortable. In particular, she has a real talent for selecting beautiful fabrics for her window treatments and bed linens. She called me because her basement was getting too messy, and she wanted some help clearing it out. Julia lives in a house built before the turn of the twentieth century. Its foundation is made of fieldstones, and the basement floor is hard-packed dirt. The whole room is damp most of the year, and it smells strongly of mildew. The only light comes from one dim window and three bare ceiling bulbs. Even though it is an inhospitable room, Julia keeps things down here because it's her main storage area.

Throughout the basement, things were stored in an almost random fashion. Some boxes were sitting on wooden pallets in an effort to keep them dry. Other things were stored on top of dusty old tables and chairs, and the remaining items filled up three sets of shelves. Only the gardening equipment—rakes, shovel, lawn mower, hand tools—appeared to have been used recently.

Methodically, we worked our way through the items on the shelves and the furniture, threw out all the trash, and put everything that remained in a pile to give away. But when we got to the eight large cardboard cartons sitting on the pallets, we discovered why the room smelled so bad. They'd gotten wet, and everything in them—beautiful curtains, comforters, bedspreads, and tablecloths Julia had saved the previous year when she redecorated—was full of mildew and ruined. Our only option was to throw them out.

Julia had put these things in the basement because she thought they were too good to give away. But the inhospitable environment had turned valuable items into trash. If she had given them away as soon as she took them off her windows and beds, at least someone else would have been able to use them. Julia felt awful about this, because she knew what a waste it was. She vowed never to store cloth items in the basement again and to give things away as soon as she stopped using them.

Before you put anything in your storage areas, ask yourself, "Will I ever use this again?" If your honest answer is no, put it in your car instead and drive it straight to your favorite charity. Decide not to keep things you really don't need, especially if someone else could make good use of them.

Wayne's corporation had downsized, and he was one of the unlucky ones. After three fruitless months of job searching among other large companies, he decided to try smaller firms. When he realized his marketing skills and experience were valuable to growing companies, he started his own consulting business and immediately got enough work to keep him busy. Wayne called me because his old home office wasn't designed to support a small business. He wanted help setting up a more functional business office in his house.

When I arrived, Wayne led me to the third floor of the spacious home he shared with his wife. He showed me the large, long room in the eaves that he was using as his office. At the far end, under a big window, was his desk. It consisted of a long counter held up by four two-drawer file cabinets. Flanking it, floor-to-ceiling cupboards filled the corners. On the left-hand wall, a shelving unit stood between two gable windows. On the right, next to the door, was a walk-in cedar closet filled with clothes. There was no other furniture in the room except Wayne's rolling desk chair and a narrow sofa to the left of the door. Every square inch of the floor was littered with a shallow layer of papers, books, file folders, and a variety of briefcases. In front of the bookshelf, there were about ten open file boxes full of papers and folders.

As soon as we entered the room, Wayne stopped short and surveyed the scene. His shoulders sagged, and he heaved a heavy sigh. He told me the mess in the room demoralized him so much it was hard to work there. He knew it was the best location in the house and had the potential to be a wonderful business office, but he had no idea how to get it from where it was to where he wanted it to be. Even though he'd been trying to work there for six months, he'd done nothing to improve its setup. So he'd called me, hoping I'd be the agent of change.

One of the most important things a professional organizer does is serve as a catalyst for clients who've been stuck in some sort of limbo. Wayne had been depressed by his inability to find a corporate job, which in turn had affected his ability to make decisions in his home office. Every time he'd thought about processing his papers, setting up file drawers, or putting his books on the shelves, he'd been so overwhelmed, he'd just tossed the next pile of unopened mail on the floor and given up this hopeless cause. Wayne was drowning under his pile of papers.

My presence in the room changed the dynamic. When we looked at the pile together, side by side, he could suddenly see the playing field from the sidelines, instead of from the line of scrimmage. From an observer's vantage point, he could view his office objectively instead of emotionally. This allowed him to use his business skills, treat the mess as an abstract problem, break down the job into doable steps, and start working on it.

In no time, Wayne was sorting, weeding, and purging papers ruthlessly. We shot out to the store to get more hanging and manila folders, and set up the file cabinets so they were ready for business. All the clothes got moved from the closet to the spare bedroom on the second floor, and the boxes went onto the closet shelves. At the end of two four-hour organizing sessions, he was fully in control and making decisions right and left. Not only that, the office looked great.

 Sometimes difficult life events can make it hard for you to make decisions, even the small ones that fill every day. This can cause a large pile to grow quickly. If you find yourself in this kind of limbo, ask someone you trust to stand next to you and help you decide what to do. Sometimes it just takes another pair of eyes (the Eyes of a Stranger) to get you going again.

Dorothy is a wonderful cook. She's also an exceedingly busy person—wife, mother, doctor, and church volunteer. Even though she loves her subscriptions to *Gourmet* and several other culinary publications, she never has time to read them all. In hopes of getting through them someday, she's been saving them for years. They've taken over the shelves in her narrow kitchen bookcase and are starting to overflow into the family room. On the coffee table, cooking catalogs are also piling up. While I was at her house working on something else, she asked me for creative ideas about storing her magazines and catalogs.

We started with the catalogs. She had multiple copies from several big chains dating back eighteen months. Dorothy said she was keeping them because she liked to leaf through them and think about ordering things. When I suggested she trim the stack by recycling all but the latest issues, she protested, "But they might have something I need!"

People have an interesting relationship with their catalogs. They think of them as being full of items they *want*. In reality, most catalogs might have one or two things you'd like to own, but *all the rest of the items* are things you *don't* want. A catalog is a sophisticated advertisement, not a magazine. Once you've looked through it, recycle it. Another one will just show up next month to try to entice you again.

When I reminded Dorothy of these facts, she decided she didn't need to clutter up her family room with advertisements for things she didn't want or need. She recycled all but the latest issue of each catalog and vowed to use the One-Comes-In, One-Goes-Out (OCI-OGO) principle with all subsequent ones.

Our next stop was the kitchen. On the shelves of a narrow bookcase, Dorothy had saved five years' worth of four different monthly cooking magazines. The stack was getting too big for the kitchen bookcase, so I asked Dorothy if we could make room for the latest copies in the bookcase by recycling the oldest ones. She looked startled and said, "But I haven't had time to read them yet!"

This is another common phenomenon. People save all kinds of reading material—books, magazines, articles, newsletters, essays, newspapers, letters—stashed around the house, sometimes for years. Some of these piles are so large, they're threatening to take over whole rooms. One client had at least a thousand magazines squirreled away in every nook and cranny of her one-bedroom apartment.

Anything left lying around unread for years is, in fact, something you *don't* want to read. If you *really* wanted to read it, you already would have. People squeeze all kinds of things they want to do into their schedules. The things that don't get done are things they're really *not* interested in doing. Reading material left lying around for a long time fits into this category.

So why do people insist they want to read things, despite all evidence to the contrary? There are several human impulses behind this phenomenon. The first is the idea that you might miss something if you don't read a certain publication. Another possibility is that you feel you *should* read it, for whatever reason. A third impulse might arise if you received it as a gift, and you want to acknowledge the gift by using it. Whatever your motivation, if you've been keeping reading material around for so long it's getting in your way, it's time for *Strategy #7*. Decide to either read it or let it go.

Dorothy recycled three years' worth of back issues. Then, because the only time she actually got to read was at night in bed, she moved the entire collection to her bedroom and vowed to make it her first reading priority.

 If you've had something in a pile for a long time, yet you never seem to act on it, recognize that you aren't going to and get it out of your way. Be honest. If you know, in your heart of hearts, that you really aren't going to say yes to something, don't pretend you will. Send it out the door immediately.

If you have piles of unread reading material lying around, admit you're never going to read it and remove it from your space. It's okay not to read things. You're just one person, and you don't have to do optional reading if you don't want to.

Rick called me bemoaning the state of his house. When I arrived, I was surprised to find it well kept, orderly, and reasonably clean. The only room that needed some attention was Rick's office. His desk was piled with papers, and he was so far behind in paying his bills that several of his utilities had been turned off. This was not a financial problem—Rick was a doctor. Instead, he was having trouble getting payments in on time because his desk was so disorganized.

As we sorted out the papers on his desk to get them in better order, Rick revealed a few facts about his life. He'd finished medical school a year ago and moved cross-country to take his first job near his girlfriend. They bought a house together and got engaged, but she left him a month before he called me. Although Rick was able to discuss these changes calmly, tears came to his eyes as he told me about the event he'd found most difficult. Just after he finished medical school, his father died suddenly and unexpectedly. Rick was still upset that he hadn't been able to get home in time to say good-bye.

Once everything was sorted into piles, we discussed Rick's attempts to organize his office. First, he set up local bank accounts and tried to get online banking, but his bank didn't allow it. He'd switched banks, but his busy schedule had prevented him from actually signing up for online services. Then Rick's first check order from the new bank was incorrect. He was still waiting for the second set, which meant he couldn't pay his bills. The third problem involved his investment accounts. They were divided between two additional banks, one local and one in his home city.

As he listed each of these difficulties, Rick kept coming back to his father's death. It seemed this traumatic and life-altering event had precipitated a chain of financial problems. Finally, I asked Rick to explain how the money issues related to the death of his father. He answered, "It's hard for me to keep on doing these little tasks of living when my father is dead." As soon as these words passed his lips, Rick fell silent. I could see the wheels turning in his mind. At last he turned to me and said, "That's the real problem, isn't it?"

Rick's real issue was deeply emotional. He was struggling to cope with the fundamental loss of his father. His limbo had come from his overwhelming sense of grief. He started to come out of it when he decided to get help organizing his office. But it was the act of speaking his grief out loud that really enabled him to face it and deal with it. Over the next few weeks, Rick got his financial affairs in order and started paying his bills on time.

If you've suffered a significant trauma or loss, it's a reasonable response to go into limbo for a while. It's important to get your basic responsibilities met—pay your bills, show up for work, eat and sleep—but it's okay to let less important daily tasks slide. When you're ready, start with small decisions and work yourself back toward your fully functioning self.

LouAnn, a thirty-five-year-old engineer, was about to get married for the first time. Because she owned her own home and her fiancé lived in an apartment, they planned to move him into her house after the wedding. She asked me to help her get the house ready for him and all his things.

LouAnn had two major projects to do before Robert moved in. First, she needed to rearrange her furniture so there was room for his. We finished this project quickly. The second job, however, was more time-consuming. LouAnn wanted to go through all her papers, page by page, and get them properly filed in a new file cabinet we bought. To prepare for this task, we figured out what file categories she would need, then drew up a master list. Between sessions, she bought file folders, labeled them, and put them in the file cabinet.

When I came back to help her sort the papers and put them away in the folders, the first thing I noticed about LouAnn's new files was the labels. Each category name was written in pale pencil strokes on a tiny Post-it note. These had been placed carefully on the tab portions of the manila file folders in the cabinet. All the stand-up tabs on the hanging file folders were still blank. I was surprised by this temporary arrangement, because we had put several hours into drawing up LouAnn's master category list. So I asked her why she'd written the labels on temporary Post-it notes. She replied, "If I used pen, it would be too permanent. What if I changed my mind?"

LouAnn was, by nature, a cautious person. She liked to take her time and do things right. This was one of the reasons she hadn't gotten married before—she was waiting for the right man. But while a slow, measured approach might be the best way to select a life partner, it can certainly bog down more mundane tasks like filing. The question that helped LouAnn figure out whether her caution was warranted was, "What's the *worst* thing that could happen if you take this step?" When she applied this standard to her file folders, she decided she could live with the risk of a bad label, even if she had to recycle a folder now and then. She started writing on the tabs with a pen.

If it's hard for you to make decisions because you're not sure the course you've chosen is the right one, ask yourself, "What's the worst thing that could happen if I do this?" If you can live with the results, go ahead and do it. If the price would be too steep, think again.

Gabriela invited me in for a general consultation. She was looking for good ideas to help her manage her active family. On our house tour, I noticed a huge mound of clothes piled on an ironing board in her bedroom. Additional garments sat underneath it in laundry baskets. The whole conglomeration took up a quarter of the floor space in the bedroom Gabriela shared with her husband, a carpenter. I asked her, "Do you iron often?" She answered, "I hate ironing." I followed up with, "Then what's all this stuff doing here by your ironing board?" She replied, "I keep thinking I should press all these clothes, but I never do it, so the pile keeps growing."

Here's another case where actions speak louder than words. No matter how much Gabriela told herself she "should" iron, no matter how many articles of clothing she piled on the ironing board to serve as incentive for getting the loathsome task done, the truth was evident. Gabriela was *not* going to iron those clothes. I encouraged her to simply admit it and let everyone wear slightly rumpled garments. Who was going to notice if a couple of little kids wore wrinkled T-shirts? No one. As soon as Gabriela admitted she wasn't going to iron anything, she freed her mind from the guilt she'd been feeling over this undone task, *and* she got her bedroom back. What a deal!

Don't burden yourself with guilt because you haven't done things that don't really need doing. Be honest, admit you don't want to do whatever-it-is and give it up. (Don't forget to get rid of the papers and things that go with it, too.)

Curt debated for a while about whether he needed my services. Finally, after a few weeks of back-and-forth phone calls, he invited me to his apartment for a consultation. The source of his indecision was that he was planning to move within the next year, and he didn't want to make a big investment in organizing his current living space.

It was clear right away that Curt didn't really know how to set up and manage a home, and he admitted as much. His mother had trained her daughters, but not her sons. So Curt's furniture was rather haphazardly arranged, there were papers littering the floor and flat surfaces, clothes were strewn around the empty second bedroom, and the kitchen was crowded with more utensils and appliances than really fit into its narrow confines. The key to getting Curt's apartment into a more livable state was its size. The whole place was small enough to clean it up quickly.

Working together, Curt and I rearranged his living room furniture into two groups: a central seating area around the wall unit holding the TV and a desk area that took advantage of the breathtaking city views you could see through the floor-to-ceiling windows. Then we straightened up the kitchen, weeded unused dishes and cooking implements from the cupboards, and arranged things neatly in all the storage areas. Finally, we cleaned up the spare room and made things look presentable. Curt transformed his apartment into a much more pleasant place to live while he looked for his own house—and he didn't have to spend a fortune to do it.

Even if you're planning major life events in the near future, keep your current life organized enough so it's comfortable for you. Don't sacrifice today in order to serve tomorrow. Live your life in the moment while you plan for the future.

Here's an unusual but telling story. During a tour of one particularly neglected home, I noticed four vacuum cleaner bags, all chock-full of dust and debris, sitting in a corner on the floor. When I asked my client about them, she said, "I think I vacuumed up an earring, so I was saving the bags just in case." In an effort to make even a small dent in the enormous mess burdening this house, I suggested we take the bags right outside, empty them out, and see if the earring was, indeed, inside one. Even if it wasn't there, this would get the dusty bags out of the house. My client's response was, "Oh no, I'm not ready for that."

 Making small decisions can help you break a decision deadlock. Start with one that has no risk at all. If you still can't decide, you aren't ready to come out of limbo. Consider getting help from a trusted friend or counselor.

 When Tyler inherited his father's house, he packed all his father's things into the garage. This created a substantial pile because Tyler's father was an inventor who amassed a collection of all kinds of gizmos and gadgets. So Tyler's garage became the repository for mysterious unlabeled boxes full of equipment, papers, memorabilia, and tools.

At first, Tyler didn't want to go through the boxes and make decisions about the contents because the idea was too emotionally painful. When he started to need the space for his own belongings, he didn't tackle the garage because it was such an overwhelming job. Finally, he called me for ideas about how to approach it. We put together a written plan that broke this large job into small tasks, and Tyler tackled it by himself. It took him a while, but getting the garage cleaned up helped him on two fronts. First, it gave him a covered place to park his car, which he hadn't had for years. Second, when he cleared out his father's physical belongings, it helped free him of some of the emotional baggage his father left behind, too.

 If a giant task is too big to take care of all at once, map out a plan for tackling it step by step and do it one step at a time. This will take longer, but it gets the job done. Slow and steady wins the race.

What a Full-Blown
Strategy #7 Crisis Looks Like

In the homes you've just peeked into, there is a pile here or there because the occupant hasn't been making decisions in one or two specific arenas. Often, the issues underlying these piles disappear as soon as the person realizes the problem will be solved by taking quick and painless action. When a person has been postponing decisions for a long time—no matter what life event(s) precipitated his or her indecision—the piles can converge and grow until they take over the whole house.

Kitty is a homemaker and artist whose story best illustrates the problems that ensue when large and small decisions are postponed over the course of years. She lives in a spacious home on a quiet suburban street with her husband of twenty-two years. Their daughter had just graduated from college, and their son was a freshman at the state university. Kitty called me because she was planning to turn her painting hobby into a business now that her children had moved away. She said her home was not set up to support this new activity, and she couldn't figure out how to rearrange everything by herself.

Kitty's home looked as if it had been built in the 1960s. It was a center-entrance colonial with a garage under the house at one end and a two-story addition at the other. A colorful flag was waving over the front door, welcoming visitors. Kitty ushered me into her kitchen, where we sat for a few minutes to get acquainted and talk about her situation. Here's what I learned.

Before Kitty met her husband, she worked as a flight attendant and did a lot of traveling. After they got married, she stayed home with their children. As a hobby, she took up painting and showed a real talent for it. Kitty occasionally accompanied her husband on business trips, but she enjoyed being at home with her children and was active at their schools and in the neighborhood. When her daughter went away to college, she started to feel at loose ends. She started several home-based businesses, but none of them took hold. Her most recent project was a major addition to the house—a new wing with a master suite above a large ground-floor studio for Kitty. This gave her the idea to turn her painting hobby into a business.

The last thing Kitty told me before we toured her home was how disorganized she was feeling. She showed me a book she'd read about people suffering from chronic disorganization and identified herself as a member of that group. Yet her kitchen seemed orderly and immaculate. When we started on our tour, I was curious to see if Kitty's house corroborated her feelings.

Space: All the rooms Kitty shared with her husband—kitchen, living room, dining room, master bedroom and bath—were reasonably furnished and neat, although knickknacks and framed photographs cluttered the shelves and tabletops. Upstairs, one spare bedroom served as a guest room; the other clearly belonged to the young man of the house. The remainder of the home—a fourth small bedroom upstairs and the studio and adjacent storage rooms downstairs— belonged to Kitty.

The new studio, a giant room at one end of the ground floor, had built-in cupboards and a sink along the original wall of the house. The remaining three sides of the room were primarily windows. It would have been a fabulous place to paint if it weren't full of old file cabinets, multiple double-pedestal desks, and an assortment of tables and chairs. These things filled up all the space in the middle of the room except for narrow pathways. From the doorway, Kitty indicated her work space, an artist's drawing board set up by the right-hand windows. To get to it, and then to retrieve her supplies and wash her brushes, she had to navigate carefully through the room. When I asked about the extra furniture, she said, "Oh, I've been putting these things here because there's room and I don't know what else to do with them." I followed up, "If you're not using them, why don't you give them away?" She replied, "I was thinking about selling them, but I haven't gotten around to it yet."

Next to the studio, Kitty and her husband had modified an existing room for Kitty's canvases and finished works. It, too, was a well-designed space—large open racks on the far wall held completed paintings standing upright, and special draftsman's cabinets with huge drawers for large sheets of paper lined the left-hand wall. Again, however, the room's design was completely nullified by a jumble of antique chairs, small tables, escritoires, and decorative items. It turned out one of Kitty's former businesses involved selling antiques, and her extra inventory had landed in this room. She said she wasn't ready to sell these things, either, so they were cluttering her space and getting in her way.

All the studio and storage space Kitty and her husband had designed to support her painting activities was virtually impossible to use.

Things: Although the living space throughout the house was relatively free of clutter, every closet was crammed with stuff. The clothes closets were bursting; in the linen closet, it was hard to get anything in or out; cosmetics and over-the-counter medicines filled the bathroom drawers and cabinets; and there wasn't room for another coat in the coat closet (Kitty draped my coat over a chair in the living room). There were more things in the house than an active family of six would have needed. Yet only two people were living there. Kitty was keeping every old towel, sheet, broken lamp, and worn-out pair of shoes she had ever owned because she couldn't bring herself to let go of them when she got new ones.

Information: The fourth bedroom on the second floor served as Kitty's home office. She kept most of her data and information stored on her computer, which sat under the window on a small desk. Although there was a small pile of unprocessed mail in this room awaiting her attention, Kitty had no trouble with papers. In this arena, she was able to keep everything moving.

Time: Her schedule, by contrast, gave her trouble on two fronts. The first problem was that she was trying to do it on her computer, and the software she was using was primitive. If she wanted to carry forward an item on her "To Do" list to the next day, she had to re-type it. Every morning, Kitty took a cup of coffee up to her desk and spent at least forty-five minutes just formatting and printing her calendar for the day. In the same amount of time, she could easily have done most of the items on the list. Instead, she postponed them from one day to the next.

Kitty's other time problem was interruptions. Whenever she set aside a block of time to paint, or read, or do any project, she was constantly being distracted by the telephone and the doorbell. Yet she didn't like to screen her calls, and she never ignored the doorbell's ring. The net effect was that her time got taken up by the demands of other people. It was hard for Kitty to turn away someone else who wanted her attention. She was used to taking care of others, and it was a hard habit to break.

Relationships: Although I never met Kitty's husband because she and I worked together during the day while he was at his office, she hinted that their marriage was going through a rocky phase. It's reasonable to assume that some of the discord was related to their son's departure for college. The two of them were left alone together, without children to distract them or serve as a shared focus of attention. But according to Kitty, her husband was distressed because the house felt messy and out of order. She blamed herself and felt pressured enough to call a professional organizer to help turn things around. She was hoping the work we did together would make him happy.

As Kitty showed me around her home, it became clear that her feeling of chronic disorganization came from her inability to decide what she wanted and then *pursue* her vision to fruition. The messes cluttering up her house—useless furniture in the studio, leftover antiques in the storage room, old worn-out clothes and supplies in all the closets, yesterday's tasks on today's schedule—were the direct result of postponed or never-made decisions. Kitty needed a stiff infusion of *Strategy #7, Decide to Decide*. When we sat down to map out her organizing strategy, I recommended immediate action.

We started with a few easy steps. Kitty began scheduling her day using a blank calendar page and a pencil, instead of her computer and printer. This saved noticeable time. Then, in lieu of transposing small tasks like telephone calls from one day to the next, she just made the calls and got them over with. Another easy change was to use the answering machine to catch incoming calls instead of always answering the phone and to ignore the doorbell. This gave Kitty the freedom to work on her projects without interruption.

From these small steps, we moved on to a bigger job—weeding out the upstairs closets. We spent hours sorting through clothes, linens, towels, stationery, games, coats—you name it. Kitty made a million little decisions, and we cleared out a lot of space for the things she was still using and wanted to keep.

We saved the biggest task for last. By the time we got to the studio and art storage rooms, Kitty was on a roll, making decisions right and left. It took a while to remove all the old furniture from her work spaces, partly because she wanted to sell it instead of giving it to charities, but eventually the studio started to serve its intended purpose.

With her children out of the house and her husband at work, the only person Kitty had to take care of every day was herself, but she was always putting herself last on her "To Do" list. As a result, she felt out of control. She initially believed this feeling came from being chronically disorganized, but its real cause was her inability to decide which way she wanted to take her life. The more she ran through different options in her mind, the more difficult it became to choose. This kept her from taking action, and put her into an unsettled limbo. Once she acknowledged it was time to put herself first, she took control and turned her life around.

Saying you want to accomplish something is not enough. Unless you back up your goals with actions, you won't be able to achieve them. Decide to decide, and take the steps that will turn your dreams into reality.

How to Put Strategy #7 Back in Place

Did any of the stories in this chapter spark the realization that you've been letting things pile up because you don't want to make decisions about them? If this is a familiar scenario, it's time to apply *Strategy #7, Decide to Decide.* The simple act of making decisions can keep your organizing system from drowning under a pile of stuff. Remember, nothing will change unless and until you make it change. And once you make up your mind to tackle a project, it'll get done. If a task you've put off is a small one, just do it. If you're procrastinating because a project is too big to do all at once, map out a plan for it and do it one step at a time. Spare yourself the mess and guilt that accompany a postponed decision. *Decide to Decide,* and get things moving again.

This section gives you concrete ways to take action and deal with the myriad issues you face every day. It also points out some of the common ways people get in trouble because they put off making decisions.

Decide to Decide
About Your Space

- If you've been wanting to rearrange your furniture for some time, but you just haven't done it, put "Rearrange" on your calendar and block off enough time for it. Then do the whole project. Avoid stopping a rearranging project in the middle because it'll be hard to finish it later. A half-done project is almost worse than no project at all.

- If you've been wanting different furniture or decorations for a while, put a budget and plan together and go shopping. Give away the old stuff as soon as the new items arrive.
- If you think you need to move, first make sure you can't achieve the results you want by making changes to your current home. If your house is still inadequate, begin looking at other places to live.

Decide to Decide About Your Things

- Don't put things in a pile to decide about them later. When you pile them, you have to think about them twice—now and when you weed the pile. This just creates double work for you. Make the decision now, and it will be done.
- If you've had something in a pile for a long time, recognize that you aren't going to act on it and get it out of your way. Be honest.
- Before you store anything, ask yourself, "Will I ever use this again?" If the honest answer is no, give yourself permission to give it away. Decide not to keep things you know you won't use.
- Once you decide to let go of something, get it out of your space as soon as possible. Put giveaway items right into your car and take them to your favorite charity.
- When things no longer have use or meaning for you, don't let them hang around cluttering up your space. Give them to someone who will value them.

- Put items you need to take elsewhere right in your car. Then, when you drive by the place you need to take them, you have them with you.
- Tidy up periodically and put things back into their places.

Decide to Decide
About Your Information

- Process your mail ruthlessly every day. Toss or recycle most of it. Don't let it pile up.
- Read your magazines right away. Then recycle them.
- Never clip articles. Clipping is a waste of time, energy, and space.
- If you never have time to read a newspaper or magazine you subscribe to, cancel your subscription and recycle the back-logged newspapers/magazines.
- If you have piles of unread reading material lying around, admit you're never going to read it and remove it from your space. It's okay not to read things.
- Skim through catalogs quickly, then recycle them. If you see something you might actually order, rip out the page and call to order the product right away. Then put the page in your "To Order" folder (kept next to your "To Pay" folder). When the item arrives, check to be sure it's what you ordered, then recycle the page.
- Take people with whom you no longer have a relationship off your mailing lists.
- Pay bills once a month. It's not necessary to do it more often. Process them all at once, and you won't have to do it again for another month.

- When your children come home from school, go through their papers ruthlessly. Display new artwork until the next batch arrives, then recycle the old items unless they're especially creative.

Decide to Decide About Your Time

- If you want to have enough time for a project, schedule it on your calendar. Then treat it like an appointment, and stick to it.
- On your "To Do" list, schedule your Have-To-Do items first. Then you can get them over with and move on to the fun stuff.
- Don't put off little tasks. Just do them. This includes phone calls, permission slips, making bank deposits—all those little jobs that add up if you let them pile up.
- Return telephone calls right away. If you get a machine, leave a message. Then the other person is "It," and it's their turn to call you.
- Schedule quiet time for yourself. Give yourself at least fifteen minutes a day to unwind. Make yourself unavailable to other people during those few minutes.

Decide to Decide About Your Relationships

- Decide to spend time with the people you care about. Don't put it off.
- If people you care about live far away from you, call them to let them know you're thinking of them.

- Invite people to visit you. Don't wait for them to drop by.
- When you're contemplating a big decision, use a "Pluses/ Minuses" list to help you keep track of all the pros and cons. Don't rush.
- If you're contemplating making a big change that affects the people you love, discuss it with them. Work together to come up with a doable plan for the change.
- Make time to sit quietly with people you love. Listen to what they have to say. This is a concrete demonstration of your care and support.

These suggestions help you identify the decisions you've been putting off and take action to get things moving again. When you *Decide to Decide*, you can make all kinds of piles disappear in no time. The result? Your organizing system will no longer be encumbered by the debris from old decisions left unmade.

Now it's time to look at a third kind of bottleneck that can keep your organizing system from functioning effectively. This bottleneck can pile up stuff when you don't apply *Strategy #8, Get Help When You Need It.*

CHAPTER 8 | **STRATEGY #8**

Get Help
When You Need It

If you don't have to do all the work yourself, why should you? Share the responsibility for tasks by delegating them. Hire people to do things you aren't good at or don't want to do. Consult experts. Avoid the trap of self-sufficiency.

Overview of Strategy #8

There are times in everyone's life when the expertise, advice, or just plain support of other people are necessary. When you need help but don't ask for it, you can trigger yet another kind of bottleneck to obstruct your organizing system. This one arises when you have more work to do than you can handle by yourself, but you don't allow anyone else to help you do it.

We expect ourselves to be self-sufficient, independent, and resourceful. American culture lionizes the pioneer spirit, the impulse that pulled people across the oceans and the frontier in search of a better life. The first settlers in America's westward expansion had to do everything themselves—there were no houses, no stores, no roads, no laws, no systems of government unless they created them. So they buckled down and got to work.

The powerful myth of the pioneer shapes our fundamental assumptions about what we can accomplish by ourselves. Throughout American history, it's been the incentive for all kinds of advancement.

In modern life, however, we don't *have* to be pioneers. We live in a highly developed civilization with myriad resources at our disposal. When a new or difficult task lands in our laps, there are plenty of other people around who can help us complete it. Nevertheless, some of us struggle along trying to do everything ourselves instead of enlisting others to help us get the job done.

Here's how the pioneer myth may be mirrored in *your* life. Let's say there's an item on your "To Do" list that never seems to get done. You've been transposing it from one list to the next, looking at it every day, then putting it off again. You may be *telling* yourself this job is still on your list because (1) you don't have time to do it, or (2) you don't know how to do it, or (3) you don't really want to do it. But that's not really why it's there. This job stays on your "To Do" list day after day because you *expect yourself* to do it, even if you don't have the time, knowledge, or desire to get it done. If you didn't feel personally responsible for it, it wouldn't be on your list in the first place—someone else would have taken it on.

This is where *Strategy #8, Get Help When You Need It*, comes into play. The basic proposition is simple.

Just because something's on your "To Do" list,
it doesn't mean you have to do it.

Its presence on your list just means you feel *responsible* for getting it done. Take a moment to consider the possibility that someone else might be able to do it better, faster, or more cheaply than you can. After all, it's the end result that counts here—not the process. Is the task completed, or isn't it? The methods you use to achieve the desired result are immaterial. If you've been putting off a job for a long time, it might be time to pass it off for someone else to complete. Then all you have to do is oversee the work. You don't have to do it yourself.

Strategy #8 helps you figure out how to share the work of running a household (or a business) and keeping everything going smoothly. Sometimes this involves delegating tasks to other members of the family. Sometimes it requires the expertise of an outside contractor or consultant. And occasionally, the only one who can help you get through a difficult bottleneck is a therapist.

No matter where the help comes from, allowing yourself to ask for assistance when you need it is an important part of getting and staying organized. If you try to do everything yourself, you're guaranteed to run up against your own limitations. No one can get all the work done alone. Each person only has so much time, energy, knowledge, and experience. When you have a hard job to complete, complement your resources by encouraging and allowing other people to help you.

Symptoms That You Need More Help

Let's take a look at some of the telltale signs that you could use a little assistance to keep everything going smoothly.

- One person does almost all the work around the house and is exceedingly busy, and that person is you.
- You don't want to do things that have to be done.
- You aren't good at doing things that have to be done.
- You don't know how to do things that have to be done.
- Your overall organizing system has bottlenecks because a routine job like doing the laundry, washing the dishes, picking up things, or cleaning isn't getting done fast enough.
- Your kids are not invited to participate in organizing and setting up their rooms.
- Your kids do not participate in routine family chores.

- Your kids need your help to take care of their responsibilities (including homework) because they don't have the proper setup to handle these tasks by themselves.
- You and your partner have conflicting ideas about how to manage clutter, storage, or ongoing projects.
- You and your partner have conflicting ideas about how much children should participate in the work of the household.
- You have physical limitations that hinder your ability to get things done.
- You have deep or unresolved emotional issues that hinder your ability to get things done.

Does your situation match one of these? Then it's time to take a look around you and see who else can be brought in to give you a hand. Help can come from lots of different directions. Here are just a few ways to *Get Help When You Need It*.

Real-Life Lessons:
Strategy #8 Missing in Action

Rita was a writer and consultant who worked from her home. She had recently moved to a two-bedroom apartment so she could put all her work activities into a room of their own. Rita set up the second bedroom as her office. But she found herself working in the kitchen, the living room, the bedroom—anywhere but in the room she'd moved to this apartment for. She called me to help her figure out what was wrong with the new arrangement.

The first thing we did when I arrived was go straight into the office. As soon as we entered, the telephone rang. It was sitting on a small table next to the room's doorway, which was on the opposite side of the room from Rita's desk. I watched Rita as she crossed to the desk, picked up a notepad and pen, and returned to the telephone table to answer the phone. For the duration of the call, which lasted about five minutes, Rita talked to her client and took notes while kneeling on the floor in the middle of the room. As soon as she finished her call, I asked her whether she got many work calls at home. When she answered yes, I asked why the telephone wasn't on her desk. She said, "The jack is over here by the door, and there's no room for the desk next to it." My final question was, "Why don't you get a new jack installed?" She said, "But then I'd have to call the phone company."

Exactly. If she called the telephone company, she would solve the problem. Everything else she was doing—kneeling on the floor to use the phone, working in the kitchen, avoiding the office—was her attempt to compensate for the problem, but it didn't make the problem go away. It was time to bite the bullet and bring in a telephone technician. Although this would cost money and might be inconvenient, it was worth the time and bother because it actually *solved the problem*. This one step allowed Rita to justify her decision to move to the new apartment.

If a single visit from a contractor can solve a problem for you, don't put it off. Call and make an appointment. If you don't know whom to call for that kind of service, ask your friends and acquaintances for referrals. Solve the problem.

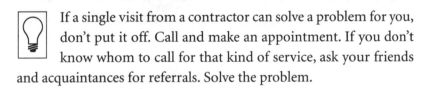 A stay-at-home mother of three teenage children, Nicole was in charge of day-to-day operations in her 6,000-square-foot home, a sprawling structure with spacious rooms, wide uncarpeted hallways, an atrium, and an enormous kitchen located in the center of the house, which served as Nicole's headquarters. I came to help Nicole streamline operations and make her house run efficiently.

One of Nicole's bottlenecks was dirty clothing. In her big laundry room, which was located at the far end of the house, most of the floor was taken up by piles of sorted clothing waiting to be washed. Other garments, clean but unfolded, were heaped on a long counter. Upstairs, all five members of the family shared two hampers, which were located in the bathrooms. None of the bedrooms had hampers, even though the children's rooms were littered with dirty clothes. Clothes were starting to pile up, and family members could be found rooting around in the laundry room trying to find items they wanted to wear. It was an issue.

To see where the laundry system could be made more efficient, I asked Nicole to explain how the process usually worked. First, she said, she went upstairs, got the hampers one at a time, and carried them down the back stairs, through the kitchen, and into the laundry room. Then she sorted all the clothes into lights and darks and began a load. Throughout the day, when she thought of it, she'd go back into the laundry room, move the washed clothes to the dryer, and start another load. When a load finished drying, she put it on the long counter. Usually, she didn't get to folding them until the next day (if then). As she folded, she separated the clothes according to their owners and put them into piles. When each pile got big enough to justify the trip, she took it upstairs to the owner's room and put it away in the drawers. At this point, it was usually time to start the whole operation over again.

Several issues were causing this process to get bogged down, as indicated by the piles of unprocessed clothing in the laundry room. First of all, the house was huge. Each trip involved several minutes' worth of walking, and nothing could be done to shorten the distances involved. The second problem came in the sorting step. Since each person's laundry was mingled with everyone else's, a considerable amount of time was spent separating clean clothes by owner. We solved this problem by giving each person her or his own individual hamper and washing each person's clothes in lots. Then, when a load came out of the dryer, it contained only one person's garments. This eliminated the separating step altogether. But the biggest bottleneck in this process—the one that was causing it to break down—was the fact that Nicole was doing *all* the work. Yet every family member benefited from having it done.

I suggested that Nicole's children were old enough to start helping with the laundry. Not only that, it was *in their self-interest* to get involved, because it would speed up the process and allow them to have clean clothes when they needed them. If each child was responsible for carrying dirty clothes downstairs in her or his hamper, bringing the clean clothes back upstairs, and putting them away again, Nicole could concentrate on getting everything washed expeditiously. The remaining kinds of laundry—sheets, towels, adult clothing—could be divided among the children so Nicole didn't have to carry these things back and forth, either.

Not only did this job-sharing lighten Nicole's burden and allow the laundry to get done faster, it set up a teaching process. Dirty clothes are a fact of life. Getting them clean is a life skill every child needs to learn. When her children started to help her, Nicole began to teach them how to manage their clothes.

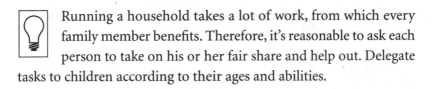 Running a household takes a lot of work, from which every family member benefits. Therefore, it's reasonable to ask each person to take on his or her fair share and help out. Delegate tasks to children according to their ages and abilities.

Douglas was partner-in-charge at a downtown law firm. After I helped his wife with some projects in their home, he invited me to his office for a consultation on ways to keep his business affairs organized.

Douglas was highly skilled at some aspects of his job. In litigation, when deadlines were breathing down his team's neck and legal issues were coming at them thick and fast, he was the star player who could tie everything together at the last possible second and win the case. He was also good at bringing clients into the firm and keeping them happy. These skills had made him a highly valued and successful attorney.

Other aspects of legal work, however, did not come easily to him. Every large case has cartons of documents that go with it. Part of the lead attorney's job is to make sure all the paperwork is cataloged, tracked, and protected as the case proceeds. Douglas's secretary managed his personal papers, but the documents that went with each case were his responsibility. He admitted he had no aptitude for the kind of administrative work his job entailed. Although he had never caused a crisis because of his lack of document-handling skills, he was worried his deficiencies would eventually cause one of his clients to lose a case.

It was interesting to hear someone so obviously successful, skilled, and prosperous talk about his lack of confidence in his own abilities. Yet every single person has a unique set of strengths and weaknesses. If you're aware of your limitations, you can figure out how to compensate for them. Douglas's strengths—his command of the law, his skill with people, his ability to galvanize a legal team—were the key to mitigating his weaknesses. I recommended he hire someone with strong administrative skills to be his documents manager. Because this person would get to work closely with Douglas, it was an enticing job offer.

Be honest about what you're good at (and what you're not). When the skills required by a crucial job are markedly different from the ones you were born with, find someone else with those skills to do that job. If necessary, hire them. Don't try to do important tasks you're not good at unless there's absolutely no one else available to help you.

As Caroline and I were touring her home and discussing ways to keep her family organized and on track, we stopped in the doorway of her four-year-old daughter's room. It was tidy and

comfortable, with a brightly covered bed, a small desk, and a combination dresser/hutch that stored the little girl's clothes and books. Making conversation, I pointed to the crowd of stuffed animals lined up
on top of the six-foot-tall hutch and said, "It's nice to have a good display place for those stuffed animals." Caroline corrected my observa-
tion. "That's not a display. Those are Megan's favorite toys. She plays
with them all the time." I responded with surprise, "How does she get
them down?" Caroline said, "I get them down for her to play with, and
then I put them back up on top of the hutch every night."

Here was a situation with an interesting twist. One of the important ways to share the work of running a household is to delegate tasks
to children according to their ages and abilities. At four years old,
Megan was perfectly capable of getting out her stuffed animals and
putting them away when she finished playing. But she could only help
clean up her play area *if* her toys were stored where she could reach
them. The inaccessible location of these toys was keeping Megan from
taking on a reasonable amount of responsibility for them, *and* it was
adding yet another task to Caroline's daily "To Do" list.

Of course, this dilemma was simple to solve. Caroline put all the
stuffed animals in a big laundry basket on the floor. Then she delegated the job of putting them away to her daughter instead of doing
this task herself.

Include your children in the work of the household by setting
up supplies and equipment so it's possible for them to help
you. In their rooms, keep toys and clothes in places that allow kids to get them out and put them away on their own. Save yourself work by teaching them to manage their own things.

On pages 63 to 64, I told the story of Olivia and Quinn,
who had just moved into an apartment and didn't know
how to set it up. They were living in chaos after the move because
their busy work schedules didn't allow them enough time to organize

their new home. Also, Olivia knew how to keep things going once they were laid out, but she was at a loss to figure out how her furniture and equipment would work best in the new space.

It only took a week for Olivia to realize her house was going to get organized much faster and better if she hired someone to do it than if she tried to get the job done herself. This was partly because she didn't really know *how* to do it and partly because she wanted it done as fast as possible. Once she decided to hire someone, she wasted no time. Olivia looked in the Yellow Pages, found the "Organizing Services" section, and called me.

In two four-hour sessions, my associate and I transformed Olivia's apartment from a chaotic mess into a comfortable home. She was thrilled to regain control of her environment so quickly. The speed with which the job was finished made the expense of hiring a consultant worthwhile to Olivia and Quinn.

The moment you realize you need a professional to tackle a task for you, get on the telephone and hire someone. Don't waste time. A trained professional will complete any job faster and better than you'd be able to do it by yourself. Not only that, the task will get done instead of lingering on your "To Do" list.

Sarah called me to see if I worked with small business owners. When I said I did, she told me she and her husband, Zachary, owned and operated two optometrist offices in neighboring communities. Each of them was responsible for one of the offices, and she handled the bookkeeping for the whole business. She was worried because she and her husband had different approaches to the company's financial records. She invited me to come talk to both of them about standardizing their administrative policies.

We met in Zachary's office. Sarah and I arrived at the same time, and the three of us got acquainted for a few minutes before we sat down to talk about their concerns. Almost immediately, it was clear that Sarah was angry at Zachary. She thought his approach to the recordkeeping was so disorganized, it was going to jeopardize the long-term viability of the whole business. At one point, her emotions were so strong she had tears in her eyes. Zachary, on the other hand, was conciliatory. He acknowledged that his style was more haphazard than hers and said he was willing to do whatever she wanted to keep the business going. But more importantly, he wanted to make her happy. Their shared life—marriage, family, and business—was his primary concern. Once Sarah recognized that Zachary was willing to make some changes, she calmed down.

My challenge with this couple was to help them without coming between them. We had to come up with a plan everyone could endorse. To do this, we started by listing all the points upon which Sarah and Zachary agreed: (1) They loved each other, so preserving their marriage was essential; (2) the business was their livelihood and needed to be managed in a fiscally responsible way; and (3) Zachary needed some help to reach the required level of fiscal responsibility in his office.

After laying this foundation of strong shared values, we moved on to the hard part—building a plan of action. This was tricky because Sarah was the one whose standards weren't being met, but Zachary was the one whose habits needed to be changed. The key question for Sarah was, "What is the minimum standard Zachary needs to meet to satisfy your concerns?" She thought about this, then listed her minimum requirements and we wrote them down. The next question was for Zachary. "Can you agree to meet these minimum requirements if you have help?" He looked at them carefully and said yes. The final question went back to Sarah. "Will you trust Zachary and his professional organizer enough to let them work on your requirements without interference?" She said yes.

Zachary and I worked together to get his records cleaned up, organized, archived, and into shape. We also rearranged some of his equipment and supplies so it was easier for him to meet Sarah's requirements and keep the store running smoothly. Sarah kept her word and didn't interfere. This meant Zachary could achieve her desired end result, but still do it his way.

 When I ask an audience, "What's your biggest organizing problem?" someone always calls out, "My spouse!" If you and your partner are having trouble agreeing about any element of your organizing system, it's important to talk through the issues. Start with your common ground. Then figure out what each of you must receive to be satisfied. Finally, establish what each of you has to do to make the other one happy. Remind each other that the things you share far outweigh your differences.

If, when all is said and done, you're not sure the things you share far outweigh your differences, see a marriage counselor together. A trained person can help enormously.

Dianne and her husband have a giant house on a quiet, tree-lined suburban street. Their four children, ages eight to sixteen, are a lively crowd involved in all kinds of school and extracurricular activities. Dianne sets the pace for the family. She volunteers at her children's schools, sits on several local boards, plays tennis, and entertains. Her lovely home carries the stamp of sophisticated interior designers, but she called me because its beauty was being marred by clutter.

During my first visit with Dianne, we made a list of projects in order of their importance and impact, and I came back several times to help her carry them out. One day, while we were sorting papers at her desk, she asked if I could come back the next week to help her organize her eight-year-old daughter Jenny's room, which was always in a state of chaos. When I asked if Dianne wanted Jenny to participate in weeding out her toys and getting things put away, Dianne replied, "Goodness, no. We'd never get anything done, and the decorator would hate it."

It had never occurred to Dianne that Jenny might be having trouble keeping her room in order because she didn't have any say in how it was set up. Dianne had chosen the original design and furniture for Jenny's room with the help of a childless male decorator. Everything in it was beautiful and expensive, but not necessarily practical for a young girl. For instance, the room didn't have a single bookcase. Once it was decorated, Jenny started to move things around and put them where she wanted them. But while she was at school, her mother would come into her room and rearrange her things. This was done with good intentions—Dianne was trying to keep the house in order—but the net effect was to quash Jenny's attempts to manage her own belongings.

As soon as I pointed out these things to Dianne, she gasped and said, "It never occurred to me that she might want to be included. I was just trying to help." Soon after that, I came over after school, and Jenny and I set up her room the way she wanted it. She was thrilled, and so was Dianne (although she still thought the decorator would hate it).

Involve your children in the organization of their rooms. Incorporate as many of their suggestions as possible. This encourages kids to take responsibility and increases their investment in making things work. Don't do things *for* them that they can do by themselves. Allow them to experiment with their clothes and things.

In the Introduction, you read the story of Terese, whose triplets arrived just before she and her husband moved into their enormous new house. I met her ten years later, when she finally got so desperate for some ideas she hired an organizer.

Although I could get her spaces cleaned out and her systems back on track, what Terese really needed was a housekeeper.

Terese certainly had the means to hire someone to manage the mundane, day-to-day details of running a home. I encouraged her to do it. If she had a full-time employee whose job was to cook, clean, do laundry, and keep everything straightened up, then she could spend her time on the fun things—overseeing the activities of her children, volunteering at their schools, entertaining, participating in her community, and doing things with her husband.

Terese, however, resisted the idea of getting help. The result? She burdened herself with too much work and impossible expectations. Her house was always in chaos, which made it difficult for the family to function. The children tried to compensate for the mess by keeping their own rooms neat. And her husband just worried—about her, about the house, and about the mess. It was worth the money to get some help.

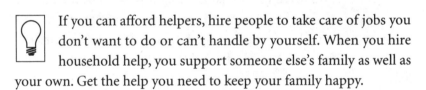 If you can afford helpers, hire people to take care of jobs you don't want to do or can't handle by yourself. When you hire household help, you support someone else's family as well as your own. Get the help you need to keep your family happy.

By the time I met Stephanie, she'd been through a string of difficult events that transformed her life. Before the first one occurred, she was a slim, vibrant, athletic young woman with her whole life ahead of her. She had a fabulous job, was well regarded in her field of work, owned her own home, was engaged to be married, and generally was enjoying herself. Then she was hurt in a car accident, and the downward spiral began.

While she was in the hospital recovering from her injuries, the trauma she'd suffered triggered a hereditary blood condition. Stephanie was in and out of the hospital for months, dealing with the systemic effects of this illness. During the six months it took to recuperate enough to resume working, her fiancé called off their engagement. Although she managed to return to her job, her energy and vitality had been drained away by her blood condition. She gained weight, her hair turned gray, and she remained partly disabled. The only things left over from her preaccident life were her house and her job.

I met Stephanie not long after she asked her employer for a transfer across the country. She was preparing to move and requested help with the packing. Over the phone, she told me her biggest problem was that she owned too many clothes and didn't know what to do with them all.

She was right to say she had more clothes than one person needed. The closets in the two bedrooms were so full, there wasn't room for another hanger. Dressers in both bedrooms held nonhanging items. Lingerie was stuffed into two trunks and several sets of rolling drawers. In the garage, the space where a car might normally be parked was filled with garment boxes and other cartons of clothing. More things were squirreled away in storage areas in the basement. Altogether, the clothes were taking up almost all of the house's storage space.

Throughout her ordeal, Stephanie had acquired full wardrobes in three different sizes, plus sports apparel she used before her accident. She even had clothing she'd worn as a young girl, although she was almost forty. Most of the things were reasonably wearable. But a few items were in terrible condition. In the garage, there were several boxes that had gotten wet, and the garments inside were mildewed and rotting. We brought all the clothes except those into the spare bedroom and started sorting.

As we worked, Stephanie told me why it was so hard for her to let go of her clothes. They were intertwined with her feelings about her mother. On the one hand, she and her mother had a difficult relationship because her mother was a formal, undemonstrative person. Stephanie craved maternal affection and approval, but these were difficult things for her mother to offer. On the other hand, Stephanie's mother was always giving her gifts of beautiful clothes. The most positive moments they shared were spent shopping. If Stephanie gave away these clothes, she felt as if she was giving away the happy memories they represented.

Therapy supported Stephanie as she tackled the difficult issue of weeding through her clothes. The work she did with her therapist helped her recognize the relationship between her attachment to her clothes and her feelings about her mother. It was still emotionally wrenching to give away any of the garments that held such meaning to her, but Stephanie knew they were getting in her way. Her therapist's support and sympathy buoyed her while she and I worked together. As soon as the unusable clothes were gone, Stephanie was freed of their hold on her emotions as well as their encroachment into her living space.

There is often a deep emotional reason behind someone's strong attachment to inanimate objects like clothes. If you know you're hanging onto things more tightly than is reasonable or rational, consider seeing a therapist. Counselors are key helpers in making your life work more smoothly.

What a Full-Blown Strategy #8 Crisis Looks Like

In most cases, it just takes one telephone call to the right person to solve an organizing problem. In a full-blown *Strategy #8* crisis, however, the problems can only be solved by calling in a squad of people with different useful skills. This situation arises when someone has been trying to operate on their own for a long time, trying to do things they either don't know how to do or are just incapable of doing. No matter what the cause of the incapacity—and there can be many—a crisis grows when a person has needed help for a long time but hasn't gotten it.

Brenda is a brilliant and successful attorney, yet she was living in chaos. One of her close friends hired me to meet with her and map out a strategy to bring order to her home.

Brenda's house is located on a short street just off the main road. Behind it, a wooded hillside rises steeply above a small creek. The backyard is secluded and tranquil. From the outside, the building looks like all the other comfortable, medium-sized houses on the block. Brenda's car was parked in the driveway when I arrived. She met me at the door and ushered me inside. The large living room and adjacent dining room were reasonably furnished, although quite dark, and there was a layer of dust on all the surfaces. The furniture was rather formal, but I got the impression of a reasonable furniture arrangement and layout.

Brenda cleared some papers from one side of the dining room table, and we sat down to get acquainted. She told me how ashamed she felt that her house was in such disorder. When she looked at each room, she could see it didn't work well. Yet when she tried to come up with a plan of action to make things better, her mind went completely blank. At home, she felt like a total failure because she just didn't know how to be a good housekeeper. Her work life, on the other hand, was completely different. There, she knew exactly how to approach her client's problems, no matter how complicated they were. The papers and procedures she needed for her cases were in perfect order. Everything worked beautifully. The contrast between her ability to function at the office and her complete inability to manage at home was stark. No wonder she spent more time at work than she did in her house! To show me what she was talking about, Brenda took me on a tour.

Space: The house had three bedrooms, a large one in front and two smaller ones facing the backyard. Brenda's bed was in the front room, which overlooked the stairs to the front door. It was sunny and bright because of the large windows in one corner, and it looked reasonably functional as a bedroom. But its proximity to the front door meant it was more public than Brenda was comfortable with. In her ideal world, she said, this room would be her home office, and she would sleep in one of the back bedrooms.

But the reason she hadn't already made this change was evident as soon as we stepped into the second bedroom. Although Brenda referred to it as "my office," it was really just a jumble. Seven large pieces of furniture were shoved into the center of the room. The biggest piece was a huge wooden cabinet designed to hold large sheets of drafting paper in flat, wide drawers. Next to it, a bookshelf lay on its side facing the drafting cabinet. Its shelves had been removed and were leaning precariously against one wall. A big roll-top desk anchored the middle of the room. Several sizable dressers and an entertainment center completed the scene. The only floor space in the room was a narrow band around the perimeter. The walls were stripped almost bare, suggesting a painting project was underway, but shreds of wallpaper still adhered to the plaster in numerous spots. When I asked Brenda how soon the painters were going to finish the project, she said, "I'm doing it myself." So I asked her how long she'd been working on it. She replied, "Eighteen months."

The second bedroom, which Brenda said she'd like to use for sleeping, was also full of massive pieces of furniture. An antique bedroom set from the 1920s was set up in a usable way. Brenda called this "the guest room" because visitors slept there. I asked Brenda why she didn't just move her clothes in here and use this furniture for herself, but she said she didn't like it. Instead, she wanted to move her current bed here, move this bedroom set into the "office," and set the office furniture up in the front bedroom. To make this happen, every piece of furniture in all three bedrooms would have to be moved.

The last room on the main living floor was the kitchen. Its layout was standard and straightforward, but the whole room appeared unused. As we started to turn back toward the dining room, I asked, "What's downstairs?" So she led me through a door and into her back hallway. "Watch your feet," she said. "I don't want you to step on anything." Gingerly, I followed her down the dark staircase. There were clumps of something on the steps, and the air smelled strongly of cat.

At the bottom of the stairs, a large room took up most of the space. At one time, it must have been a comfortable family room. When I saw it, it was filthy. The linoleum floor was covered with a thick layer of silt, there were pieces of broken furniture scattered here and there, none of the lights worked, and Brenda's cat was using the floor as a litter box. Brenda said the room had been flooded several years before, during a rare overflow of the creek behind the house. After that, she stopped using it for anything.

Things: Except for the excessive amount of furniture, Brenda's house wasn't overflowing with things. She didn't really spend enough time at home to cause this category to be a problem, nor did she spend much time shopping.

Information: Obviously, Brenda was not doing her paperwork in her "office." Instead, she had her mail, bills, and reading material spread out on the dining room table and in her bedroom. She said she took care of most of her business affairs at work. After she got the furniture moved around and turned the front bedroom into a functional home office, she planned to bring her financial records home with her. In the meantime, the current arrangement was satisfactory.

Time: Because her home was so dark, disorganized, and unwelcoming, Brenda didn't like to spend time in it. Yet she spoke wistfully about how nice it would be to have everything set up comfortably and functionally. Until that happened, her life was skewed toward work. She was spending a disproportionate amount of time at her downtown office because she just didn't want to come home.

Relationships: The disorganization of Brenda's home was affecting her relationships in two important ways. First of all, she didn't like to invite people over because she was ashamed of her home. This curtailed her friendships. Most of the people she socialized with were from work, and the relationships were conducted during business hours. The second and more important result of Brenda's disorganization involved dating. Brenda said she was lonely and would like to have a relationship, but she was afraid any man would be scared away by the condition of her house. As a result, she didn't date at all.

For years, Brenda had been stymied by her house. Although she had good ideas for setting it up comfortably and functionally, she wasn't able to make them happen on her own. Together, we made a list of the tasks she wanted to accomplish. Then, using the Yellow Pages as our reference guide, we picked out several possible companies for each task. Here's what she needed help with.

Movers: She needed a moving crew to carry her heavy pieces of furniture from their current locations into the right rooms. If any of these heavy items were superfluous, the movers could take them down to the garage.

Charity Organization: Once the movers got all the extra furniture out of Brenda's living space, she could call a local charity and arrange to have these items picked up and taken away.

Painter: A professional painter could make short work of Brenda's new guest room. If she wanted to brighten up her main rooms, the painter could take care of that, too.

Heavy-Duty Cleaning Company: There are companies dedicated to cleaning things that require more than the usual vacuuming and dusting. Brenda needed one of these to get her downstairs back in shape. Even if she chose not to use the space for much, at least it would be clean.

House Cleaner: If Brenda arranged to have her house cleaned once every two weeks while she was at work, it would be a big improvement. There's a lot to be said for coming home to a clean house.

Professional Organizer: Once the furniture was moved and the house was clean, Brenda could use assistance getting all her things—

papers, decorations, clothes, and so forth—organized to support the way she was using her house. This wouldn't take long if she got help.

Foundation Specialist: Although Brenda thought the creek overflow that flooded her basement was a one-time occurrence, it was prudent to get an expert to check out her foundation and make sure there was no long-term damage. After all, her house was her most valuable asset.

Once we put the whole list together, Brenda was concerned about how much these different services would cost. When I pointed out that she could afford the services and that they'd produce the results she wanted, she nodded thoughtfully. Then she asked how to decide which contractor to hire for each job, as there were several names to choose from in all the categories. In my experience, the one to hire is the one who calls you back, talks knowledgeably about the job, comes to the appointment on time, and gives you a written estimate. It's better to pay more and get good service than to save a few dollars.

When I left Brenda's house, she had all the information she needed to turn it into a comfortable home. Recently, I learned from our mutual friend that she got married a few years later. Good things happen if you get help when you need it.

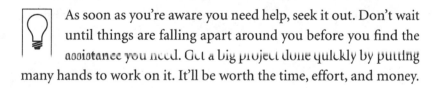 As soon as you're aware you need help, seek it out. Don't wait until things are falling apart around you before you find the assistance you need. Get a big project done quickly by putting many hands to work on it. It'll be worth the time, effort, and money.

How to Put Strategy #8 Back in Place

If you recognized yourself in any of the preceding stories, your system is out of sync with your life because you aren't getting the help you need. Despite any cultural or internal pressures to the contrary, it's all right to share the work instead of trying to do it all yourself. In fact, sometimes it's imperative to delegate. If your children don't help you around the house, for instance, how will they learn basic life skills? Running a household or business takes a lot of work. When you get someone else to take care of tasks you don't have time for or don't know how to do (or simply don't want to do), everything gets done, and the system operates smoothly.

Strategy #8 helps you prevent the messes that grow when tasks aren't getting the attention they need. It's also a fine rule of thumb if you find yourself suffering from difficult emotions that prevent you from fully participating in life. A professional counselor can help you work through your feelings so you can start living again.

Everyone needs help with something. No one can take care of everything alone. Here are some ways to figure out what kind of help you need and where to get it.

Get Help for Your Space When You Need It

- If someone else has made a mess in your space, ask *them* to clean it up. If that person is too young to do it alone, ask him or her to help. Everyone needs to know how much work it takes to keep things clean and neat.
- If you're planning to make changes in your furniture arrangements, discuss them with other members of the family. Involve everyone in changes that affect them.
- If your rooms are too dark, hire an electrician, lighting consultant, or painter to help you brighten up the place.
- If things aren't flowing well through your space, hire a space planner or professional organizer to rearrange things and improve your environment.
- Involve the whole family in routine cleaning. Even if you hire

someone to do the heavy work, teach your children how to do basic cleaning tasks. This is an essential life skill.
- Set up your children's rooms so it's possible for them to get things out and put them away by themselves. Save yourself work by teaching them to care for their own rooms.

Get Help for Your Things When You Need It

- Ask your partner to pull his or her weight in keeping everything working smoothly.
- Set up your children's clothes and things so they can manage them on their own.
- If you've been saving a broken or torn item to fix, but you never get to it yourself, pay someone else to mend it. If the item isn't worth the expense, throw it out.
- If you have too many things and it's hard for you to weed them out by yourself, ask a friend to trade weeding sessions with you—you'll help them if they help you. If that doesn't work, hire a professional organizer to help you go through your stuff.
- If you have strong emotional attachments to things, and they're starting to overflow into your living space, consider consulting a therapist to help you sort out your feelings.

Get Help for Your Information When You Need It

- If you feel you don't know enough about any given topic, read about it. Get books from the library, a bookstore, or the Internet and bone up on the subject.

- Use Quicken to help you manage your finances. It makes all your money-handling work go faster and makes retrieving information simple.
- If your finances are complicated or hard to manage, consider hiring a bookkeeper.
- Consult an attorney, accountant, and/or financial planner for help buying a house, saving for college, planning for retirement, or reaching other major financial goals.
- Make a list of local contractors—electricians, plumbers, painters, engineers, carpenters, contractors, insurance agents, and so forth—and keep it handy. Ask your friends for referrals and add their suggestions to your list.

Get Help for Your Time When You Need It

- Don't do things for other people that they're perfectly capable of doing by themselves.
- Make time for yourself by sharing the work with others who benefit from it being done.
- Get a big project done quickly by putting many hands to work on it.
- If you're struggling to fit everything you have to do into your schedule, use the Require/Desire Grid on page 66 to figure out where to weed. If that doesn't work, read a book on time management for more ideas.
- Hire a professional organizer or time management consultant to go through your schedule with you and figure out where to make changes.
- If you have enough money to afford helpers, hire people to take care of jobs you don't want to do. Use the time you save to do something worthwhile.

Get Help for Your Relationships
When You Need It

- If you're struggling with your own deep issues, treat yourself to therapy. A therapist or counselor is like a trusted friend you can confide in, except you don't have to reciprocate by listening to his or her confidences. Seeing a therapist is a sign of courage, not weakness.
- If your children are struggling in school, arrange for special tutoring or a visit to the school counselor to help them keep up with their peers.
- If you and your partner are struggling with deep issues, seek out a licensed therapist. Go alone if you can't get your partner to come with you.

These suggestions give you an idea about what help is available and where you can get it. Whether you invite others to do some of the work or allow others to support you as you do it yourself, your system will keep working smoothly if you *Get Help When You Need It.*

Now it's time to move on to *Strategy #9, Evaluate Honestly and Often.* This final strategy gives you guidelines for looking honestly at the system you've set up and figuring out when it needs to be adjusted.

CHAPTER 9 | **STRATEGY #9**

Evaluate Honestly
and Often

Organizing your life is like hitting a moving target. Even when things are working smoothly, it's reasonable to expect life to change. Pay attention as life evolves, and change your system to make it keep up. Maintain your system so it's lean, flexible, and attuned to your life.

Overview of Strategy #9

In the last several chapters, we looked at three possible bottlenecks that can cause a clog in your organizing system and keep it from working efficiently. Piles start to spring up all around the house when (1) your procedures get too complicated, (2) decisions don't get made, or (3) you don't have the help you need. Fortunately, these kinds of messes are preventable. *Strategies #6 (Keep It Simple)*, *#7 (Decide to Decide)*, and *#8 (Get Help When You Need It)* keep everything moving so it doesn't have a chance to build up and get in your way. The fourth kind of pile, on the other hand, is guaranteed to happen in every organizing system ever assembled. It's the one that takes root when your life begins to diverge from the way it was when you set up your system in the first place.

Things change. It's an immutable fact of life. Since there's absolutely nothing you can do about this, it's impossible to prevent the messes that spring up when life takes a turn. But if you react quickly, you can nip them in the bud using *Strategy #9, Evaluate Honestly and Often.*

Creating an effective organizing system is like building a new house. First, you figure out what activities you want to incorporate into it, design a structure to accommodate those activities, and draw up a blueprint. Then you frame the structure, fill in the interior, and set up the spaces so people and things can move into, through, and out of your home. As soon as the building is finished, you move all your belongings in and begin to live there. Only then, when all the dust has settled and life resumes its normal course, can you begin doing routine maintenance. *Strategy #9* is the routine maintenance component of an effective organizing system.

The trick to keeping your system running smoothly, even as life changes around you, is to pay close attention to how everything is working. Employing *Strategy #9* is like doing an appraisal of your life, but on a smaller scale. You're looking for signs that things are *beginning* to get out of whack. You want to catch each problem while it's little and easy to deal with. That's where the word *honestly* comes in. If you try to ignore a potential issue, hoping it'll go away by itself, you're bound to cause yourself big trouble. Don't just look at your system—let yourself see it with clarity. Find the problems so you can fix them. The moment to invoke *Strategy #9* is the moment you notice a pile growing anywhere in your system. As soon as you see one, put on your Eyes of a Stranger and take a good, hard, honest look at it. Ask yourself, "Why is this pile here?" If you need to, consult Appendix A: "Evaluation Questions to Ask Yourself," to see which strategy is playing hooky. Put that strategy back in place, solve the problem, and get your system on track again. The faster you recognize and deal with each problem, the easier it is to keep the whole system running like a top.

If you practice *Strategy #9* consistently, most issues will never get big enough to get in your way. It's a "tweak as you go" plan. But life can still surprise you with difficult, unforeseen events that change everything. If something big happens to distract your attention, your whole system can fall apart while you're not looking. When you turn back to it, an honest evaluation will alert you that it's time for a brand-new design. In these circumstances, *Strategy #9* brings you full circle back to *Strategy #1, Make Your Systems Fit You and Your Life.*

Symptoms That Your System Needs Tweaking

There are a number of different ways to tell if your organizing system is starting to get off track. Here are some indicators that your system needs to be looked at closely and adjusted.

- Piles are starting to grow in your house.
- Something doesn't feel right or is making you uncomfortable.
- Your organizing system used to work smoothly, but now the exact same setup is giving you trouble.
- You recently tried a new organizing tactic, but it's causing more problems than it's solving.
- You've lost track of what's in your storage areas.
- You've exquisitely fine-tuned your system, and now each task has so many steps it's hard to get everything done.
- People you live with are complaining about how things are working.
- A life event you consider minor has left you feeling more upset and overwhelmed than you anticipated.
- You know a major life event is going to happen in the next six months (a move, wedding, new baby, job change, empty nest, retirement), and you don't feel ready for it.
- You're reeling from the effects of a major life event, and your old systems don't fit your life anymore.

When one of these applies to you, it's time to scrutinize your organizing system, see which of the Nine Strategies has gone missing, and figure out how to put it back in place.

What a Full-Blown Strategy #9 Crisis Looks Like

The previous eight chapters started with stories about people who were having small-scale problems, then went on to describe a full-blown crisis caused by the strategy in question. This time, we're going to depart from the usual format and start with the crisis scenario. The next story will demonstrate how essential *Strategy #9* really is. Then, in contrast, you'll see how other people used *Strategy #9* effectively to adapt their organizing systems to their lives during periods of transition.

In my professional experience, the worst organizing dilemmas arise when *Strategy #9* is missing, because it's impossible to fix a problem unless you acknowledge it exists. People who turn away from their messes, ignore the piles, or insist an obvious problem isn't an issue can't make things better. In the long run, a well-established pattern of denial can cause an entire system to fall into ruin.

Very few people I've worked with fall into this category. Even though many clients tell me they feel totally disorganized, we usually discover most elements are working much better than they realized. All they need to do is put one or two strategies in place to make the whole system function reasonably well. This is because they've been good at applying *Strategy #9, Evaluate Honestly and Often*. With a pinch here and a poke there, they identified and fixed many small problems as soon as they arose. The projects we worked on together simply complemented what they'd already been doing on their own.

Once we got everything set up, they were able to maintain their systems on their own using *Strategy #9.*

Unfortunately, this is not how things worked for Miriam, whose enormous and overwhelming problems resulted from long-term denial. She lives with her sister in a three-bedroom home she inherited from her parents, who in turn inherited it from her maternal grandparents. This means Miriam and her sister are the third generation to inhabit the same house. It must have taken her a great deal of courage to pick up the telephone and invite me over for a consultation. As I discovered, asking for help was not her normal practice.

At first glance, Miriam's house looked like all the other ones on the block. A fairly large right-entrance colonial, it had a detached garage and small front porch. I climbed the stairs to the door, which was flanked by several broken pieces of garden equipment, and rang the bell. There was no answer. Finally I knocked, and Miriam came to let me in.

The first thing that struck me about the house was its natural light. The rooms I could see—the entrance hall, the living room to my left, and the staircase going up on my right—were bright and nicely proportioned. The next thing I noticed was the clutter. Every flat surface in the entrance hall, including the floor, was heaped with a one-foot-high pile of stuff. The only walking spaces were paths going from doorway to doorway. Miriam draped my coat over the banister, which already held four similar garments, and led me down the path into the living room. In this large space, clutter also reigned. The sofa, which faced the television, had two sofa cushions left uncluttered, but the third was piled with magazines and newspapers. Obviously, this was where the occupants of the house watched TV.

Sitting on the sofa side by side, Miriam and I spent a few minutes getting acquainted. She told me she grew up in the house, moved away, then came home after her father's death. Although her sister lived there, too, the house belonged to Miriam. When she wasn't working at her full-time job as an administrator, she spent most of her time at home. She liked to shop, sew, and watch television, and she confirmed that the sofa we were sitting on was where she relaxed in the evenings. On that note, we started to tour the house.

Space: Just off the living room, at the end of the house, Miriam led me into a small den. Its windows were covered with cracked, yellowed shades that must have been thirty years old. Curtains hung in tatters from ancient rods. I asked Miriam how this small room was used. She said she was thinking about making it into a sewing room. Currently, it was so full of miscellaneous piles—papers, books, pillows, junk—it was impossible to identify the furniture underneath. When I offered to take the curtains down right then, just to take a positive action, she demurred, saying she'd do it later. We proceeded with the tour.

In the dining room, the walls were taken up by six floor-to-ceiling china cabinets full of numerous sets of fine china. The table was heaped with sewing projects, although one corner was clear. Miriam said she and her sister ate their meals in the two chairs placed there at that corner. Clutter was piled two feet deep on all the other surfaces.

In the kitchen, a giant smoke stain marred the wall above the stove. When I asked her about it, Miriam revealed that something had caught fire and burned fiercely before it was extinguished, but this had happened two years ago. As far as I could tell, the wall had not been cleaned since. Like every room I'd seen so far, the kitchen was heaped with things. It was impossible for Miriam and her sister to eat in the breakfast nook because there was so much stuff on the benches. An overflowing cat box on the floor contributed to the general mess.

After we toured the front hall, whose closet was so full that coats had to be hung on the banister, we carefully climbed the stairs, where each step had a pile of new purchases on one side. At the top of the stairs, Miriam showed me three bedroom doors. Her sister's room was behind one. But Miriam said her sister didn't want me to look in there, and of course we respected her wishes. Across from her room was the "spare bedroom." When Miriam turned the handle and pushed it open, it only went about a foot before it was blocked. When I peered around the door, I realized the entire room was full of things piled five feet deep from wall to wall. The only thing you could do with this room was toss something inside and shut the door again.

Miriam's room, while reasonably furnished, was just as cluttered as the rest of the house. Her clutter was clothing. She also pointed out a trap door in the hallway ceiling—the kind that pulls down and unfolds into stairs—and said she kept most of her wardrobe in the attic.

The last stop we made before returning to the living room was the basement. Here, the entire space was full of junk—large pieces of furniture, ancient bicycles, the remains of a workshop, and so on. Everything was heavily layered with dust, and every single item appeared to be broken beyond redemption. When I asked Miriam what all this stuff was, she said it belonged to her parents and her grandparents, so she didn't feel she could get rid of any of it.

Things: Obviously, the two people who lived in this house owned more things than the house could reasonably contain, and way more than they needed. For instance, they had every piece of fine china ever bought by anyone in their family going back generations. But when I asked her which dishes they ate on, Miriam indicated a cupboard in the kitchen. Inside was a mismatched hodgepodge of chipped and inexpensive dishes and glassware. "Why don't you use some of this nice china?" I asked. She replied, "It's too nice for every day. I'm saving it."

The same kind of conversation took place about Miriam's clothes. In her bedroom, the closet was full, and there were clothes hanging on hangers from the curtains, the tops of the doors, and the dressing table mirror. More clothes were evidently stored in boxes and on garment racks in the attic. It wasn't even possible to retrieve some of these items without moving piles of things first. Yet when I asked

Miriam whether she wore all these clothes, she looked me right in the eye and said, "Oh, yes."

Despite all the items already piled up around the house, Miriam was obviously continuing to buy new things and bring them home. The shopping bags from clothing and household goods stores lying around in the front hall and on the stairs indicated as much.

Information: Although loose and piled papers made up a portion of the general mess in every room, the dining room seemed to be the place where bills were paid. Piles of mail could be seen poking out from underneath the sewing projects on the dining room table. There were also some papers in the living room. Miriam did not ask for advice about paper processing issues.

Time: Miriam and her sister both spent much of their spare time in the house. They didn't try to escape the mess by spending their time elsewhere, as many people tend to do. Instead of trying to create space for their activities by getting rid of the extra stuff, they pared their activities down to fit into the two small, cleared areas in the living and dining rooms. Anyone who wanted to be alone would have to retreat to a bedroom.

Relationships: Miriam said both she and her sister were single and had never been married. While she was living on her own, she had more of a social life. Since she'd moved back into this house, her activities with friends had dwindled. She expressed interest in dating and having a serious relationship, but didn't really know how to go about finding someone she might like. So she stayed home with her sister.

After the tour, we returned to the living room and sat back down on the sofa. As I usually do, I asked her, "What do you want for your house?" She reached down, picked up a *House Beautiful* magazine from the top of the nearest pile, and showed me the gorgeous living room pictured on its cover. "I want a house in perfect order, like this one," she told me.

When Miriam said this, I chose my reply carefully because her answers to my questions during the tour were so jarringly out of touch with the reality of her life. Her house belied her words in so many ways. The clothes, the tattered curtains, the dishes, the "sewing room," the "spare bedroom," the junk in the basement—perhaps these things were so daunting she just wouldn't let herself see them. But they indicated she might not want to hear the truth spoken bluntly. So I answered her statement carefully. "You can't have a house in perfect order *and* still keep all these things."

I wrote out a plan for Miriam suggesting several ways to approach the massive job of getting her house closer to "perfect order." Before I left, we set up an appointment to start weeding the following week. She called to cancel the appointment three days later. I never heard from her again.

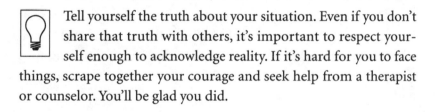

Tell yourself the truth about your situation. Even if you don't share that truth with others, it's important to respect yourself enough to acknowledge reality. If it's hard for you to face things, scrape together your courage and seek help from a therapist or counselor. You'll be glad you did.

Real Life Lessons: Strategy #9 Missing in Action

Now it's time to turn your attention toward people who respected themselves enough to face the future and adapt to it. Each of these individuals did a good job of applying *Strategy #9, Evaluate Honestly and Often*, during a time of transition. All of them reacted to the life event in question—no matter how they felt about it—by changing their organizing systems to fit their new reality. If you're facing one of these common life transitions, take some tips from them.

Moving to a New Home

In Chapter 8, you read about Curt, who invited me to help him organize his apartment even though he was planning to move in the near future. Six months later, he called to tell me he'd found the house he was looking for. Knowing he didn't have the skills to organize his new space by himself, Curt invited me to help him unpack and get settled (*Strategy #8, Get Help When You Need It*). Together we designed the layout of the new place by deciding which room would hold each of Curt's regular activities (*#1, Make Your Systems Fit You and Your Life*). Then we arranged his furniture to support each function and sorted all the boxes into the right rooms (*#2, Sort Everything by How You Use It*).

Because the new place was three times bigger than the old apartment, we made a list of the other furniture he would eventually need. Curt also put together a punch list of supplies to get right away (shelf liner, hooks, shower curtain, light bulbs, and other sundries). Then, while he was at work, I unpacked all his things and put them away in the spots where he wanted to use them (*#4, Use the Right Containers and Tools*).

When he came home, we went through everything so he knew where each item was located (*#5, Label Everything*). He was settled in his new house in no time.

When you move from one space to another, the different room configuration and layout *require* you to design a whole new organizing system. Do this right away. First figure out which activities will be done in each room. Then move all the furniture and boxes that go with those activities into the designated spaces. Unpack things and put them away, then purchase the tools and supplies you need to equip yourself properly. Finally, give everything a name—rooms, storage areas, closets, furniture groupings—so you can find things you're looking for. All these activities are facilitated if you pack and label your boxes by room.

Starting a New Job

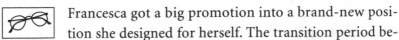 Francesca got a big promotion into a brand-new position she designed for herself. The transition period between her old job and her new one was tricky. Until a successor was named, she was still in charge of the people and projects that fell under the old title. But she had already begun to take charge of her new responsibilities. Time management was becoming a big issue.

Francesca and I sat down together for a few hours to talk about her time crunch. She wanted help figuring out how to manage the change from one set of responsibilities to the other. First we listed the responsibilities in her old job (*#2, Sort Everything*). Task by task, we went down the list to see if there was anyone else who could handle it. If another person already on her staff could take over that task, Francesca delegated it to him or her (*#8, Get Help When You Need It*). Some of the remaining items could wait for her successor (*#7, Decide to Decide*), but a few of them stayed on Francesca's plate.

When we finished with the old list, we made a corresponding one for the new job. She picked out some tasks that had to be done right away (*#7*). Others could wait until Francesca was doing the new job full time. Our last step was to set up a timeline for the entire transition period. By the end of our meeting, Francesca had pared down her daily responsibilities to a set she could handle (*#3, Weed Constantly*). She knew what she had to do to close out her old job and jump feet first into her new one (*#1, Make Your Systems Fit You and Your Life*), and she was ready to get back to work.

When you get a new job, it can affect your schedule in unforeseen ways. It's a good idea to map out your old and new responsibilities so you can move smoothly from one set to another. If you have a family (which Francesca didn't), it's also wise to sit down with your partner and list the ways the new position will affect family life.

Remodeling Your House

Connor, an architect, bought an old townhouse to gut and renovate. In his spare time, he designed a whole new layout (*#1, Make Your Systems Fit You and Your Life*). Just before the contractors were due to arrive, he called me for a consultation. He wanted to walk through the new design to make sure he hadn't left out any important organizing elements. Together we went through each room in his house and compared it to the blueprints. Using a tape measure, Connor showed me where the new walls and doorways were going to be placed, as well as the places he planned to put key pieces of furniture. Then we moved a chair to each of those spots—where the bed, sofa, entertainment center, desk, and dining table were going to be—and Connor sat in it, envisioning his new surroundings. We made only one change to the plans—we added a laundry chute from his bedroom down to the washer/dryer (*#6, Keep It Simple*)—but when we finished, Connor was sure his new design was just right.

When you're planning a construction project, whether it's a remodel or a new building, it's really helpful to go to your site and walk through the proposed design. Using a tape measure and some kind of line (string, rope, or a mark drawn in the dirt), block out the new spaces. Put yourself in key spots and imagine the building around you. If that's not possible, consider buying home design software that lets you visualize your plans. Make changes if you find something that doesn't work as well in real life as it does on paper.

Working from Home

The desk in Elise's bedroom was perfectly adequate for writing letters and holding her stationery, but when she decided to quit her job and start working from home, she knew it was going to be inadequate for the needs of her home-based business. She asked me to help her figure out where to set up a real office.

Walking from room to room, we talked about the elements Elise required for a functional setup (*#1, Make Your Systems Fit You and Your Life*). First, she didn't want to feel enclosed. This made a potential spot in the spare bedroom untenable. Second, she craved natural light. So we needed to find a spot with at least one window. Third, she needed good storage so her papers wouldn't look like a mess all the time.

Although it hadn't occurred to Elise to assemble an office in her living room, this turned out to be the perfect location. We picked a spot for her desk between two windows. From there, she could see the whole room, monitor the front door, participate in her family's conversations (this was an active room for them), and still get her work done. We purchased an inexpensive but functional desk, two file cabinets, and a task light (*#4, Use the Right Containers and Tools*), retrieved all Elise's papers from around the house (*#2, Sort Everything by How You Use It*), and got the phone company to install a new jack (*#8, Get Help When You Need It*). In no time, she was set up and ready to get to work.

 When you're planning to work from home, your office requirements are different than they are for doing family paperwork. Where you put your desk is the most important factor. Since you need to make a living from that spot, find the place in the house that best supports your work activities. Consider *every* room as a possibility and factor in such subtle elements as light, public space versus private space, and how each location feels. When you find the right spot, shop around until you find a desk and file cabinets that fit. These elements are key to setting up a home office that really works well for you.

Getting Ready for Your First Child

Ryan and Samantha were expecting their first child in four months. They were thrilled about this enormous, life-transforming event, but they knew their house wasn't ready for it. They asked for advice on setting up a nursery and incorporating a small third person into their three-bedroom home.

You really don't know all the ways your first child will transform your life until after it happens, so planning is difficult. In the prebaby stage, the first task is to find space for all the paraphernalia that comes with an infant. In Samantha and Ryan's case, allocating one room to the nursery caused a domino effect. To put the nursery in the room next to the master bedroom, they had to move the office furniture into the third bedroom. This was already full of someone else's stuff. Ryan called him and told him to come get it, then it went into the garage until he arrived. This put a strain on the garage, which was already crowded with old furniture. So Samantha called the Salvation Army and requested a pickup (*#7, Decide to Decide*). Finally, we made a list of baby items they definitely needed (there is so much baby paraphernalia available, it's overwhelming to shop if you don't have a good list), and they went to the store (*#4, Use the Right Containers and Tools*). The whole process took weeks, but finally the room and the house were ready (*#1, Make Your Systems Fit You and Your Life*).

The postbaby stage also requires some thought and planning. Once the baby arrives, your schedule will be completely altered. It's smart to look at your activities when your first child is a few months old. See if there are things you're no longer doing, or if you need to rearrange your house to support new functions. Plan to look at your space, things, and time fairly frequently until your family gets into a routine pattern (*#9, Evaluate Honestly and Often*). Life picks up speed after your first child is born.

Your first baby will transform your life in every way. Talk to your partner often about all the implications of parenthood. Keep an eye on all the elements of your organizing system to make sure things don't get bogged down. Aim for simplicity in the first few years.

Dealing with a Disability

Erica has multiple sclerosis. When I met her, she needed a cane to get around, and one side of her body was visibly weaker than the other. She felt pretty organized, but she needed help with papers. Because her disease was progressive, she didn't like to let anything pile up (*#3, Weed Constantly*).

Erica had already made her life as simple as possible (*#6, Keep It Simple*). She lived in a building that had reliable management, handicapped parking, and a fast elevator. She moved there because of these features and the fact that the local hospital was close by. It was easy for Erica to come and go, and help would arrive quickly if she needed it (*#8, Get Help When You Need It*). In her apartment, everything was already streamlined and elegant. The only clutter was a pile of bills and papers on the dining table. We tackled that together by setting up a rolling file cart on a leash so Erica could pay bills in front of the TV.

She could pull it out easily, then put it back in her office when she was finished with it (*#4, Use the Right Containers and Tools*).

Once that task was done, Erica felt she had her life as much under control as was possible, given the reality of her disease. She promised to call again if the disability worsened and another pile started to grow (*#9, Evaluate Honestly and Often*).

Chronic or terminal illness will have a profound effect on every aspect of your life, including your organizing system. Although it's difficult to face the loss of your physical (and sometimes mental) powers, denying the symptoms of your illness will not make them go away. Many people find their lives transformed in positive ways when they are able to face and accept their illnesses. Consult a counselor or therapist to help you get through the rocky periods, then set up your system so it helps you make the most of your life.

Preparing for Retirement

Annie and Frank are friends of mine, not clients, but the way they approached Frank's retirement from his longtime teaching job is a wonderful example of *Strategy #9* at work. Frank taught high school for forty-five years. His wife, Annie, stayed home with their children, then devoted her time to doing volunteer work and visiting a small crowd of elderly relatives in their respective nursing homes. As Frank's retirement date drew near, he and Annie sat down to assess their finances and figure out how they were going to manage on his pension. Right away, they realized their postretirement monthly income was barely adequate to cover their expenses. If they wanted to do anything fun or extra, something would have to change.

Because they couldn't do anything about the income side of their retirement equation—Frank's pension amount was already fixed—they turned to their expenses to see what they could cut. The most obvious thing was the mortgage payment (their house payments were expensive). Annie and Frank lived in a suburban town with an excellent school system, yet they no longer needed the schools. So they made a big decision (*#7, Decide to Decide*) to sell their house and move one town over, where housing prices were more reasonable. This would sharply reduce their monthly costs.

After a few months spent weeding out all their closets and storage spaces (*#3, Weed Constantly*), Frank and Annie put their house on the market. It sold in no time for a very good price. Right away, they used some of the proceeds to buy an affordable house in the next town and put the rest into savings. The new house cost them much less, suited them well, and was just as close to friends and family as the previous one. As an added bonus, it was bigger.

With their financial affairs in order, Frank and Annie were ready to retire in style. They settled into their new home and figured out all kinds of fun ways to spend their new free time (*#1, Make Your Systems Fit You and Your Life*).

If you're getting ready to retire, look carefully at your financial situation to make sure you have enough income to support yourself comfortably. Consider both sides of the equation—income *and* expenses—to find a balance that gives you enough cushion to enjoy your free time. Sit down with your partner and talk about all the implications of this major life change so you can take care of your responsibilities and still have some fun.

Preparing for Death

After George's wife died of cancer, he realized he was ill-prepared for his own death. His affairs were not in good enough order to enable his children to handle his estate easily (*#9, Evaluate Honestly and Often*). First, he worked with his attorney and accountant to consolidate his finances, make lists of all his assets and insurance policies, bring his will up-to-date, and create a health care power of attorney in case he got too ill to make medical decisions himself (#8, *Get Help When You Need It* and #7, *Decide to Decide*). Next, he bought a cemetery plot and prepaid for his funeral and cremation.

Finally, George sat down with his adult children, gave them copies of his financial statements, and explained the arrangements he'd made. He made sure they understood his wishes so there wouldn't be any conflict or arguments. When he was suddenly hospitalized and discovered he had terminal cancer, George was ready to let go (#7). He gathered his family around him, said a special good-bye to each person, and died two days later. The only thing his children had to worry about was their grief at the sudden loss of their father. George had already taken care of everything else.

None of us know when the hour of our death will arrive, but we know it's going to happen sometime. Get your affairs in order so your family doesn't have to suffer more than necessary if something happens to you. Put your wishes in writing and share them with the people who are important to you. Don't leave a mess for your loved ones to muddle through while they're trying to grieve.

How to Put Strategy #9 Back in Place

The people whose stories you just read were all going through major life events, the kind that can wreak enormous havoc on an organizing system. Yet their systems didn't fall apart. Why? Because they recognized that life was changing, and they took steps to actively manage the transition from the old phase to the new one. The end result? All of them *remained* reasonably organized after the life event was over.

Strategy #9, Evaluate Honestly and Often, is the ongoing maintenance component of the Nine Strategies of Reasonably Organized

People. When you put on the Eyes of a Stranger and look at your system honestly, with clarity, you'll recognize the places it's starting to get off track, and you'll be able to fix the things that aren't working. If you do this often enough, your system will only require an occasional tweak to continue running smoothly. The frequent, honest evaluations required by *Strategy #9* enable your organizing system to stay attuned to your life as it changes.

This section focuses on ways to *Evaluate Honestly and Often* so you can stay reasonably organized over time.

Evaluate Your Space Honestly and Often

- Know what activities you do in each of your spaces.
- Pay attention to the way things flow through your spaces. If something about your space is bothering you, figure out what it is and solve the problem using the Nine Strategies.

Evaluate Your Things Honestly and Often

- Know what you have.
- Know what's in all your storage spaces.
- Don't let your things get in your way, or in the way of the people you care about.
- If some of your things are bothering you, figure out what the problem is and address it using the Nine Strategies.

Evaluate Your Information Honestly and Often

- Know where your key data is.
- Know how to retrieve it.

- Teach other important people to retrieve it, too.
- If some of your information is causing you trouble, figure out what the problem is and fix it using the Nine Strategies.

Evaluate Your Time Honestly and Often

- Know how you're spending your time (because that's how you're spending your life).
- Know your long-term goals so you can work toward them.
- If life is changing and you feel as if you're caught in a whirl-wind, set aside time every day (even five minutes is helpful) to think about what's happening to you. If other people are in-volved, talk to them, too.
- If you're unhappy about the way you're spending your time, fill out a Require/Desire Grid, figure out what the problem is, and apply the Nine Strategies to it.

Evaluate Your Relationships Honestly and Often

- Know whom you care about.
- Know who cares about you.
- If you know a change is coming, set aside time to think about it and its implications. If you have a partner and/or family, talk things over together. Figure out what you need to do to mini-mize the negative effects of the change.
- If your relationships aren't fulfilling, figure out what the problem is and see if any of the Nine Strategies will help you address it.
- Pay attention to your life and the people you love. These are your greatest gifts.

Strategy #9, Evaluate Honestly and Often, encourages you to put on the Eyes of a Stranger from time to time and scrutinize how things are working. If your system needs tweaking, use Appendix A: "Evaluation Questions to Ask Yourself" to figure out which of the Nine Strategies of Reasonably Organized People will close the gap. And if the whole system has gotten totally off track because your life has undergone a major change, *Strategy #9* points you full circle back to *Strategy #1, Make Your Systems Fit You and Your Life.*

Now that you've read about the Nine Strategies of Reasonably Organized People, you're ready to apply them to your life so you can be *organized enough.*

Conclusion

Now that you've peeked into the lives and homes of other people, you know something I learned not long after I started my business:

> *There is* no such thing
> *as a perfectly organized person.*

It's time for this myth to be debunked. The powerful cultural forces that promote this fallacy are just plain *wrong*. Even professional organizers, people who are hardwired to seek order and consistency, have messes piling up here and there. If you feel disorganized, you're in excellent company. It's simply *not possible* to be in control of every facet of your life at every moment.

Why? Because *life is messy*. The beast we're always trying to organize and bring under control keeps changing on us. It takes unexpected twists and turns, creates piles of stuff right and left, and occasionally does something so outrageous or unexpected it leaves us gasping. We can't stop it, we can't control it, and we don't know what it's going to do next. The best we can do, as mere mortals, is keep our chin down, roll with the punches, and try to stay upright until the match is over. We don't need to be perfectly organized; we just need to be *organized enough*.

So what does that mean?

You are organized enough when your systems fit your life *as you're living it right now*. You're an organized enough person if you're ready to react when life throws a left hook. You could have been lying on the mat a minute ago, or be flattened by the next punch, but at the moment, you're standing up and circling the ring with fists at the ready.

The project of getting *organized enough* never ends. As soon you put an effective system into place, life changes. Unless you change the system, too, things get out of whack. The tactics that allow you to be organized enough to keep your balance over time are the ones that make your organizing system into a lean, mean fighting machine. These tactics are the Nine Strategies of Reasonably Organized People.

Let's look again at the steps involved in getting organized enough. First you scrutinize your life through the Eyes of a Stranger to figure out what you're actually doing and design your organizing system so it supports those activities.

#1, Make Your Systems Fit You and Your Life

Then you set up a structure that tailors the elements of your system to conform to your design.

#2, Sort Everything by How You Use It

#3, Weed Constantly

#4, Use the Right Containers and Tools

#5, Label Everything

Finally you implement streamlined policies that keep everything moving through your system.

#6, Keep It Simple

#7, Decide to Decide

#8, Get Help When You Need It

#9, Evaluate Honestly and Often

Once your organizing system is in place, you use *Strategy #9* and the Eyes of a Stranger to help you keep your system and your life on the same track. If things get really out of sync, *Strategy #9* will let you know it's time to go back to *Strategy #1* and put together a new design.

Before you delved into the details of the Nine Strategies, you used the Eyes of a Stranger to pick out the one organizing issue that bothers you the most—your unique #1 Challenge. Then you wrote down a list of the underlying problems you'd have to solve to make this #1 Challenge disappear. Now that you've read about all the strategies and know how each one works, you know how to address every item on your "To Solve" list.

It's time to ask you the question I ask all my clients when we finish the appraisal tour: *What do you want?*

You get to choose. Would you rather be an active participant in your life, taking steps to keep things balanced and running smoothly? Or do you prefer to just lie on the mat, flattened, and hope you never have to get up?

- If you want to live your life smoothly and efficiently—
- If you want to spend your time on people and projects you care about—
- If you want to get your responsibilities taken care of without wasting your precious time and energy—
- If you want to deal with things as they come along instead of waiting until the molehills turn into mountains—

then *decide to decide*, and commit yourself to putting the Nine Strategies of Reasonably Organized People to work for you.

If you need some fine tuning to get everything running at optimum performance levels, this shouldn't take long. Address the items on your "To Solve" list, make the necessary adjustments, and start using *Strategy #9, Evaluate Honestly and Often*, to keep things operating smoothly.

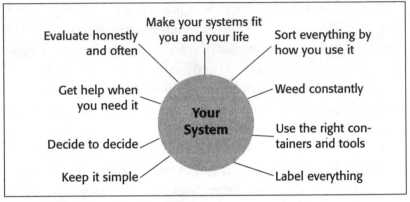

Conclusion: Full Circle of Strategies

If you have more than one strategy missing in action, think about what you'd need to do to put them back to work. Could you use a little help? Figure out the best (and fastest) way to put those strategies back into place. Then do it. Soon you'll be ready to start applying *Strategy #9*, too.

If you're like Leo, and your whole system has fallen apart while you were distracted by overwhelming life events, take a few deep breaths. Ask yourself whether you're really ready to get back into action. Try making a few small decisions just to get yourself started. Throw out some junk mail, move a piece of furniture, call a professional organizer—do just *one thing* to jump-start the process. Then, if it feels okay, call someone and ask for help. Wouldn't it be nice to get up off the floor and start living again?

Whichever group you find yourself in, the Nine Strategies of Reasonably Organized People are the stepping-stones that lead you back into the ring. Use them to get *organized enough* to keep your life running smoothly over the long haul. Make up your mind to get and stay organized for life.

What *do* you want?

Evaluation Questions to Ask Yourself

This section gives you questions to ask yourself during an appraisal tour so you can pinpoint which of the Nine Strategies of Reasonably Organized People is missing from your organizing system. When you turn the Eyes of a Stranger inward, the questions offer guidelines about what you're looking for. You'll want to consult them whenever you use *Strategy #1, Make Your Systems Fit You and Your Life*, to set up a new design. They're also useful when you do routine maintenance using *Strategy #9, Evaluate Honestly and Often*.

If you can answer yes to a question, you'll know which strategy is starting to slide. Go back and review the chapter that covers it, and consult the tips at the end of the chapter for ideas about how to solve the problem.

Does Your System Fit You and Your Life? (Strategy #1)

Make Your Systems Fit You and Your Life is the first and foremost of the Nine Strategies of Reasonably Organized People because you need to know what's happening in your life in order to get yourself organized. If you can identify the things you're *actually doing*—your activities, responsibilities, priorities, and natural tendencies—then you'll know exactly what functions your organizing system needs to support to be effective *for you* in the life you're living today.

Here are some questions to ask yourself to pinpoint the places your systems might be out of sync with your life.

Has My Life Changed?

- Have recent life events affected my ability to be organized?
- Am I hanging on to things from my past that are getting in my way now?
- Am I expecting my life to change and putting things on hold until after that?
- Do I have my system set up to support things I'm no longer doing?

Do My Systems Match My Skills?

- Is there any part of my organizing system that really doesn't work for me?
- Am I trying to change myself in order to make any of my organizing tools work for me?
- Do I feel I "should" organize things differently even though they work well for me?
- Is any part of my organizing system not used because it requires different skills or personal traits than I actually have?

Do My Systems Match My Real Activities?

- Is there something I never do, even though I love doing it, because my system makes it hard for me?
- In my home, are some rooms holding lots of activity while other rooms stand unused?

- Are my systems set up to support the *people* in my life or the *things* in my life?
- Do I have trouble taking care of tasks I'm responsible for because there isn't a well-designed place to do them?

Is There Anything About My Setup That I Intensely Dislike?

- Do any of my rooms or seating areas make me feel uneasy or uncomfortable?
- Is my space too dark for my activities, especially at night?
- Do I find myself doing an activity in one place when I have a perfectly good setup for it someplace else?
- Do I ever use the words *I hate* to refer to any part of my organizing system?

If you answered yes to any of the questions above, you would benefit from an infusion of *Strategy #1: Make Your Systems Fit You and Your Life*. Go to the introduction and reread pages 22 to 23 describing how to appraise your life using the Eyes of a Stranger. Then review Chapter 1 and read the Strategy #1 tips on pages 50 to 54.

But if you can honestly answer no to all these questions, then your organizing systems are a good match for you and your life. Congratulations! Pat yourself on the back, and feel free to skip ahead to *Strategy #2, Sort Everything by How You Use It*.

Have You Sorted Everything by Use? (Strategy #2)

Sort Everything by How You Use It follows the principle of *Making Your Systems Fit You and Your Life* for a good reason. Sorting is the second step toward getting your systems to match your life as you're living it right now. After you use *Strategy #1* to figure out where your life and your systems have diverged, *Strategy #2* allows you to move things into place so they work better for you.

 The following questions will highlight the spots where some sorting might improve your efficiency.

- Do I do lots of activities in a few rooms in my house, while other rooms are rarely or never used?
- Do I have the tools, supplies, equipment, and information I need for each of my major activities spread out around the house?
- If I have rooms with multiple activities, are the things that go with each activity—its tools, supplies, equipment, information, furniture—spread messily across the room?
- Do I have things stuffed in a jumble in containers, drawers, closets, and piles around the house?
- Do I have more than one junk drawer?
- Are there any piles in my house that come from storing something in a different room than the one where I'm using it?
- Am I often frustrated because it takes me a while to find something I'm looking for?
- Do I leave things in a pile anywhere because putting them away is too inconvenient?
- Am I collecting things without knowing what I already have in each collection?
- Are there any collections taking up storage space in multiple locations around the house?
- Are there activities I enjoy that I never do because it takes too long to gather the supplies and equipment needed?
- Is my desk covered with miscellaneous piles of paper, and I don't know what's in them?
- Is it impossible for my children to put their toys away by themselves?

- Once my children put their toys away, do they have trouble finding them again later?
- Do I have lots of little bits of free time scattered throughout my schedule, but no big blocks I can really use to get things accomplished?
- Do I ever get home from a round of errands, only to discover I have to go out again because I forgot something?
- Is anyone in my family trying to do a task without the tools and equipment they need?
- Are my kids' rooms set up so they can't possibly manage their stuff by themselves?
- Is my schedule keeping me from spending enough time with the people I care about?

If you answered yes to any of the questions above, you could benefit from an infusion of *Strategy #2, Sort Everything by How You Use It*. Go back and review Chapter 2, then read the *Strategy #2* tips on pages 79 to 83.

But if you can honestly answer no to all these questions, then you've sorted your space, things, information, and time to adequately support the life you're living right now. Good for you! It's time for you to jump ahead to *Strategy #3, Weed Constantly* to see whether you're keeping things you don't need.

Are You Weeding Constantly?
(Strategy #3)

Weed Constantly is the third step in getting your overall organizing system to support the life you're actually living. Once you've figured out a workable design for your systems, then sorted everything into functional groupings, you may find you have a lot more stuff than you really need. Weeding helps you get things you're not using out of your way and makes room for the activities you're actually doing.

 Here are some questions that'll let you know your system is burdened with too much stuff and could use a little weeding.

- Do I have more stuff than I can keep track of and put away?
- Do I have to move piles of stuff out of the way to do things I have to do or want to do?
- Are my storage spaces full of stuff I never use?
- Do I discourage people from visiting me because my home is so cluttered?
- When someone comes over, do I have to move things out of the way so they can sit down?
- Do I have things that need to be put away just sitting around in my house because my storage spaces are full?
- Are there clothes floating around in my bedroom because my drawers and closets are too crammed to put them away?
- Am I trying to find a place for things I've inherited from someone I loved, even though I don't really like them or need them?
- Do I come home with something new every time I run out to do a few errands?
- Do I ever have to run out and buy something I know I already have, because I can't find it when I need it?
- Do I have any collections that are so big, they're getting in my way?
- When I get new things, do they sit around in piles because there's no place to put them?
- Do I spend good money every month to rent a storage locker I never take anything out of?
- Is there anything in my house I never use, but I'm keeping it because it's too good to give away?

- Is there anything in my house I never use, but I'm keeping it because I might need it someday?
- Do I have piles of paper sitting around on flat surfaces because my file cabinet is so full I can't stuff another piece of paper into it?
- When someone drops in unexpectedly, do I have to run around tossing things into closets and behind furniture before I open the door?
- Do I spend more time taking care of all my stuff than I do with the people I care about?
- Am I feeling resentful because I've taken responsibility for something that keeps me from spending time on the people and activities I care about?

If you answered yes to any of the questions above, it's time to take a hard look at your surroundings and start now on *Strategy #3, Weed Constantly*. Go back and review Chapter 3, then read the *Strategy #3* tips on pages 109 to 114.

But if you can honestly answer no to all these questions, then you've been effective at keeping a balance between new things coming in and old things going out. You're already weeding constantly. Good job! It's time for you to move on to *Strategy #4, Use the Right Containers and Tools* for a discussion about how to contain all the stuff you've decided to keep.

Are You Using the
Right Containers and Tools?
(Strategy #4)

Using the Right Containers and Tools is the fourth step in getting your organizing system to support your life. After you finish sorting and weeding your belongings, this strategy helps you figure out how to contain everything that's left so you can use it. Good containers and tools make things easier for you. If you're having trouble putting things away, it may be because your tools and containers aren't helping you.

 If any of the following questions rings a bell, you may need to make some changes in your inventory of containers and tools.

- Do I have boxes stacked on top of each other in any of my storage spaces?
- Have I been saving all my photographs until I have time to put them into photo albums?
- Is it hard to take a telephone message because there's never a pen or notepad by any of my telephones?
- Do I have food and drink stains on my carpets because people don't have any place to put their food and drinks when they sit down?
- Are my file drawers hard to open and close?
- Do I wear the same jewelry all the time, even though I own lots of other nice pieces?
- Do I ever miss appointments because I didn't write them in my calendar?
- Are there dirty clothes littering the floors in my bedrooms and bathrooms?
- Am I always finding damp towels on the floors and doors?
- Is it hard to find a pair of scissors or a stapler or some tape when I need it?
- Are people in my family always squabbling over the most comfortable chair in the family room?
- Do any of my closets have a jumble of shoes on the floor?
- Do I need a desk?
- Do I hate sitting at my desk?
- Are my file drawers hard to open, close, and/or use?

- Am I always wiping up drips from my kitchen and bathroom floors?
- Do I have clothes piled up in my bedroom or closet because I don't like to put things in the drawers where I can't see them?
- Do I have to get up when I want to throw something away or recycle it?
- Are there videotapes and/or game cartridges on every flat surface next to my television?
- Am I always tripping over the backpacks and jackets my children dropped on the floor when they got home from school?
- Do I like to pay my bills somewhere besides my office?
- Do I have to spend five minutes every night picking up the books my preschooler has scattered all over the bedroom floor?

If you answered yes to any of the questions above, it means your containers and tools are getting in your way instead of helping you. It's time to look at them with a ruthless eye and make some changes. Go back and review Chapter 4, then read the *Strategy #4* tips on pages 138 to 144.

But if you can honestly answer no to all of these questions, then your containers and tools are effectively supporting you instead of hindering you. No shopping trips are required! It's time to turn your attention to *Strategy #5, Label Everything.*

Are You Labeling Everything? (Strategy #5)

Label Everything is the fifth step in getting your organizing system to support your life.

It is the necessary culmination of the sorting, weeding, and containing you've done using *Strategies #2, #3,* and *#4.* Without accurate labels, you won't be able to retrieve your sorted, weeded, and contained things to use them or share them with other important people. The names you choose for all the elements of your organizing system give you visual and vocal clues about their content and their use. If you're finding it hard to locate things, or you're not using all your space and resources to support your activities, you may be experiencing a conflict between your labels and your life.

 Ask yourself the following questions. If they match your situation, you may need to add some new labels or change a few of the old ones.

- Do I have any rooms whose name or label doesn't match the things I'm actually doing inside that room?
- Are there any rooms in my house still set up for activities I no longer do in them?
- Do I ever look in my storage area and wonder what's in all those boxes?
- Are any of my collections spread out among miscellaneous closets, cupboards, and containers instead of being stored in their own location?
- Once I file a given piece of paper, is it impossible to find it again?
- Do I have to play the beginning of a bunch of videotapes in order to find the one I want?
- Do I ever miss appointments because I haven't written them down in the right spot in my calendar?
- Is anyone in my family ever surprised or upset because they didn't know an activity was on the schedule?
- Are toys jumbled together in all the containers in my kids' rooms, even though the collections were recently sorted out and stored together?
- Do my children have trouble finding the clothes they want in their dressers and closets after they've been put away?
- Are my kids always arguing about which thing belongs to whom?

- Do I ever hear myself saying, "Never mind, I'll find it," because it's easier to locate something myself than it is to explain where it is to someone else?
- If something happened to me, would my family have to struggle to find things they need in order to keep everything going?

If you answered yes to any of the questions above, it means the labels in your life may be keeping you from functioning smoothly and efficiently. Go back and review Chapter 5, then read the *Strategy #5* tips on pages 160 to 164.

But if you can honestly answer no to all of these questions, then everything in your life is labeled well enough to support you and your activities. Nice work! It's time for you to move on to *Strategy #6, Keep It Simple,* for ideas about streamlining your policies and procedures to prevent bottlenecks from causing clogs in your organizing system.

Are You Keeping It Simple?
(Strategy #6)

Keep It Simple is the sixth step in getting your organizing system to support your life. Once you've sorted, weeded, contained, and labeled all the elements of your system, check everything and make sure you can retrieve it, use it, and put it away without wasting time and energy. *Strategy #6* helps you find and eliminate bottlenecks caused by extra steps in your system. When you use it to trim your system so it supports your life with the least possible effort, you give yourself the flexibility you need to handle whatever life throws at you.

Look closely at your policies and procedures, then answer the following questions. If they remind you of your situation, it may be time to simplify.

- Do I ever put off doing something I need to do because it takes too much effort?
- Do any of the jobs I often do take me a long time to complete because they're so complicated?
- Are there piles of things around my house that I don't put away because it's hard to get them in and out of their containers?
- Do I have more activities on my "To Do" list than I have time to really do?
- Do I have things that belong in my drawers strewn around my living space even though the drawers are empty?
- Is it hard to get papers into and out of my file cabinet?
- Do I have things sitting around on top of the containers they belong in, instead of stored inside?
- Am I always wiping up drips and footprints from the floors around my house?
- Do I ever find stray food in odd spots around the house, making a mess and attracting pests?
- Do I have trouble finding all my bills when it's time to pay them?
- Do I have to keep filing extensions with the IRS because I can't find all my tax receipts?
- Do I have any horizontal stacks of books, magazines, catalogs, boxes, or papers on the flat surfaces in my home?
- Is my schedule too full because my kids all participate in lots of activities, each one of which requires work from me?
- Have I ever put a paper into a pile instead of a file because I didn't have the right color folder or label for it?
- Does my planner include any sections I never use?
- Do I have trouble saying no when people ask me if I have a minute, even if I'm busy?
- Have I been wanting to put those photographs into albums for years, but I never get to it?
- Are my kids' bedroom floors covered with stuff because they

have trouble getting things back into their proper containers?

- Are my kids' backpacks and jackets always spread out around the kitchen or family room?

If you answered yes to any of the questions above, it means you could subtract some steps from your policies and procedures and still achieve the same results. It's time to figure out how to *Keep It Simple.* Go back and review Chapter 6, then read the *Strategy #6* tips on pages 186 to 190.

But if you can honestly answer no to all of these questions, then the elements of your system are already streamlined and efficient. It's time for you to see whether your system has any obstructions caused by postponed decisions. The next section focuses on keeping everything moving using *Strategy #7, Decide to Decide.*

Have You Decided to Decide?
(Strategy #7)

Decide to Decide is the seventh step in getting your organizing system to support your life. The decisions you make keep things moving through your system and help you operate smoothly. When you postpone decisions, especially the myriad little ones that come through day after day, you start to build logjams of papers and stuff just waiting for you to deal with them. The more you procrastinate, the bigger the pile grows. Postponed decisions don't go away—they just fester and make you feel guilty. But if you use *Strategy #7*, you can prevent these bottlenecks from cluttering your space and your consciousness.

The following questions will tell you whether things are piling up in your house because they need your attention or require a decision.

- Do I have a big pile of mail (mostly junk) lying around in my house because I hate dealing with it?
- Do I have a pile of things I know I want to give away sitting around anywhere in my house?
- Is my desk covered with papers I know I should do something about, but I don't want to?
- Do I set aside clothes because I think they need ironing, but I never actually iron them?
- Am I setting aside all kinds of things, telling myself I'll get to them later, but I never actually come back and do anything with them?
- Are any of my file folders labeled with Post-it notes?
- Have I got piles of things I want to read, but I never make time to read all of them?
- Am I putting off making a change I know I need because it's too hard or scary to actually do it?
- Am I piling up things in my house because I plan to have a yard sale someday?
- When I get new things, do I hang on to the old ones they're replacing, even though I have no use for them any more?
- Is there a big project I know would make everything work better if I finished it, but I can't seem to find a big enough block of time to get it done?
- Am I planning to make a big change—a move, a wedding, a new job, anything—so I don't want to waste time getting this place into good shape?
- Do I ever find myself wishing life could go back to the way it used to be?

If you answered yes to any of the questions above, it means your system is clogged with the debris from postponed decisions. It's time to *Decide to Decide*. Go back and review Chapter 7, then read the *Strategy #7* tips on pages 214 to 218.

But if you can honestly answer no to all of these questions, then you're already making enough decisions to prevent your organizing system from getting clogged with elements needing attention. Hurray! It's time to move on to *Strategy #8, Get Help When You Need It* to see how other people can help you get things done better and faster than if you did them by yourself.

Are You Getting Help When You Need It? (Strategy #8)

Get Help When You Need It is the eighth step in getting your organizing system to support your life. Like *Keep It Simple (#6)* and *Decide to Decide (#7)*, it addresses one of the common bottlenecks that can choke your system and keep it from operating smoothly. *Strategy #8* helps you figure out how to share the responsibility for running a household and making everything work. When you allow and encourage (and sometimes pay) other people to help you, you get a lot more done than you could accomplish by yourself.

 The following questions will help you decide whether you're trying to do too much work all by yourself.

- Is almost all the work that needs doing around my house done by only one person?
- Do I avoid doing something I have to do because I just don't want to do it?
- Do I avoid doing something I must do because I'm not good at it?

- Do I avoid doing something I have to do because I don't know how to do it?
- Are piles building up around my house because routine jobs like doing laundry, washing dishes, picking up, or cleaning are not getting done fast enough?
- Do my kids' rooms get organized and cleaned up without their participation or input?
- Do our routine family chores get done by adults without help from children?
- Do my kids have trouble being responsible for their own things and responsibilities (including homework) because they don't have a setup they can manage by themselves?
- Do my partner and I have conflicting ideas about storage, clutter, or ongoing projects?
- Do my partner and I have conflicting ideas about how much children should participate in the work of the household?
- Do I have physical limitations that hinder my ability to get things done?
- Do I have any deep or unresolved emotional issues that hinder my ability to get things done?

If you answered yes to any of the questions above, it means your system doesn't have enough people working in it to handle all the issues that come up. It's time to invoke *Strategy #8, Get Help When You Need It*. Go back and review Chapter 8, then read the *Strategy #8* tips on pages 239 to 243.

But if you can honestly answer no to all of these questions, then you've already invited other people to help you get your work accomplished. Good thinking! It's time to turn your attention to *Strategy #9, Evaluate Honestly and Often*. The last of the Nine Strategies of Reasonably Organized People, it shows you how to figure out when your system needs tweaking.

Are You Evaluating Honestly and Often? (Strategy #9)

Evaluate Honestly and Often is the ninth and final step in getting your organizing system to support your life. The work of getting organized doesn't end when you unclog the last bottleneck. Because life is always changing, the effectiveness of your system is always changing, too. By examining it with honesty and objectivity—in effect, by using the Eyes of a Stranger on it periodically—you can see how it's gotten out of whack and figure out which strategy has gone missing. Then you can put it back in place and solve the problem so your system gets back into line with your life. If more than one strategy is missing, it might be time to go back to *Strategy #1, Make Your Systems Fit You and Your Life* to put together a new design for your whole organizing system.

 The following questions will let you know if it's time to tweak your system so it works better.

- Is a pile starting to grow anywhere in my house?
- Is there something about my organizing system that's making me feel uncomfortable?
- Did my organizing system used to work smoothly, but now the exact same setup is giving me trouble?
- Have I recently adopted a new organizing tactic that's causing more problems than it solves?
- Have I lost track of what I'm keeping in my storage areas?
- Have I fine-tuned my system so much that it's gotten complicated and hard to use?
- Is anyone in my household complaining that something isn't working well?
- Has a minor life event left me feeling upset and overwhelmed (even though I don't think I *should* feel this bad about it)?

- Am I anticipating a major life change in the next six months (move, wedding, new baby, job change, empty nest, retirement), but I feel completely unprepared for it?
- Has my household recently undergone a major life change, and the old systems don't fit the way things are going now?

If you answered yes to any of the questions above, it means your overall organizing system is suffering for want of your attention. It's time to apply *Strategy #9, Evaluate Honestly and Often.* Go back and review Chapter 9, then read the *Strategy #9* tips on pages 262 to 265.

But if you can honestly answer no to all these questions, then your system is honed, refined, and ready to support your life as you're living it today. At this moment, you are an Organized Person! You've been effectively using the Nine Strategies of Reasonably Organized People to stay *organized enough* to keep your life on track. Keep up the good work!

What's Your
Organizing Style?

If you want an organizing system that will work smoothly *for you*, you need to design it to match your unique operating style. For example, if you're a visual person who needs to see something in order to remember to act on it, a "To Do" folder in your file cabinet is not going to work for you. Conversely, if you like to keep your environment visually uncluttered, then a closed storage system like a file cabinet will work better for you.

To help you get a handle on the way your personality affects the way you approach the task of getting organized, look at the chart on page 291. It shows eleven different spectrums, each one a sliding scale depicting a single quality. Where do you fall between the opposite traits at either end? Rank yourself on the scale for each of these personality traits. Remember, there are no right or wrong answers. You are who you are. So be honest! Then look at the pattern your rankings has made on the page. What does your unique pattern tell you about your operating style?

Leaning to the Left

If most or all of your marks fall between the left edge and the center, your natural tendency is to thrive on chaos, live a lively life, and constantly add new elements to your systems. Your biggest organizing challenges revolve around keeping your schedule simple enough so you can manage it, and saying no to more than you can handle. The strategies that are hardest for you to apply are *#6 (Keep It Simple)* and *#3 (Weed Constantly)*. Study *Strategies #6, #3, #2 (Sort Everything by How You Use It)*, and *#5 (Label Everything)* for ideas about how to walk the fine line between your love for change and your tendency to let things descend into chaos. Apply *#8 (Get Help When You Need It)* by stepping back, delegating, and sharing the work with other people.

Leaning to the Right

If most or all of your marks fall between the center and the right edge of the scales, your natural tendency is to keep things quiet and tightly controlled. Your biggest organizing challenges revolve around incorporating change into your life and keeping your systems from getting too complicated. The strategies that are hardest for you to apply are *#1 (Make Your Systems Fit You and Your Life)* and *#6 (Keep It Simple)*. Work on subtracting unnecessary structure. Make your systems simple, flexible, and up-to-date using *#1, #6, #4 (Use the Right Containers and Tools)*, and *#7 (Decide to Decide)*. Use *#8 (Get Help When You Need It)* to involve other people in your life instead of doing everything yourself. Even if you do a better job than anyone else does, it's good to spread the work around and get involved with other people. Don't let your love of order keep you from enjoying the opportunities life events can bring you.

Centrist

If most or all of your marks fall close to the center, your natural tendency is to keep things in balance. Your biggest organizing challenges

Organizing Personality Test Scale

|----------------------------------|--|

← Free-form *or* Structured →

|----------------------------------|--|

← Spontaneous *or* Methodical →

|----------------------------------|--|

← Sentimental *or* Stoic →

|----------------------------------|--|

← Extrovert *or* Introvert →

|----------------------------------|--|

← High Energy *or* Low Energy →

|----------------------------------|--|

← Intuitive *or* Intellectual →
(Your bottom line: *How do I feel?*) (Your bottom line: *What do I think?*)

|----------------------------------|--|

← Sensualist *or* Ascetic →
(You like to pamper yourself) (You like to challenge yourself)

|----------------------------------|--|

← An "Outie" *or* An "Innie" →
(If you can't see something,   (You like things put away
it doesn't exist)   out of sight)

|----------------------------------|--|

← Living in crowded quarters *or* Living alone →

|----------------------------------|--|

← Involved in many activities *or* Focused on a few activities →

|----------------------------------|--|

← Constantly changing *or* Fixed in stone →

revolve around tweaking your systems to keep things balanced as life changes. Use *Strategies #1 (Make Your Systems Fit You and Your Life), #3 (Weed Constantly),* and *#9 (Evaluate Honestly and Often)* to maintain your steady course. Use *#8 (Get Help When You Need It)* to check in with supportive friends for advice when things start to get off kilter.

Snake

If your marks are all over the chart, from left to right and back again, there are two possible scenarios at work:

1. It could be that your living situation is at odds with your natural tendencies. For instance, you might be an introvert in charge of a family of free-form children, or a free-form person whose partner likes everything orderly and just so. If this is your situation, your biggest organizing challenges revolve around maintaining a balance between your needs and the needs of others. The strategy that is hardest for you to apply is *#1 (Make Your Systems Fit You and Your Life),* because what works for you does not necessarily work for those you love. Use *#2 (Sort Everything by How You Use It)* and *#5 (Label Everything)* to create separate spaces for different conflicting values— for example, set aside a room for you, call it Your Room, design it for your style, and keep others out—and *#7 (Decide to Decide)* to help you be a firm advocate for yourself and those you're responsible for. Use *#8 (Get Help When You Need It)* when you need to escape and be yourself for a little while. Try to strike a balance between your needs and the needs of the people you love.

2. The other possible reason your marks range all over the chart is that your natural tendency is to resist classification. If this is you, keep in mind that the chart is for you, not for anyone else. No one is going to use it but you. No one else will even see it unless you choose to show it to them. And no one is going to judge your answers. So

give the exercise another shot, and be honest. Where do you really fall on these scales?

Once you know your own unique organizing style, you can incorporate it into the overall design of your organizing system. Using *Strategy #1, Make Your Systems Fit You and Your Life,* figure out a setup that suits your style. Then put it in place using the Nine Strategies of Reasonably Organized People. Voila! A custom-designed organizing system that fits you.

Two Aids for Sorting and Weeding

The Weeding List

Questions to Ask as You Sort and Weed

1. Why have I been keeping this?
2. Is it still doing something for me?
3. If I have more than enough of these, how many do I really *need*?
4. Am I tired of seeing it? thinking about it? cleaning it? moving it around?
5. If I'm going to keep this, is there a better place for it?
6. If I'm not going to keep this, would someone else find it useful?
7. If I get rid of this and I need it again, can I get another one?

Boxing Day

How to Weed Out a Single Space

1. Pick a single space to weed out.
2. Empty it onto a flat surface.
3. Get five paper bags (for a small space) or roomy boxes (for a large space).

4. Label your boxes as follows:

BELONGS ELSEWHERE

This is everything you find that goes somewhere else in your house. *After* you're finished weeding, put away all the things in this box. *Do not* put them away now.

TO FIX/MEND

This is anything you *know* you want to keep, but which needs repair. When you're finished weeding, put this box in the car and get everything *fixed*, or give it away.

TO GIVE AWAY

This is every useful thing that *you* don't need, but someone else might. When you've finished weeding, put this box right in the car and take it to the nearest charity drop-off. Get a receipt and deduct the donation from your taxes.

TO DISCARD/RECYCLE

This is all the stuff you've been keeping that has no real use or value. When you've finished weeding, put this box at the curb for the trash collector, or put it in the car to take straight to the dump.

BELONGS TO SOMEONE ELSE

This is anything that belongs to someone else, which you've been storing for them free of charge. When you've finished weeding, put this box in the car and take everything back to its rightful owner *pronto*!

5. Go through the pile, sorting into the boxes.
6. Everything that's left belongs where it was.
7. Put it back neatly.
8. Doesn't that look great?

Recommended
Reading

It is easy to find books on organizing but hard to tell which ones offer truly helpful information. The following books contain a wide variety of tips to augment the lists provided in this book.

ASLETT, DON. *Is There Life After Housework?* Cincinnati: Writer's Digest Books, 1981. Focus: fast, efficient cleaning tactics.

BERENSTAIN, STAN & JAN. *The Berenstain Bears and the Messy Room.* New York: Random House, 1983. Focus: a story for kids.

CHUEN, MASTER LAM KAM. *Feng Shui Handbook.* New York: Henry Holt & Company, 1996. Focus: overview of feng shui.

CULP, STEPHANIE. *How to Conquer Clutter.* Cincinnati: Writer's Digest Books, 1990. Focus: general tool/container tips.

DORFF, PAT. *File . . . Don't Pile!* New York: St. Martin's Press, 1986. Focus: paper tips.

FELTON, SANDRA. *Messie No More.* Grand Rapids, Mich.: Baker Book House, 1989. Focus: personality nuances

HEMPHILL, BARBARA, *Taming the Paper Tiger at Home.* Washington, D.C.: Kiplinger Books, 1998. Focus: information management.

KOLBERG, JUDITH. *Conquering Chronic Disorganization.* Decatur, Ga.: Squall Press, 1999. Focus: personality nuances.

LEHMKUHL, DOROTHY & DOLORES COTTER LAMPING. *Organizing for the Creative Person.* New York: Crown Publishers, 1993. Focus: personality nuances.

LINN, DENISE. *Sacred Space.* New York: Ballantine Books, 1995. Focus: simplicity.

MORGENSTERN, JULIE. *Organizing from the Inside Out.* New York: Owl Books, 1998. Focus: general tips.

PASSOFF, MICHELLE. *Lighten Up! Free Yourself from Clutter.* New York: HarperCollins, 1998. Focus: clutter tips.

ST. JAMES, ELAINE. *Simplify Your Life.* New York: Hyperion, 1994. Focus: simplicity.

SAPADIN, DR. LINDA. *It's About Time.* New York: Penguin Books, 1997. Focus: time tips.

SCHOFIELD, DENIECE. *Confessions of an Organized Homemaker.* Cincinnati: Betterway Books, 1994. Focus: household tips.

STODDARD, ALEXANDRA. *Creating a Beautiful Home.* New York: Avon Books, 1992. Focus: interior design.

WINSTON, STEPHANIE. *Getting Organized.* New York: Warner Books, 1991. Focus: general tips.

Index